Optimizing Teaching and Learning

To those who take the time and energy to care about teaching and student learning

Optimizing Teaching and Learning
Practicing Pedagogical Research

Regan A. R. Gurung and Beth M. Schwartz

WILEY-BLACKWELL

A John Wiley & Sons, Ltd., Publication

#X89385

This edition first published 2009
© 2009 Regan A. R. Gurung and Beth M. Schwartz

Blackwell Publishing was acquired by John Wiley & Sons in February 2007. Blackwell's publishing program has been merged with Wiley's global Scientific, Technical, and Medical business to form Wiley-Blackwell.

Registered Office
John Wiley & Sons Ltd, The Atrium, Southern Gate, Chichester, West Sussex, PO19 8SQ, United Kingdom

Editorial Offices
350 Main Street, Malden, MA 02148-5020, USA
9600 Garsington Road, Oxford, OX4 2DQ, UK
The Atrium, Southern Gate, Chichester, West Sussex, PO19 8SQ, UK

For details of our global editorial offices, for customer services, and for information about how to apply for permission to reuse the copyright material in this book please see our website at www.wiley.com/wiley-blackwell.

The right of Regan A. R. Gurung and Beth M. Schwartz to be identified as the authors of this work has been asserted in accordance with the Copyright, Designs and Patents Act 1988.

Library of Congress Cataloging-in-Publication Data

Gurung, Regan A. R.
  Optimizing teaching and learning : practicing pedagogical research / Regan A. R. Gurung and Beth M. Schwartz.
    p. cm.
  Includes bibliographical references and index.
  ISBN 978-1-4051-6179-4 (hardcover : alk. paper) 1. College teaching. 2. Reflective teaching. 3. Learning. I. Schwartz, Beth M. II. Title.
  LB2331G797 2009
  378.1′2–dc22

2008028047

A catalogue record for this book is available from the British Library.

Set in 10.5 on 13 pt Minion by SNP Best-set Typesetter Ltd., Hong Kong
Printed in Singapore by Fabulous Printers Pte Ltd

1 2009

Contents

Preface

Where do you start when you think about teaching and learning? Conventional storytelling would suggest the beginning. But this is about telling a different kind of story. Research and advice on how to optimize student learning and teachers' teaching suggests that the best place to start is at the end. If you know what you want your students to leave your class with, you are in a better position to design your course content and delivery to get them there. You are also well positioned to assess your students' journey to learning and study the detours, pitfalls, or shortcuts along the way. Commonly referred to as "backward design" (Wiggins & McTighe, 2005, and discussed in more detail later), this approach provides a helpful framework for examining teaching and learning and makes clear the need for the two main goals of this book: 1) collecting, summarizing, and prioritizing for you, what is known about teaching and learning; and 2) providing you with easy ways to catalyze your own scholarly investigations into teaching and learning.

Research on teaching and learning (pedagogical research or the Scholarship of Teaching and Learning, SoTL) is one of the most energizing areas of research in the field of higher education today, in which faculty continuously evaluate the quality of their teaching and its effect on student learning. Galvanized by the efforts of the Carnegie Academy for the Scholarship of Teaching and Learning (CASTL; in particular individuals such as Lee Shulman, Pat Hutchings, and Mary Huber), the Lilly Foundation (especially Laurie Richlin, and the Preparing Future Faculty program), the Visible Knowledge Project, and the Peer Review of Teaching Project, the banner of SoTL has been taken up by academics from diverse fields. Educators are beginning to notice the fruits of SoTL labors, and a growing number of publications and directives within the academy are drawing attention to the importance of taking a close look at how we teach and how students learn.

As emphasized by both Seldin (2004) and Hatch (2006) faculty are being held accountable for the effectiveness of their teaching and in turn they are starting to engage in intellectual exchanges, not only on their research agendas but also on the ways in which they teach their students in the classroom. Huber and Hutchings (2005) called this type of intellectual exchange a "teaching common." At the heart of this new movement, there is a simple idea: *take a close look at how you teach and how your students learn, use the same methodology that you would use for formal investigations (be it in the humanities or science), and hold your research to the same standards, most notably peer review.*

What exactly are methodologies of pedagogical research? What do we already know about how students learn and optimal teaching? What are the best practices for optimizing teaching? This book will answer all these questions and provide practical ways to bridge the gap between research on teaching and learning and the practice of teaching. As well as summarizing the vast literature on teaching and learning and providing a source of information on topics such as what the master teachers do and what is known about how students learn, we also provide tools to facilitate pedagogical research. This book takes the reader beyond intellectual discourse on SoTL: The case for SoTL has been and continues to be made by vocal and noted leaders in the field. This book will provide specific techniques to put these findings into action together with a clear guide on how to assess the fruits of your labor.

Why should academics care, given all else we have to care about? One of the most critical deterrents to doing this sort of methodological inquiry into teaching and learning has been the lack of a clear reward structure for such work and a corresponding lack of motivation on the part of those interested. As Fink (2003) notes throughout his work, research on teaching and learning takes a great deal of time and effort. Without an institutional culture in which this type of scholarship is recognized and valued, faculty will spend that time and effort elsewhere. Now universities, colleges, and high schools nationwide are not only beginning to recognize and value educators who are interested in SoTL, but are also starting to require that teaching and learning be studied (O'Meara and Rice, 2005). Researchers in the field of education and psychology have been particularly active in taking basic research from each of their fields and applying it to the classroom, and their theories and methods are inspiring faculty in many other diverse areas. All SoTL must incorporate the qualities of any good science, which includes an objective assessment based on data that is verifiable and that holds up to peer review (Richlin, 2006; Weimer, 2006). Unfortunately, there is currently no adequate resource that serves as a guide both to demonstrate how to conduct pedagogical research within any field of study and to provide best practices based on the existing pedagogical research findings. This book will do just this, providing a resource for anyone who is interested in improving their teaching, the learning of their students, and, correspondingly, contributing to the scholarship of teaching and learning. In short, this book will bridge the gap between the research on pedagogy and the practice of pedagogy, with explicit instructions on how to design, conduct, analyze, and write up pedagogical research. It will also explore the advantages and disadvantages of various pedagogical practices and present applications of SoTL using case studies from a variety of disciplines. To this end we review and summarize the current writing on pedagogical research and provide examples of questionnaires or explicit research protocols to help guide the design of investigations into teaching or learning. The surveys or questions can be directly taken and used to catalyze personal investigations into one's teaching and one's students' learning.

Although the rigor of the scientific method or the varieties of ways of knowing in the humanities are valid and necessary parts of how teaching and learning should be viewed, many faculty are trained to apply these methods to their research endeavors and not to student learning or to their teaching. Furthermore, although one's discipline can be applied to investigate the problems of teaching and learning, the resistance of these same problems to the discipline's familiar modes of inquiry can limit the motivation to conduct SoTL and even contaminate its efforts (Huber & Morreale, 2002). In essence, as more and more faculty are being encouraged to assess the effectiveness of their teaching, they will in turn need the tools necessary for that type of assessment. Only when those tools are made available will faculty be more comfortable stepping outside their research comfort zone and into the forum of SoTL. When instructors learn the importance of going beyond the content and better understanding the process of teaching and learning, students in their classroom in turn learn more material and learn that material more effectively. Unfortunately a large number of teachers enter the classroom without a background in the very essence of what makes good teaching and learning. However, as Bain (2004) illustrates, the best teachers continually collect evidence to assess the effectiveness of their teaching. Similarly, SoTL scholars such as Davis and Buskist (2006) illustrate that when one understands and believes that assessing teaching effectiveness is essential, one can then become a more effective teacher. This book will serve as a resource for all faculty to conduct this type of continuous assessment – both seasoned faculty and new faculty who are just beginning to assess their teaching methods and learn how to think beyond the content.

This book is designed to be a resource for faculty who are engaged in SoTL projects and for faculty developers who promote SoTL. It should also be useful to any faculty member who is interested in examining their own teaching and their students' learning as part of becoming a more effective teacher. A number of books on the market provide readers with how to present or organize one's teaching accomplishments through use of a teaching portfolio (e.g., Bernstein et al., 2006, Seldin, 2004) or are driven to strengthening the case for SoTL work (e.g., Huber & Hutchings, 2005). This book builds upon these existing books by providing faculty with methodologies for conducting SoTL in order to strengthen the supporting data used in one's teaching portfolio. This book can be a part of graduate courses on teaching and learning in higher education and can be especially useful reading for new and midlevel faculty. Given that higher education is being called on to demonstrate the effectiveness of what it is doing, the pressure for more scholarship on teaching and learning is going to increase. Faculty development programs nationwide have already been holding training sessions to increase SoTL, and more and faculty are interested in this area. Journals such as *MountainRise*, and *Inventio* and others publishing the results of these investigations have originated in almost every discipline, and many junior faculty are learning of the importance of SoTL for tenure and promotion.

Each section will first summarize years of work in pertinent areas to provide a foundation for scholarly investigation. In chapter 1, we clarify the nature of pedagogical research and distinguish between the different labels currently in use (e.g., Scholarly Teaching, SoTL, Action Research) and review the history of the field. In the two consequent chapters we focus on teaching (chapter 2) and learning (chapter 3), first reviewing and summarizing the relevant literature and then providing guidelines on how to conduct scholarly research on the questions we raise. Once you have caught the excitement of conducting research on your teaching and student learning, been convinced it is a good idea, or even if you are strong-armed into doing it, you will probably be faced with one of two big problems. You have no idea what to look at? You have *too much* to look at? The first is an illusion: You will almost certainly discover there is a lot you want to examine once you know how to look. The second problem is a blessing not even in disguise. Having a plethora of research questions ensures you will not get bored. No matter which of these two problems may be yours, chapters 2 and 3 will provide you with a roadmap to getting starting, offering reviews of the literature that will serve to bring you up to date with some of the best prescriptions for conducting research on teaching and learning while providing you with options for further reading. Once you have collected your data- measured student learning or assessed whether your changes have worked- you need to be able to analyze what you have and establish if you have significant findings. Chapter 4 describes the basic statistical methods for evaluating your findings. We walk you through the main considerations in designing studies and provide explicit instructions on how to analyze your data using a commonly used statistical package (with clear examples and screen shots of commands and results).

In chapter 4 we provide what, as far as we can tell, is the only explicit and straightforward guide to the statistical analysis of pedagogical research on teaching and learning. Finally, we provide the reader with a wealth of information related to setting up pedagogical research centers and connection with colleagues also interested in examining their own teaching. Chapter 5 will be especially useful for those who are setting up a teaching and learning center on their campus. In the end, we hope you find that you have found the answers to many of the teaching and learning questions you have always wondered about and gained the knowledge to create your own pedagogical research program. Doing your own pedagogical research will help you answer even more questions and allow you to share your findings to others in the field. We also hope we will help you ask the right questions about your teaching and your students' learning, to find the tools needed to analyze your data and interpret your findings in relation to existing knowledge in the field. Importantly, we hope that this guide will provide the tools needed to be more effective in the classroom.

Acknowledgments

Neil Lutsky and the other wonderful faculty at Carleton College (MN) showed me what it means to be a passionate teacher. Neil took the time to make sure that I realized that it is worth it to care about teaching and introduced me to a world of wonderful passionate teachers within the Society for the Teaching of Psychology, Jane Halonen, Bill Buskist, and Bill Hill, amongst others. I thrive on my friendships with them and am a better teacher because of it. Colleagues both in the University of Wisconsin System and on my own campus and department (especially the Teaching Scholars and Fellows, members of OPID, and my faculty friends and collaborators) catalyzed my interests in pedagogical research, and I am grateful to them for putting up with my constant search for the empirical answers to any and every classroom quandary. Denise Scheberle and Fergus Hughes, Founding Co-Directors of the UWGB Teaching Scholars Program, were particularly instrumental in fostering my growth as a pedagogical scholar. I also owe a debt of gratitude to my teaching and research assistants with whom I had many a stimulating pedagogical conversation especially Amanda Jeske, Angie Roethel, and Janet Weidert.

R. A. R. G.

As a student in class at Colby College, with faculty who were dedicated to teaching and learning, I was inspired to continue my education and to learn how to create the same stimulating learning environment for my own students. Since the day I first set foot on campus, my colleagues at Randolph College (founded as Randolph-Macon Woman's College) exemplified the joy of teaching. I am particularly grateful to my colleagues in the psychology department over the years, Dennis Goff, Rory McElwee, Rick Barnes, and Holly Tatum, who all have provided mentoring, friendship, and discussions about their own teaching experiences and ideas, which to this day continue to make me strive to be a better teacher and scholar every time I step into the classroom. I also thank my many students, who continue to bring to the classroom their energy and interest, which inspire me to be the best that I can be as a teacher, providing for them an optimal learning environment. These are the people who lead me to continually rethink, refine, and improve as an educator.

B. M. S.

We both would like to thank Chris Cardone at Wiley-Blackwell and her editorial staff for cultivating the ideas for this book and helping to make it a reality.

1

What Is Pedagogical Research?

How do we know if our students are learning? How do we know if we are teaching well? Do research methods really exist that allow us to answer these questions? We all realize the importance of understanding if our students are learning and whether we are teaching well. However, the process by which to answer these important questions is often outside the area of expertise of many academics, though if given the tools we could all head into the classroom with a greater understanding of how our methods of teaching influence students' learning.

In addition to learning the tools and methods available to conduct pedagogical research, we also need to gain an understanding of the existing literature in which many scholars have emerged as pioneers in the field of scholarship of teaching and learning. We must identify those pioneers and use the knowledge gained from their research and use that to develop our own pedagogical investigations. When examining student learning and optimal teaching, the disciplines of education and educational psychology provide a good starting point for our look at how to examine teaching and learning. Although we will draw strongly from these areas, we will also be tapping into many other disciplines that focus on how teaching and learning can be improved. As much as the field of education and educational psychology seem to have cornered the pedagogical research market, the big difference is that researchers in those areas treat the classrooms of others as their laboratory. The pedagogical research we will examine puts *your own* classroom, teaching, and learning under the microscope. But we digress. What is pedagogical research? Why should you care?

Pedagogical research can be easily defined as research on teaching and learning. It can provide the answer to a wide range of questions, such as why a class goes awry, or why students fail to grasp the concepts taught, or why despite our best efforts students exhibit no signs of creative thinking or higher learning. Changes in higher education are also driving up interest in teaching and learning. The composition of our classes is changing, there are different national priorities, greater public accountability, and changing pedagogical techniques (Huber & Morreale, 2002). Clearly, we need to pay attention to pedagogical research. It is the umbrella term that encompasses a number of other terms such as *action research, scholarly teaching*, and, a term we hear more and more often, *SoTL*.

By now you have probably heard the acronym SoTL. Some pronounce each letter and call it S-OH-T-L, others So-till, and still others, Su-till (as in "subtle"). Although it may look like yet another of the myriad acronyms that dot the educational landscape, in recent years we have seen a number of publications heralding the worthiness and proliferation of the scholarship of teaching and learning (e.g., Becker & Andrews, 2004; Cambridge, 2004; Hatch, 2006; McKinney, 2007; Savory, Burnett, & Goodburn, 2007), though few publications place SoTL into the greater context of educational research. This introductory chapter traces the development of pedagogical research from *before* the time Boyer first coined the phrase SoTL in 1990 (there was pedagogical research long before the use of the phrase) to the present day. Along the way we will provide critical reviews of the extant literature on SoTL and also disentangle the many related terms that have been used to describe similar pursuits (i.e., action and teacher research and scholarly teaching).

First a little more on why we use the phrase *pedagogical research* for describing the systematic investigation of teaching and learning. After reading a variety of sources and being exposed to a number of terms (to be reviewed briefly), we believe pedagogical research is the phrase that best captures the essence of scholarly work that is conducted to optimize teaching and learning. We also believe that this term is less value-laden than SoTL and other variations on the theme. In our view, pedagogical research encompasses SoTL, action and teacher research, scholarly teaching, and essentially any other phrase used in this arena. There is a lot of debate about what constitutes SoTL, and, rather than getting into the detail of that we will focus on what we know about optimal teaching and optimizing learning, and the steps needed to achieve it. This optimization is what teachers care about. Our goal is to show you how to do it in the easiest, most reliable and most valid way possible. Along the way we will also expose you to the results of years of pedagogical research as well as highlight many unanswered questions and issues. We hope to stimulate your intellectual curiosity in elucidating quandaries, which will catalyze both your teaching and your own pedagogical research.

A number of different academic areas explore pedagogical research with an emphasis on research from the fields of education and psychology and the work of a wide array of scholars (e.g., Entwistle, Hestenes-Hake, Huber, Perry, Shulman). Just as a rose by any another name is still a rose, so too research on teaching and learning is still essentially *pedagogical research*, no matter what discipline the research is based in. In many disciplines, the methodologies formerly used by faculty for research are now recognized as valuable resources to assess methods of teaching. This transformation has only slowly emerged over the last decade but it is spreading and growing exponentially. as general questions of inquiry lead to more and more refined questions.

Multidisciplinary Roots of Pedagogical Research

Research on teaching and learning has a long history in various disciplines and is more widespread than one may have imagined. In a recent review of the history and diversity of pedagogical research, Maryellen Weimer (2006) notes that almost all the major disciplines have pedagogical journals. By giving one of the most comprehensive listings of publication outlets for pedagogical research, Weimer's work clearly shows that, if one wants to learn more about how to optimize teaching and learning, there are many places to look. There are also many outlets to publish your own pedagogical research. There are journals and magazines written for higher-education audiences such as *Academic Medicine*, *Journal of Economic Education*, *Teaching Philosophy*, and *Teaching Sociology*, and a number of discipline-based pedagogical journals written for educators at various levels. Some examples of this second group include *Art Education*, *History Teacher*, *Business Education Forum*, and *Physics Teacher*. Weimer also identifies cross-disciplinary publications written by and for faculty in different fields (e.g., *Journal of College Science Teaching*) and theme-based journals written by and for postsecondary educators (e.g., *Active Learning in Higher Education*).

As a testament to the (mostly unknown) longevity of pedagogical research, the earliest journal articles on teaching and learning were published back in 1924 with the first edition of the *Journal of Chemical Education*, a publication still in press today. Many of the journals that began a long time ago started as newsletters (e.g., *Teaching of Psychology;*, conversely, many pedagogical publications are not published on paper at all: a number of outlets exist in online form only. A recent example is the *International Journal for the Scholarship of Teaching and Learning (IJSOTL)*, a peer-reviewed electronic journal published twice a year by the Center for Excellence in Teaching at Georgia Southern University, the first issue of which appeared in January 2007.

Examining Definitions of Scholarship

Do you want to optimize student learning but don't know how to do it? If you have always wondered if your efforts to improve your teaching and trials and errors in the classroom actually have a name, this section is for you.

We introduced the term pedagogical research to avoid the snares and snafus of definition arguments. But as academics we cannot shy away from a good debate. What is SoTL? Is SoTL the same as education research or teacher research? Is it different from pedagogical research? The phrase Scholarship of Teaching and Learning entered the national higher-education consciousness in 1990. It is not that this type of work did not exist before then. It is just that the events taking place that year, and Boyer's (1990) exploration of the diverse nature of scholarship, raised awareness of pedagogical research. SoTL is often referred to as a new field, in which research focuses on the assessment of student learning in connection to particular teaching practices, but (as we will illustrate shortly) research on student learning or pedagogical research in one form or the other has been taking place from the beginnings of formal education. In fact, the view that scholarship is primarily synonymous with research and does not encompass the examination of teaching and learning is a relatively recent (postwar) phenomenon (Rice, 2005).

People have been talking about pedagogical research and SoTL (though not using the same terms) for over a hundred years. The Harvard psychologist William James was asked to give a few public lectures to Cambridge teachers in 1892. In his talk, he not only expressed how knowledge of psychology could help the teachers teach better and understand their students better, but he asked teachers to "deem it part of your duty to become contributors to psychological science or to make psychological observations in a methodical or responsible manner" (James, 1899/2006, p. 9). The concepts and ideas were present, but no term was coined at the time or specific field of research identified. Some years later, in his inaugural address as the fifth president of the University of Chicago in 1928, Robert Maynard Hutchins essentially suggested faculty should carry out pedagogical research on their students (Thompson, Nelson, & Naremore, 2001). These two examples suggest that the concept of SOTL existed long before Boyer popularized the term.

The emergence of the now ubiquitous acronym SoTL is more the reflection of a political uprising of sorts. As the story goes, there were rumblings of discontent in the academy. The late 1980s saw issues such as assessment, active learning, cost containment, and accountability coming to the fore (Edgerton, 2005). In addition, colleges and universities began to take a closer look at faculty priorities. In early 1990 a study of 23,000 faculty, chairs, and administrators showed that teaching received too little emphasis in comparison to research (Gray, Froh, & Diamond, 1992). This project helmed by Syracuse University showed that this sentiment was commonly held across universities (Diamond & Adam, 2000) and led to major institutions such as Stanford University and the University of California System taking a close look at faculty rewards and what constituted scholarship.

Boyer's (1990) somewhat incendiary *Scholarship Reconsidered*, which used the phrase "scholarship of teaching," was released into this whirlpool of change. His thesis that scholarship needed a broader definition catalyzed extensive examination of the work done on teaching and learning and flexed the political muscle of organizations such as the Carnegie Foundation for the Advancement of Teaching. The results are staggering (O'Meara & Rice, 2005). For example, shortly after its publication 62 percent of chief academic officers in colleges reported that *Scholarship Reconsidered* had influenced decisions regarding faculty reward (Glassick, Huber, & Maeroft, 1997). National studies also illustrated that Boyer's report influenced the reform of the faculty reward system and especially the recognition of scholarship on teaching (e.g., Braxton, Luckey, & Holland, 2002). Most recently, the American Association for Higher Education (AAHE, now defunct), building on strong testimonies at its annual Forum on Faculty Roles and Rewards conferences, launched a two-year project that both surveyed chief academic officers nationwide and gathered best practices of encouraging the scholarship of teaching from entire institutions. The result, *Faculty Priorities Reconsidered: Rewarding Multiple Forms of Scholarship*, nicely illustrates how the scholarship of teaching and pedagogical research is fostered nationwide (O'Meara & Rice, 2005).

The call to give teaching a place in the broader vision of scholarship was enthusiastically acted on by many eager to increase a focus on teaching and learning and was soon supported by a rich body of publications. For example, Lee Shulman wrote a motivating piece in *Harvard Educational Review* (1987), Angelo and Cross (1993) jumpstarted classroom assessment with their classic compendium of Classroom Assessment Techniques (CATs), and more attention was paid to developing new ways of evaluating teaching, giving rise to the greater use of teaching portfolios (Seldin, 1997). Near the end of the decade, Bransford, Brown, and Cocking (1999) at the National Research Council released *How People Learn: Brain, Mind, Experience, and School*, a tour de force report on what was known about cognition and learning that provided additional dimensions for pedagogical research.

It has been nearly twenty years since *Scholarship Reconsidered* was published, and today SoTL is a well-known phrase used by multiple national and international organizations such as the International Alliance for Teaching Scholars (IATS) and the International Society for the Scholarship of Teaching and Learning (ISSOTL). Labels are empowering entities. Akin to the political force, visibility, and ownership that the politically correct terms such as Asian American and African American gave members of the related ethnic groups, SoTL has provided faculty interested in pedagogical research a rallying cry and a flag to follow. As the following chapters will show, with the publicizing of the phrase SoTL in response to Boyer and subsequent work of his Carnegie colleagues (e.g., Shulman and Hutchins) among others, this type of research has been recognized only recently in most disciplines as a legitimate area of scholarship, worthy of recognition equal to that of more traditional lines of research and inquiry. However as Kuh (2004) notes, this "new" line of research, is really a new spin on what researchers in certain fields of study have focused on for decades. So what has been going on in other fields? It is time for a short excursion into the history of pedagogical research.

The Other SoTL: Action Research and Teacher Research

As previously stated, educators have been examining their own teaching long before the advent of the phrase SoTL. Two major movements, *action research* (as it is more commonly referred to in North America) and *teacher research* (as a similar movement is more often referred to in the United Kingdom), also involve the systematic examination of teaching and learning. These investigations primarily conducted in K-12 settings are consequently off the radar of most higher-education faculty but provide many useful parallels and procedures.

Action research. Action research is any systematic inquiry conducted to gather information about how schools operate, how they teach, and how well their students learn (Mills, 2007). The origins of action research are obscure, but Kurt Lewin in the mid-1940s constructed a theory that described action research as "proceeding in a spiral of steps, each of which is composed of planning, action and the evaluation of the result of action" (Kemmis & McTaggert, 1990, p. 8). Lewin argued that in order to "understand and change certain social practices, social scientists have to include practitioners from the real social world in all phases of inquiry" (McKernan 1991, p. 10). This construction of action research theory by Lewin made action research a method of acceptable inquiry, and it grew in prominence worldwide. In the United States, action research had its roots in the progressive education movement and the work of John Dewey. In the United Kingdom action research fostered curricular reform and increased professionalism in teaching, and in Australia, action research brought about collaborative curriculum planning (Mills, 2007). Currently, action research is the preferred modus operandi for teacher-researchers.

The teacher-researcher movement. The simple combination of the words "teacher" and "researcher" serve as an upfront indicator of the twin thrust of this movement. While teachers educate as subjective insiders involved in classroom interaction, researchers traditionally design studies to answer questions of interest and are merely objective outside observers of classroom processes (MacClean & Mohr, 1999). But when teachers become teacher-researchers, the "traditional descriptions of both teachers and researchers change. Teacher-researchers raise questions about what they think and observe about their teaching and their students' learning. They collect student work in order to evaluate performance, but they also see student work as data to analyze in order to examine the teaching and learning that produced it" (Maclean & Mohr, 1999, p. x).

Originating in the United Kingdom with the work of Stenhouse (1975) and the Humanities Curriculum Project, teacher-researchers are now found worldwide. Stenhouse felt that all teaching should be based upon research, and that research and curriculum development were the preserve of teachers (McKernan, 1991). Other significant teacher-researcher developments include the Ford Teaching Project, the Classroom Action Research Network, and work supported by the National Writing Project.

How is action or teacher research different from SoTL? Apart from the superficial labeling difference where the former terms are more often used for K-12 and secondary-school-level research on teaching and learning whereas the latter is applied to higher education, SoTL tends to emphasize the use of disciplinary-specific methodologies. As we move into the next generation of SoTL research, these disciplinary differences are diminished. Faculty are more likely to want to use the best method to answer their pedagogical questions and not limit themselves to the methodologies of their home fields, which can prove limiting. In fact, the current literature documents traditional and traditionally problematic pedagogies. We hope this book will inspire the movement toward re-envisioning disciplinary-based pedagogies through the lens of how students actually learn and seeking evidence for that learning. We present a framework for the next stage of SoTL whereby scholars connect their own work on teaching and learning to the work already out there on traditional pedagogies and learning in their disciplines.

Beginnings

Although the term SoTL is a somewhat relative newcomer to the scene, people have been thinking about how to improve teaching and learning for centuries. In a recent history of the field of educational psychology, Berliner traces the modern trend of thinking about individual differences, development, the nature of the material being taught, problem solving, and assessment to the ancient Jewish rite of the Passover (2006, p. 4). The leader of the Passover service told the story of the Passover each year but differently to each of his sons according to the sons' own specific aptitudes. Plato and Aristotle discussed such topics as the role of the teacher, the relations between teacher and student, and the means and methods of teaching (Watson, 1961). Berliner (2006) similarly describes how writers down the centuries from the Roman Quintilian (first century), Juan Luis Vives (fifteenth century), Comenius (sixteenth century), Herbart (eighteenth century), to the philosopher Joseph Scwhab (1973) have given serious thought to, and written about, education. Education psychologists also have identified a "father of research on teaching," Joseph Mayer Rice

(1912), who conducted empirical classroom-based research, and a "grandfather," William James (1842–1910), mentioned previously, who was asked to present Cambridge educators with lectures on the new psychology (James, 1899/2006). Other psychologists have tackled education. G. Stanley Hall, the first president of the American Psychological Association, was professor of psychology *and* pedagogy at Johns Hopkins University. John Dewey, like Hall, was a former classroom teacher who respected the complexity of teaching and also contributed greatly to the methodological study of education (Dewey, 1910).

Researchers in the area of student development take a completely different tack. focusing primarily on the psychosocial development of the student and how the level of development influences student learning. To measure student development, a number of inventories were developed to assess how students change and develop during their college years, including the Iowa Student Development Inventory (Hood, 1986) and the Student Developmental Task Inventory (Prince, Miller, & Winston, 1974). However, this field includes a wide range of areas of study, and some of particular interest to us, including an examination of the knowledge and cognitive skills that students are expected to acquire during the college years. In this area of the field of student development we measure the development of cognitive skills such as higher-order thinking and reasoning abilities. Research by Perry (1970), Gilligan (1982), and Wood (1983) led to the development of assessment tools to measure higher-order thinking. Interestingly, results from this line of research illustrated the limited cognitive skills of most entering first-year college students. This in turn led to discussions of how to teach these students given their level of cognitive development when entering college. Therefore, the question of pedagogical choices and their impact on student learning is not a new field of inquiry. However, in past decades the majority of those involved in this area of scholarship were in the field of higher education and/or psychology. In particular, students at the undergraduate level who are "majoring" in the field of education learn how one chooses effective teaching strategies, focusing on the questions of interest to scholars in the area of SoTL. Interestingly, this is rarely a component for students at the graduate level who are obtaining a doctoral degree, many of whom will be teaching at colleges and universities across the globe.

Fortunately, in more recent years, this line of research is one of interest to academics across all fields who are interested in determining just how effective they are at teaching.

The foremost champion of SoTL is undoubtedly the Carnegie Foundation for the Advancement of Teaching, which, since 1905, has carried out a wide range of activities and research that has helped to support and advance the work of teachers at all levels. In 1998, the Carnegie Academy for the Scholarship of Teaching (CASTL) was established when Lee Shulman became president of the Carnegie Foundation. CASTL was formed to provide faculty with ways to optimize postsecondary teaching and learning. The program has three parts. CASTL funds faculty as "Carnegie Scholars" and has them conduct research on specific pedagogical topics, offers campus programs for colleges and universities to foster SoTL, and provides initiatives with disciplinary groups aimed at fostering SoTL within their disciplines. The first program has involved over 150 faculty as fellows at the CASTL advanced study center in Palo Alto, California, and the other two initiatives have initiated a number of publications and conferences (see Huber and Hutchings, 2005, for a detailed report). A great deal of the advancement of the field of SoTL can be credited to the many individuals involved with CASTL. This foundation started the support, and continues to do so, necessary for this line of line of research to become a viable component of the academic culture on campuses both nationally and internationally. Through the efforts of those involved with CASTL, teaching is no longer a private endeavor but instead a topic of discussion that involves critical analysis of how we foster learning in the classroom.

Why is this is an important questions for all instructors to ask? As Shulman states, "an educator can teach with integrity only if an effort is made to examine the impact of his or her work on the students" (2002, p. vii), an obligation that he refers to as the pedagogical imperative. Like many others who are active in the field of SoTL, Shulman points out that assessment of our pedagogical choices should be an inherent component of our teaching.

There are other champions of pedagogical research. The Lilly Foundation has long been a supporter of teaching enhancement and has been funding faculty scholars nationwide since the 1970s. It also supports an international conference, as well as four national conferences around America. Although now defunct, the AAHE (American Association of Higher Education) also sponsored many initiatives over the years to advance teaching and its scholarship, as has the Pew Foundation.

Still others have greatly contributed to pedagogical research, but are not linked to foundations such as the Carnegie and Lilly Foundations. Maryellen Weimer for example, one-time associate director of the National Center on Postsecondary Teaching, Learning, and Assessment and editor of the *Teaching Professor* newsletter on college teaching, has greatly helped guide and foster pedagogical research (see Menges, Weimer & associates, 1996; Weimer, 2006). Going beyond the previously discussed traditional sources, it is important to also include a look at how SoTL is conducted and defined outside America. For example Hounsell and Entwistle spearhead the British Enhancing Teaching and Learning (ETL) Project, which seeks to develop subject-specific conceptual frameworks to guide institutional and faculty or departmental development of teaching-learning environments. This group has developed a number of useful tools for pedagogical research and has also mapped out key variables that influence learning. We shall discuss work from the ETL Project in greater detail in later chapters.

Why Is Pedagogical Research Important?

Every discipline survives by training new minds to carry on the work. Although only a small number of majors may go on to graduate work, research, and teaching in the same area as their undergraduate degrees, it is upon their shoulders that academic traditions rest. Every discipline gathers and creates knowledge in different ways. The art historian combs through ancient manuscripts in foreign tongues. The chemist titrates liquids and analyzes mass spectrometry. For the philosopher, logic reigns supreme, whereas for the biologist empirical data may be the Holy Grail. That said, research is only one part of what we do as educators in academic settings. We all teach. We all step into classrooms (or virtual realities if teaching online) to help our students learn.

Those who teach far outnumber those who do basic or applied research. For example whereas only about 3,000 Ph.D.s in psychology are granted in a given year, one and a half million students take introductory psychology every year. Those who teach therefore carry a great responsibility. It is upon them that we rely to convey the basics about our various disciplines. Through general education and via requirements for the majors and minors, teachers nationwide help students learn about the different areas that make up the academy. But it is not only on the doctorate holders that we rely on to educate. Men and women with many levels of education – those in K-12 education, secondary schools, community colleges and four-year colleges and universities – all work to teach students and help them learn. This shared common goal, to educate our students no matter what the discipline or topic, is what unites all educators. Yes, there are those who *want* to teach and others who just *have* to teach, but at some level all teachers want their students to learn. You can vary in what evidence you will accept to say that learning has taken place. You can vary in how much you care about whether learning has taken place. You can vary in the extent to which you assume learning has taken place. But at the heart of it all is still the goal to have students learn. How do we know if the students are learning? Beyond the simple rubric of exam grades and appreciative nods of understanding lies the challenge we all face as teachers: the challenge to establish that our teaching is working and our students are learning.

A Teaching Hierarchy

Is pedagogical research for everyone? If you want to optimize your teaching and your students' learning you will want to do pedagogical research at some level. Doing this research (and calling it "research") does not have to entail the use of complex statistical models (chapter 4 will give you an introduction to the varieties of statistics that can be used) or hours of interviewing or content analysis of student writing. You could do all that, but the method you use will depend on your question (chapter 2 will discuss how to make that important connection). It is more important to decide where you want to be on the teaching hierarchy (see figure 1.1).

We have little doubt that if you're reading this book, you reside higher up on our pyramid. However, there are many instructors who are essentially just *going through the motions* of teaching. They pick a textbook for their classes with little thought of the quality of the textbook but perhaps go on what they have heard many others use or the urging of a particularly persuasive textbook representative. Their syllabi contain only the most basic information and they do not really pay too much attention to what a good syllabus should contain and less attention to what students need to get from a syllabus. They go to all their classes and make their way through the material often using lecture materials they have written a long time before and reused, and material written more with an eye towards what they find interesting and capable of teaching than what the course and students really require. They mostly lecture, include little if any active learning strategies, and make no effort to improve their teaching. They are often sticklers for rules, not willing to take the time to listen to students

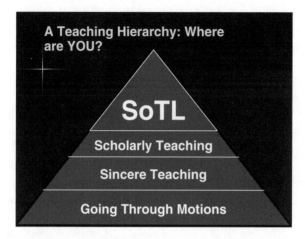

A Teaching Hierarchy: Where are YOU?

SoTL

Scholarly Teaching

Sincere Teaching

Going Through Motions

Figure 1.1: A teaching hierarchy

who may have valid reasons not to stick to their mostly ambiguous but still rigid syllabi, and once a lecture, class period, or the semester is over, they do not think much of the class and may not even read their course evaluations (if they even use them). This scenario may seem somewhat extreme but we have both heard of and even talked to some instructors who are truly just going through the motions.

A nice notch up are instructors who are involved in *sincere teaching*. These instructors care about students and are sincere about doing a good job at teaching. They spend time looking at all the textbooks available for their classes and then take the time to read through textbook options before deciding on one. They make sure they check their university requirements to ensure their syllabi include everything they should. They check the syllabi of colleagues and spend time revising their syllabi with an eye towards the students who read and rely on such documents. They also spend time on their lectures. They may change lectures often to make sure they are including the most up-to-date material. They take pains to search for visuals and examples to bring the lectures to life and they also try and ensure that their students have an opportunity to participate in class, allocating time to discussion of the material. They may also willingly incur the load of grading by assigning papers and using short-answer or essay-exam questions in lieu of the easier-to-process multiple-choice exam. These instructors reflect on their performances and adapt and change in response to bad days or lectures that do not go well. Instead of plodding on ahead with their set plans for the class, they take the time to modify delivery or format to better serve their students. Not only do they pay close attention to their student evaluations, they may even have students evaluate them at many times during the semester to make sure they are doing a good job. They keep good tabs on the grade distributions and take pains to examine the causes of anomalous student performance. We believe that a significant portion of educators are teaching as described here. As you can see, this location on the hierarchy sounds pretty good and is clearly a far cry from the person going through the motions.

But there is more. Some instructors go beyond their gut reactions and the counsel of friends and colleagues in course design, the syllabi, what they do in class, how they prepare lectures, and how they evaluate learning by actually conducting formal or informal studies of their teaching. These instructors often rely on the published literature on teaching and learning to modify their own teaching and almost always use some basic rudiment of the scientific method. Essentially, they start by identifying a problem, then review the literature to see if and how the problem has been dealt with, then modify what they do, and then measure student outcomes to see if the changes they have made have resulted in changes in student learning. This basic process, which we shall elaborate on in the next two chapters, is the core of the scientific method and is one that provides rigor. Instructors who are not only teaching (such as those in level two) but who are methodologically working to improve teaching and learning are *scholarly teachers*. Well described by Richlin (2001, 2006), this type of teacher may create a course design portfolio to document their systematically collected observations for further reflection and course modification. This allows for the identification of problem areas, and, unlike the teacher who may also informally analyze student problem areas, the scholarly teacher takes pains to venture into the pedagogical publications in search of solutions. This use of an organized methodology is primarily done for the teachers' own benefit, to make their next class better. The results of their reflections and course modifications may be written up in a teaching portfolio (Seldin, 2004) and may be used to review the instructor for merit or promotion, but is not sent out for publication or even shared with peers.

Conducting formal investigations of teaching and learning (regardless of method), placing the results in the context of relevant published pedagogical literature, and then submitting it for peer review and subsequent publication makes the scholarly teacher into one involved in the Scholarship of Teaching and Learning (SoTL). Currently, it is the actual dissemination of one's own investigations using a peer-reviewed procedure (as compared to posting your own work on your own website and emailing it to a listserve or colleagues) that entitles one to the SoTL stamp. Does one need to climb to this level of the hierarchy? Given that the only real distinction between scholarly teaching and SoTL is peer-reviewed publication, students will probably be as well served by scholarly teachers and teachers as by practitioners of SoTL. That said, the exposure to best practices, innovation, and pedagogical literature that being in the top two levels affords will undoubtedly make one a better teacher and hence serve students better. Furthermore, it is likely that exposing one's work to the scrutiny of peer review of SoTL will ensure that flaws are minimized, loopholes are identified, and methodologies are watertight.

The disciplines of conducting SoTL and being a scholarly teacher have many benefits, and both fall squarely into our conceptualization of pedagogical research. We believe it is important to use the best methods possible to examine your own teaching and to optimize your students' learning. If you are not familiar with the methods you need to test your specific questions or are unsure of what sort of observations or evidence of learning you need to collect, the key is find the resources to fill the gaps. That is where this book comes in. If you are in the second level, a passionate, caring teacher who wants to conduct pedagogical research, regardless of whether you want only to optimize your class and students (and be a scholarly teacher) or to publish your findings to add to the knowledge base of the discipline and field (and conduct SoTL), the ensuing chapters have all you need to get started. Scholarly teachers can take pains to read the pedagogical literature and change the way they teach based on what they find, but if they do not do any systematic assessment of whether the changes they implemented made a difference, then they are not really doing pedagogical research. Even if the scholarly teacher does decide to do pedagogical research, unless they disseminate their findings to a wider audience (preferably via a peer-reviewed publication), few would consider their own classroom innovations and assessments SoTL. In this book, we will refer to any peer-reviewed pedagogical publications or work aimed for wide dissemination as SoTL. Personal investigations of one's own teaching or one's students' learning (even formal examinations and assessments) will be referred to by the more general term "pedagogical research," as it need not be published or planned for publication (though one hopes the work is robust enough to be publishable).

A Caveat

We would be remiss if we urged SoTL without a word of warning. We must acknowledge the existence of resistance towards SoTL at different levels in different institutions (whether the faculty, the administration, or the Board of Regents). There are schools where doing pedagogical research is seen as a distraction from the "main area of research." There are schools where tenure decisions are not aided by SoTL. In the last chapter we will discuss some of the possible reasons why SoTL has generated resistance and discuss institutional contexts that have embraced SoTL, including works by Cox (2001, 2004) in which transformation of higher-education institutions into learning communities is discussed.

The academic community is changed when SoTL becomes a valued priority, both at the undergraduate level, where faculty use SoTL in the classroom, and at the doctoral level, where programs are shaping the next generation of faculty. We believe that pedagogical research in general and SoTL in particular can lead to new models of teaching and learning and in turn can create an environment in which discussion of teaching and learning is the norm and these exchanges can further improve the academy.

What do you want your students to learn before leaving your class? This is perhaps one of the most prudent questions that teachers should ask. There are clearly others (e.g., How can you get students to pay attention? How can you get students to read the book?). All of these questions can be asked and then addressed using pedagogical research.

How Can Pedagogical Research Be Useful to You?

After the preceding caveat some good news is in order. There is a veritable bounty of benefits to doing pedagogical research.

Effective teaching. By its very nature, SoTL directly influences how effective your teaching is in terms of student learning. Engaging in pedagogical research will help you become a more effective teacher, as you become increasingly aware of your classroom practices and make strides toward systemic change. You will learn to be mindful of your teaching practices and gear everything you do to clearly assessable outcomes. Another big benefit to thinking about how you teach and diving into the literature on teaching is that it will serve to energize you for the classroom. A number of our mid-career colleagues have reported that engaging in pedagogical research has given them a fresh look at the classroom and injected their teaching with new life and energy. You may be surprised by what even reading the literature on teaching and learning can do for your own attitude towards teaching and your course design.

Research opportunities. Being energized to teach from reading the literature can also make you really want to do pedagogical research of your own and on your own classes. Pedagogical research is real, quantifiable, and rigorous research. More and more departments are counting SoTL publications toward decisions about tenure and promotion, though this is not yet universal (McKinney, 2007).

Tenure and promotion. Teaching effectively is one thing, but proving your effectiveness is quite another. Pedagogical research makes it easy to demonstrate your practices in the classroom and highlights your active interest in improving your teaching. Outcomes from pedagogical research make natural components of teaching portfolios, which are often used in tenure and promotion decisions. What are the methods of your discipline? What are the shortcomings? What are the advantages? The portfolio and your mindful consideration of teaching in your discipline can provide all the answers.

Beyond these major benefits, engaging in pedagogical research can be very satisfying. It allows you to solve the mysteries that may plague your non-conscious mind, those little things you wonder about after you leave a class (more so after a really difficult class – why did it go that badly? – but also after a particularly exceptional one – why did that go so well?). Most of us wonder about our techniques, our course designs, and how our students perform and behave, but not all of us take the time to investigate the issues in depth. Pedagogical research provides us with an understanding of a myriad of issues and helps us gain perspective on the complex interplay of factors that is education. If you take your explorations into the realm of SoTL (beyond scholarly teaching) you also stand to inform your colleagues in academe, the administration, and the tax-paying public.

Whether you are someone who has been teaching for 30 or more years or are someone who has still to step in front of a classroom of students, we hope the topics discussed in this book will give you a lot to think about and at least something to work on. You will probably run into some things you are familiar with, but we trust you will also encounter many things that will be somewhat new.

2

Pedagogical Research

Focusing on the Teaching

Have you every walked out of the classroom and wondered if you chose the right teaching approach? Have you ever said to a colleague, "I have no idea if they understood a word I said," or, "It seemed like everything I said was going right over their heads"? Given the assessment techniques available, there is no reason to leave the classroom without knowing what the students learned or did not learn that day. Angelo and Cross (1993) point out that using classroom assessment techniques (CATs) on a regular basis can eliminate the uncertainty that often occurs before giving a test in your class. If throughout the semester you are aware of what the students understand, you should find that students do well on the tests that are developed to evaluate student learning outcomes. You should be able to eliminate that unwanted surprise of finding out that most students were unable to answer certain questions on a final exam. Of course, this is just one of the many benefits to doing pedagogical research on your teaching. Choosing the appropriate tools to answer the questions above is also the first step toward your pedagogical research program, where your area of scholarship and teaching can come together through systematic evaluation of your teaching and student learning. These tools are also useful when you are interested in evaluating a particular teaching technique you are using in your classroom. Is this technique improving your students' understanding of the material?

But how exactly does one assess teaching effectiveness? Once you have identified your learning goals, you can identify the appropriate assessment to use. How do you determine which assessment tool is the appropriate one to use? What tools are available? How does one use the results of those assessments to make changes? How do you start the process of conducting this type of research? How do you share your findings with others in the field of pedagogical research, including how to present this type of scholarship to your colleagues, your institution, and to others in the field of SoTL?

This chapter will provide you with answers to these many questions and demonstrate the steps needed for a successful pedagogical research program. We focus here on the "what works" questions, one area in the taxonomy of questions in the field of SoTL (Hutchings, 2000). Below, we review much of the literature on what is known about effective teaching including how to connect one's teaching goals with the types of teaching techniques chosen, and how to develop valid assessment tools to determine the effectiveness of that choice. Finally we also focus on how to reflect on the outcome of these assessments and decide which changes in teaching strategies might be worthwhile. In the end you will know how to create a coherent teaching experience and base your choice of teaching method on your own pedagogical research findings.

To accomplish this goal, we first discuss how to validly assess if your pedagogical approach and assessment choices are accomplishing your learning goals. As Hutchings (2000) points out, there is no method or approach that works for everyone. In other words, one size does not fit all, which makes sense since we have different priorities when it comes to the learning goals we create for our classrooms. Our discipline-specific training often shapes the way we think about our teaching, allowing us to apply a particular approach to answer the questions that are most important to a particular topic matter. Many disciplines may even have "signature pedagogies" (Gurung, Haynie, and Chick, in press; Shulman, 2005), specific ways of teaching. However, although our disciplines do influence what we teach and often how we teach, the process of determining the most appropriate methods is applicable to all regardless of the type of institution where one teaches or the field in which one is trained. Interestingly, as Huber (2001) points out in her chapter that focuses on disciplinary styles in the scholarship of teaching, we differ from one discipline to the next with regard to our traditional teaching practices, but so often the effectiveness of these traditional practices have not been examined. Are we making the right choice?

As we stated in the first chapter, conducting pedagogical research to assess your teaching is beneficial at many levels. First and foremost, this type of assessment should theoretically make you a more effective teacher, and in turn your students will more likely achieve your intended learning outcomes. When conducting pedagogical research on your own teaching, you also create an objective measure of the effectiveness of your teaching that can be presented within the confines of your institution, when questions of tenure and promotion are raised, in relation to questions of assessment for an accrediting agency, and also within the context of your field of study, when awards of teaching excellence are obtainable and documentation concerning your teaching is essential. Your need for developing pedagogical assessment tools might be based on a new expectation at your institution of some type of assessment of your teaching or their departmental goals. As Berk (2006) points out, the information available for these types of decisions is often weak, or, as he so eloquently puts it, "BLECCCH" (p. 2). Finally, in addition to creating valid measures of your effectiveness as a teacher, you also broaden your scholarship beyond your discipline-specific research area and create scholarly work that contributes to the SoTL body of literature.

Assessing Our Teaching Effectiveness

On many occasions, educators discuss their teaching strategies and the degree of success they feel they achieve when using a particular teaching technique. However, the degree of success is often measured not through carefully designed observations, by carefully development assessment tools, or by an empirically based collection of data to measure the degree of success. Instead, teaching effectiveness is most often determined through anecdotal comments made by students on course evaluation forms or by reflection on experiences in the classroom (Weimer, 2006). In fact, as Berk (2006) points out, student evaluations come first to mind when one brings up teaching assessment or evaluation. Some do believe the evaluation forms provide valuable information for making decisions regarding the effectiveness of teaching techniques, when at the end of the semester students have the experience in the course needed to provide comments (McKeachie, 1997). However, the end of the semester, and in particular the last week of class right before finals, might not be the best time for students to assess each course they take. One must keep in mind that the last week of classes is also the time when students are most anxious about studying for their upcoming finals or completing papers for numerous classes before finals begin. They might not take the time necessary to complete the entire form or to even provide valid responses. In addition, because they are completed at the end of the semester, these comments can be useful for future courses but do not allow you to monitor learning throughout the semester or make changes during the semester at hand (see also our discussion of formative versus summative assessments below).

As is true for any construct we are interested in measuring, it is best to include multiple sources of assessment to increase the likelihood that the sources of information we use are valid and reliable indicators. Conducting pedagogical research throughout the semester provides the multiple indicators of effectiveness and allows you to determine student learning not only at exam time, but when you wish to check that the level of understanding meets your learning goals at any point in time. Therefore, student evaluations can provide valuable information but are not necessarily a sufficient source of information for your pedagogical research. Rather, you are better off using additional assessments in your classroom to answer the precise questions you have about your teaching and student learning. Choosing and/or developing these assessment tools will be discussed below.

So why assess? Including measures of teaching effectiveness is a valuable undertaking on several grounds. You are more aware of what your students are learning in your classroom, you create coherence between your teaching goals and teaching techniques, the results provide you with valuable data for a discussion of your pedagogy beyond the standard course evaluations in place, and this line of inquiry can be used to develop an interesting line of scholarship based on your pedagogical research. As the definition above indicates, scholarly activity focused on pedagogy goes beyond creating a teaching portfolio, or reflecting on the effectiveness of our teaching techniques, or using course evaluations to improve our teaching. Hutchings and Shulman (1999) point out the important distinction that differentiates teaching from scholarly teaching from scholarship of teaching and learning. As they note, mirroring the teaching hierarchy we introduced in chapter 1, all faculty are expected to teach well, but that is different from scholarly teaching. Scholarly teaching includes use of SoTL findings in the classroom, peer observation of teaching, and classroom assessment techniques. Finally, those engaged in SoTL conduct original research focused on teaching and student learning and share findings with others in the field. One could argue that any faculty member, even those deemed "the best college teachers" (Bain, 2004), could benefit from careful reflection on the choice of teaching strategy and how one assesses the effectiveness of that choice. As Fink (1995) states, we need to make the distinction between thinking we are doing a good job to knowing we are doing well through use of valid objective assessment methods that eliminates biases. As Ludy Benjamin so eloquently stated "If you teach, learn to do it well; if you do it well, learn to do it better" (Buskist and Keeley, 2005).

Despite its value as an important tool to increase our success in the classroom and in our role as faculty, many of us are not trained to develop the appropriate methods needed for such an undertaking because so often our graduate training does not include a teaching component. Fortunately, a paradigm shift occurred during the last decade, in which institutions and faculty were asked for evidence of student learning. This in turn required the development of learning assessment tools in order to provide the assessment data needed to illustrate that students were in fact achieving the stated learning goals. As Zhao and Kuh (2004) point out, this shift towards requiring assessment data has led to an established field of assessment at the postsecondary level. This established field of assessment should be the perfect resource as we attempt to choose the appropriate tools to assess the effectiveness of our teaching.

When faculty are hired, they are expected to provide effective classroom instruction, and this expectation remains throughout their tenure. In the past, this assumption was often accompanied by the notion that effective teaching required little assistance from colleagues or anyone else at the institution. Far too often, colleges and universities touted the excellence of their faculty, yet rarely was this backed by any resources to assist with obtaining that level of excellence or any method of determining whether teachers were effective. In fact, in many cases at institutions labeled as "Research I," faculty members were often discouraged from taking time away from their scholarship/research to improve their teaching. Too often, assumptions were made that anyone making efforts to improve teaching skills was not spending enough time on scholarly efforts. Fortunately, over the last two decades many institutions have embraced the idea of providing support to assist faculty in teaching effectively and developing pedagogical research programs. For many institutions, building a campus culture that supports SoTL was greatly assisted by CASTL. One component of this effort was coordinated by the American Association for Higher Education (AAHE), titled the Teaching Academy Teaching Program, which focused on creating a campus culture where SoTL can thrive when the scholarship of teaching and learning is an inherent part of the teaching process (Hutchings, 2000). More details about these initiatives are included in chapter 5 in this text, which discusses faculty development/teaching and learning centers.

Engaging in the scholarship of teaching and learning can serve to inculcate new faculty into the academic life as well as reenergize mid- and late-career faculty. New faculty are often faced with the overwhelming task of preparing course material for courses they have never taught before, often focusing on the content that must be covered rather than the way in which the content is taught. Seasoned faculty are often comfortable with their teaching methods, which they believe have passed the test of time.

A Degree without the Teaching Tools

With a Ph.D. in hand, many of us leave our graduate work behind and head on to a new institution as faculty members who will be teaching a number of courses as well as continuing our scholarship in our chosen field of study. We are brimming with enthusiasm at the thought of teaching students how to think critically about the mass media in an Introduction to Mass Media course or theories of the electronic structure and bonding of molecules in a course on Molecular Structure. As we search for faculty positions, most of us hear during the interview process that reappointment and tenure decisions are based on the areas of teaching, scholarship, and service, with the emphasis on each determined by the type of institution we decide is the best fit for us (e.g., research I vs. liberal arts vs. community college).

For most of us, our program of scholarship continues the work we began in graduate school, which of course makes perfect sense given that much our time in graduate school is focused on our research and in particular our dissertation. For many new faculty members that part of the transition from student to faculty is not too daunting. However, as we start off our careers in the classroom on the "other side of the desk" we are constantly faced with questions of how to teach students in the classroom and what is the best approach given our teaching and learning goals. For some, who have only taught as teaching assistants, complete ownership of a course is a new experience. For many others, teaching one course at a time was a very common experience as a graduate student or post-doc. Some graduate programs have incorporated learning how to teach as a requirement in the doctoral program, incorporating programs through an initiative called "Preparing Future Faculty," which provides graduate students with opportunities to observe and experience faculty responsibilities. But most people complete graduate school with extensive knowledge of the content of their discipline and very little training in how to effectively teach others about that discipline, not to mention learning how to assess whether they are effective at teaching beyond the use of student evaluations. We would never assume that you cannot teach something you don't know, but many make the assumption that you can teach what you know well without learning how to teach. This may be true of someone "going through the motions" (see figure 1.1), but this is surprising to many unfamiliar with the world of academia. After all, if a majority of those obtaining doctorates are going to become faculty members at our colleges and universities, wouldn't most assume that they have also learned how to teach and how to determine whether they are effectively teaching their students? Although the questions about how to teach are more obvious when we start out as faculty, we believe that how we teach and how our choices in the classroom significantly change our students' learning potential should be part of our "teaching conscious" throughout our academic careers. As Fink (1995) states, we need to make the distinction between thinking we are doing a good job and knowing we are doing well through use of valid objective assessment methods that eliminates biases.

Many faculty members have never tested the effectiveness of a chosen teaching method or whether an alternative would be better. Why? The most common response would be: "There is not enough time to teach, continue scholarly activity, provide service to the college, *and* evaluate my teaching methods." This is exactly why combining one's teaching and scholarship might be the perfect solution (or at least applying the skills of the latter to inform and test the former). When faced with the challenge of showing promise as both a teacher and a scholar, why not combine these two avenues of professional development, which will allow you to do best in the classroom and at the same time produce scholarly work based on this pedagogical research? This type of scholarly activity focused on pedagogy goes beyond creating a teaching portfolio, or reflecting on the effectiveness of your teaching techniques, or using course evaluations to improve your teaching. It also takes you from being a scholarly teacher to a practitioner of SoTL.

Acquiring the Necessary Tools

Let's face it: unless one is obtaining a doctorate in cognitive psychology or education, rarely are new faculty members exposed to the field of cognitive science, in which thinking and learning are systematically examined (National Research Council, 2001). In fact, many faculty interested in conducting pedagogical research will need to learn a set of investigative techniques that are very different from the research methods used in their own area of expertise and are often not knowledgeable about the type of methodology and design techniques used when examining teaching and learning. If you are a social scientist you likely completed a number of classes in research methods and design as well as statistical analyses that are very applicable to a research program examining pedagogy. However, for those of you trained in disciplines such as the arts or humanities, your research training is quite different and possibly not applicable to a research program focused on teaching and learning. In addition to learning methodology, you may be interested in learning how to create the important connections between learning goals, teaching techniques, and assessment tools. Understanding how to make these connections is also an essential tool for conducting pedagogical research.

If we aren't provided with formal training on how to teach or to determine how well we are teaching, how then do we determine if we are reaching our stated learning goals? Many faculty members learn about effective teaching strategies through trial and error during their first appointment on the faculty. As they teach each course, certain strategies are deemed successful, while changes are often made when other strategies clearly need to be rejected or transformed. Success and failure are often determined by how well students perform on exams or how much they rant or rave on course evaluations. For most faculty, the idea of systematic inquiry of teaching effectiveness is very new (Hutchings, 2002). Once again, this would likely be a surprise to those outside the academic world. We all know the cost of attending college; should it not be assumed that those teaching the young men and women attending those colleges assess how effectively they are teaching and students are learning?

What Can We Learn from the "Best" College Teachers?

Before we discuss what needs improvement, let us think about what it really means to be an effective teacher. A number of researchers have focused on identifying those behaviors and characteristics believed to be qualities of effective teachers. Bain (2004) identified what he called "the best college teachers" and was interested in determining what they do to help their students achieve exceptional learning in their classrooms. After determining how to identify these outstanding teachers, Bain then conducted interviews with students and teachers, videotaped and observed class meetings, and reviewed course material to determine exactly what these teachers do and how they think. The qualitative data led to a number of conclusions, which Bain pointed out cannot simply provide a "to-do-list" for those interested in improving their teaching methods. On the contrary, his findings illustrate the fact that effective teaching requires, not surprisingly,

Box 2.1: Major Conclusions from Bain's Research Defining the Best Teachers

What they know and understand
  active and accomplished scholars in their field can simplify and clarify complex
    subjects
  intuitive understanding of human learning

How they prepare to teach
  see teaching as intellectually demanding
  equal priority to teaching and scholarship

What they expect of their students
  create high expectations for their students
  create expectations that require real-life thinking

What they do when they teach
  create a challenging learning environment
  provide students with a sense of control of their education
  create collaborative learning conditions
  provide feedback prior to performance evaluation

How they treat students
  with a great deal of respect
  with an assumption that students want to learn
  share their own intellectual experiences

How they check student progress and evaluate their efforts
  use of systematic assessment
  focus on learning objectives

"careful and sophisticated thinking, deep professional learning, and often fundamental conceptual shifts" (p. 15).

So what was discovered about the "best teachers?" In box 2.1 we show the categories under which Bain's conclusions fall and then list some of the characteristics identified within each category. For a description of each, we point you to Bain's easy-to-read book, which provides details for each category and findings within each category. Of particular interest to us is the finding that Bain's exceptional teachers all used a variety of assessment tools to measure student learning and that assessment results were examined in terms of intellectual and personal development and the nature of that development. In other words, these teachers were more interested in finding out about how well their students understood the material and were less interested in using assessment to measure student performance. This is an important distinction to think about as you develop your pedagogical research program. Are you interested in student learning, student performance, or both?

The types of behaviors found by Bain are similar to those discovered by Buskist, who also conducted research on what he called "master teachers" to determine what teaching behaviors are associated with effective teaching (Buskist, 2004). Buskist et al. (2002) then developed the *Teacher Behavior Checklist* (TBC), which identifies one's overall teaching score, followed by a score for one factor that measures interpersonal caring and supportive skills, and a second subscore that examines one's professional competency and communication skills. You can find a copy of this checklist in box 2.2.

Box 2.2: The Teacher Behaviors Checklist

Instructor Evaluation – Dr. _____

Instructions: On the back of this sheet of 28 teacher qualities and the behaviors that define them. Please rate Dr. _____ on the extent to which you believe she (or he) possesses these qualities and exhibits the corresponding behaviors. Please use the following scale for your ratings by bubbling in the corresponding space in your scantron for each question/item number.

A   Dr. _____ always exhibits/has exhibited these behaviors reflective of this quality

B   Dr. _____ frequently exhibits/has exhibited these behaviors reflective of this quality

C   Dr. _____ sometimes exhibits/has exhibited these behaviors reflective of this quality

D   Dr. _____ rarely exhibits/has exhibited these behaviors reflective of this quality

E   Dr. _____ never exhibits/has exhibited these behaviors reflective of this quality

In addition, please use the space below on this side of the page to write any comments regarding Dr. _____'s teaching. These comments may include both what you find positive and negative about Dr. _____'s teaching.

Please be sure to read each item in this list carefully. Thank you.

(see next page)

Continued

Item Teacher Qualities and Corresponding Behaviors

1	*Accessible* (Posts office hours, gives out phone number, and e-mail information)
2	*Approachable/Personable* (Smiles, greets students, initiates conversations, invites questions, responds respectfully to student comments)
3	*Authoritative* (Establishes clear course rules; maintains classroom order; speaks in a loud, strong voice)
4	*Confident* (Speaks clearly, makes eye contact, and answers questions correctly)
5	*Creative and Interesting* (Experiments with teaching methods; uses technological devices to support and enhance lectures; uses interesting, relevant, and personal examples; not monotone)
6	*Effective Communicator* (Speaks clearly/loudly; uses precise English; gives clear, compelling examples)
7	*Encourages and Cares for Students* (Provides praise for good student work, helps students who need it, offers bonus points and extra credit, and knows student names)
8	*Enthusiastic about Teaching and about Topic* (Smiles during class, prepares interesting class activities, uses gestures and expressions of emotion to emphasize important points, and arrives on time for class)
9	*Establishes Daily and Academic Term Goals* (Prepares/follows the syllabus and has goals for each class)
10	*Flexible/Open-Minded* (Changes calendar of course events when necessary, will meet at hours outside of office hours, pays attention to students when they state their opinions, accepts criticism from others, and allows students to do make-up work when appropriate)
11	*Good Listener* (Doesn't interrupt students while they are talking, maintains eye contact, and asks questions about points that students are making)
12	*Happy/Positive Attitude/Humorous* (Tells jokes and funny stories, laughs with students)
13	*Humble* (Admits mistakes, never brags, and doesn't take credit for others' successes)
14	*Knowledgeable About Subject Matter* (Easily answers students' questions, does not read straight from the book or notes, and uses clear and understandable examples)
15	*Prepared* (Brings necessary materials to class, is never late for class, provides outlines of class discussion)

16	*Presents Current Information* (Relates topic to current, real-life situations; uses recent videos, magazines, and newspapers to demonstrate points; talks about current topics; uses new or recent texts)
17	*Professional* (Dresses nicely [neat and clean shoes, slacks, blouses, dresses, shirts, ties] and no profanity)
18	*Promotes Class Discussion* (Asks controversial or challenging questions during class, gives points for class participation, involves students in group activities during class)
19	*Promotes Critical Thinking/Intellectually Stimulating* (Asks thoughtful questions during class, uses essay questions on tests and quizzes, assigns homework, and holds group discussions/activities)
20	*Provides Constructive Feedback* (Writes comments on returned work, answers students' questions, and gives advice on test-taking)
21	*Punctuality/Manages Class Time* (Arrives to class on time/early, dismisses class on time, presents relevant materials in class, leaves time for questions, keeps appointments, returns work in a timely way)
22	*Rapport* (Makes class laugh through jokes and funny stories, initiates and maintains class discussions, knows student names, interacts with students before and after class)
23	*Realistic Expectations of Students/Fair Testing and Grading* (Covers material to be tested during class, writes relevant test questions, does not overload students with reading, teaches at an appropriate level for the majority of students in the course, curves grades when appropriate)
24	*Respectful* (Does not humiliate or embarrass students in class, is polite to students [says thank you and please, etc.], does not interrupt students while they are talking, does not talk down to students)
25	*Sensitive and Persistent* (Makes sure students understand material before moving to new material, holds extra study sessions, repeats information when necessary, asks questions to check student understanding)
26	*Strives to Be a Better Teacher* (Requests feedback on his/her teaching ability from students, continues learning [attends workshops, etc. on teaching], and uses new teaching methods)
27	*Technologically Competent* (Knows now to use a computer, knows how to use e-mail with students, knows how to use overheads during class, has a Web page for classes)
28	*Understanding* (Accepts legitimate excuses for missing class or coursework, is available before/after class to answer questions, does not lose temper at students, takes extra time to discuss difficult concepts)

Source: Keeley, Smith, and Buskist (2006).

Essentially, the checklist breaks down the qualities of a master teacher into three categories, which include knowledge, personality, and classroom management skills using a 28-item instrument. In the area of knowledge, master teachers illustrate not only their expertise in the content area but also illustrate to students how the content relates to other subject matter, and they demonstrate to their students how to think critically about the content. In terms of personality, there are a number of characteristics associated with the master teacher including approachable, genuine, humorous, respectful, and adaptable to the situation at hand in the classroom. However, the one characteristic that is most often associated with a master teacher is enthusiastic. Master teachers convey a genuine passion for the subject and in turn communicate a genuine joy for teaching. These personality characteristics are present both inside and outside of the classroom. Finally, Buskist discovered that master teachers also convey to their students a level of control in the classroom. They are very adept at handling the day-to-day problems faced in the classroom as well as the more difficult, though admittedly uncommon, situations one sometimes must face. Importantly, these teachers promote an academic culture of cooperation, making students feel at ease to speak their mind and be respectful of the voices of others. To help create this type of learning environment, active learning is often incorporated in the classroom to motivate students during the learning process.

The lesson from this line of research is that if one is aware of the types of behaviors most common among faculty who are identified by others as the best teachers or as master teachers, those of us who are interested in becoming more effective in the classroom can use this inventory to identify how our own teaching behaviors match those of the master teacher and/or attempt to incorporate those specific behaviors in our teaching if we find some of those behaviors are absent. Importantly, Buskist and Keeley (2005) point out that these are learnable behaviors. This is in contrast to suggestions that technique has little to do with good teaching (Palmer, 1998) or that some factors shown to contribute to the degree of learning are not learnable. For instance, findings from one recent study that examined non-instructional factors indicate that students learned more, had higher grades, and liked the class better when the instructor was not only likeable, well dressed, and approachable, but also attractive (Gurung & Vespia, 2007). In fact, in this study in which instructional variables such as the professor's knowledge of the topic was not included, attractiveness was the best predictor of student learning. So, why not take a look at the Teacher Behavior

Checklist and perhaps use it in your classroom to take control of the factors or behaviors we can amend and which we know influence student learning. You'll then be able to identify for yourself which behaviors and corresponding qualities you exhibit in the classroom. At this point you might be thinking, "Oh no, not another evaluation that will provide unreliable and/or invalid information regarding my teaching performance!" In fact, this is not the case. Evidence collected thorough psychometric analysis demonstrates both the validity and reliability of this sound teaching assessment instrument (Buskist, 2006). Wouldn't it also be an interesting exercise to fill out the TBC on your own in an attempt to determine what behaviors you believe you exhibit in the classroom and compare your responses to your students' responses? You might be surprised by the results, and perhaps this would provide an interesting starting point for your pedagogical research. Also of interest is whether the results of this checklist match your teaching philosophy. Do your behaviors in the classroom, fit your teaching philosophy? Next, we discuss the construction of teaching philosophies.

Creating your Teaching Philosophy Statement

As a faculty member, at some point during your career you will likely be asked to compose a statement on your philosophy of teaching. For some, writing this statement is needed during the job search process, as many are asked to include it within their materials when applying for a faculty position. When applying for a grant or a teaching award, a teaching philosophy is often required or recommended. Finally, for others, the reappointment process and tenure materials require a statement that illustrates self-reflection on your teaching. For our purposes, a teaching philosophy can be a guide to what is most important to you in the classroom and in turn what aspects of your teaching you are most interested in assessing. You could even create assessments to see whether in fact your classroom teaching matches your philosophy of teaching. Are you using the active learning you emphasize as an important component of your teaching? Are students actively engaged in your classroom? Keep in mind, your teaching philosophy statement should not be another presentation of your accomplishments listed on your CV. This statement should allow the reader to understand what you are like in the classroom. It should provide a clear understanding of how you structure your classes, your style of teaching, your thoughts on student learning, and how the two are related. This statement is also very useful to you as you determine how you can assess whether you are meeting the expectations you put forth in your teaching philosophy statement and consequently is a cornerstone of pedagogical research on teaching. To optimize your teaching, you should have a good sense of where you stand and what your own idea of optimal teaching is. By continually reviewing your statement on teaching you can change teaching behaviors when necessary and ultimately foster your professional and personal growth.

For many, writing this statement starts off as a difficult task. However, if you are given a set of questions for guidance, the difficult task of writing the statement becomes so easy your task changes to attempting to keep the statement to no more than two pages. Questions that are particularly helpful include the following:

Why do you teach?
What do you find rewarding about teaching?
What standards do you set in you classroom to define effective teaching?
What is unique about your teaching?
What works for you in the classroom and why?
What are your expectations for your students?
What effect are you having on your students and on their learning?
What would you like your students to learn?
Do you focus on content, skills, or both?
What do you use to test the effectiveness of achieving your student learning goals?

You should also consider including examples of classroom activities or teaching techniques that best illustrate your philosophy. In other words, it is not enough to say you focus on encouraging an active learning environment. You should provide ways in which you create that type of learning environment. These examples not only provide detail to the more general statements of teaching but often place your ideas within your discipline. Using examples allows readers to separate you from the pack. In the context of a job application, you can imagine the number of applicants that discuss creating a classroom of collaborative learners, making it difficult to distinguish one statement from the next. However, if you include specific ways in which you accomplish collaborative learning, you have identified your own way of teaching and not just a statement made by the masses.

In addition, many faculty include thoughts on strengths and weaknesses in the classroom: what do you believe you do best and what do you still need to work on with regard to your teaching? After all, you do not want to create a statement that sounds as if you are all-knowing about teaching. Instead, you want the statement to illustrate that you provide time for self-reflection with regard to your teaching and that this process allows for continual change in your pedagogical choices as you continue to improve how effective you are in the classroom. Do you have assessment data that led to these beliefs about strengths and weaknesses? Finally, when writing your statement, always remember that students are an important component of your teaching. Therefore, it is imperative that you provide an understanding of how students fit within your philosophy of teaching.

How Do I Teach?

So, our teaching philosophy provides a reflection on the type of teacher and teaching we hope to provide to our students and the Teaching Behavior Checklist allows us to obtain some information from our students (and perhaps even our peers) as to what we actually do in the classroom and how we are perceived by others as we teach. Almost every institution also requires faculty to use an evaluation form at the end of each semester for each course. This form is often a universal form, used by all faculty members, and in many cases allows administrators to obtain some type of assessment of your teaching in comparison to others. In this situation, the evaluation of your teaching is a summative one in which a personnel decision is often the outcome (e.g., promotion, tenure, merit pay). As we've expressed on a number of occasions in this book, we should also reflect on our teaching for reasons of formative evaluation, for which the information generated is used to provide us with ways in which we can improve our teaching. In comparison to summative evaluations, which are used at various points during one's career, formative evaluations are ongoing and are the basis for one's continuing professional development as a teacher and the content of pedagogical research.

How do you obtain the necessary information for either type of evaluation? Again, your home institution likely has a clear standard set of resources used to make the summative type of evaluations described above. However, the format or resources used for formative evaluations are usually less prescriptive. In the following section, we include a number of methods available to gather information about your teaching. As many in the field of teaching evaluation point out, the most valid and reliable way to assess one's teaching is to use multiple methods and multiple sources. Keep in mind that not all methods are appropriate in all instances of teaching assessment. Rather the methods you choose should be determined by the specific questions you have about your teaching and/or by the purpose of the evaluation. To choose the most appropriate evaluation methods, assessments that best fit your teaching, you should first determine your teaching style and teaching goals.

Using Teaching Inventories

As one begins to develop a research program focused on pedagogy, it is common to ask oneself, "How exactly do I teach?" or, "What is my style of teaching?" Even though many of us have taught for a number of years and therefore have a great deal of teaching experience, attempting to describe your own teaching style can be a difficult task. Often responses to this question focus on the way we teach our students. So for instance one faculty might respond by saying he uses primarily lectures in my classroom, while another faculty member might comment that she teaches using discussions. While the way in which we teach is an important component of how we teach, there are many other factors to consider in order to obtain the full picture of exactly "how" we teach. To get the full picture, the easiest way to examine your teaching is to start with an existing inventory developed to tap the many facets of teaching.

Anthony Grasha (1996) developed the *Teaching Style Inventory*, which consists of a series of questions that are rated on a Likert scale ranging from 1 to 5 (see box 2.3). This inventory can also be accessed online at http://www.iats.com/publications/TSI.html. If you take a look at the inventory, you will notice that your responses to the 40 statements generate a score for the five different types of teaching styles identified by Grasha. These five styles are described according to the prevalent behaviors associated with each category: expert, formal authority, personal model, facilitator, and delegator. We've included a description of each type in box 2.4. Usually, no one fits neatly into one category. Instead, most of us are a mix of these five different styles of teaching. Our mix of teaching style also often changes

Box 2.3: Grasha's Teaching Style Inventory

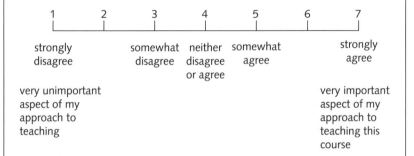

1. Facts, concepts, and principles are the most important things that students should acquire.
2. I set high standards for students in this class.
3. What I say and do models appropriate ways for students to think about issues in the content.
4. My teaching goals and methods address a variety of student learning styles.
5. Students typically work on course projects alone with little supervision from me.
6. Sharing my knowledge and expertise with students is very important to me.
7. I give students negative feedback when their performance is unsatisfactory.
8. Students are encouraged to emulate the example I provide.
9. I spend time consulting with students on how to improve their work on individual and/or group projects.
10. Activities in this class encourage students to develop their own ideas about content issues.
11. What I have to say about a topic is important for students to acquire a broader perspective on issues in that area.
12. Students would describe my standard and expectation as somewhat strict and rigid.
13. I typically show students how and what to do in order to master course content.
14. Small group discussions are employed to help students develop their ability to think critically.
15. Students design one or more self-directed learning experiences.
16. I want students to leave this course well prepared for further work in this area.

Continued

17. It is my responsibility to define what students must learn and how they should do it.
18. Examples from my personal experiences often are used to illustrate points about the material.
19. I guide students' work on course projects by asking questions, exploring options, and suggesting alternative ways to do things.
20. Developing the ability of students to think and work independently is an important goal.
21. Lecturing is a significant part of how I teach each class session.
22. I provide very clear guidelines for how I want tasks completed in this course.
23. I often show students how they can use various concepts and principles.
24. Course activities encourage students to take the initiative and responsibility for their learning.
25. Students take responsibility for teaching part of the class sessions.
26. My expertise is typically used to resolve disagreements about contentious issues.
27. This course has very specific goals and objectives that I want to accomplish.
28. Students receive frequent verbal and/or written comments on their performance.
29. I solicit student advice about how and what to teach in this course.
30. Students set their own pace for completing independent and/or group projects.
31. Students might describe me as a "storehouse of knowledge" who dispenses the facts, principles, and concepts they need.
32. My expectations for what I want students to do are clearly stated in the syllabus.
33. Eventually, many students begin to think like me about the course content.
34. Students can make choices among activities in order to complete course requirements.
35. My approach to teaching is similar to a manager of a work group who delegates tasks and responsibilities to subordinates.
36. I have more material in this course than I have time to cover.
37. My standards and expectations help students develop the discipline they need to learn.
38. Students might describe me as a "coach" who works closely with someone to correct problems in how they think and behave.
39. I give students a lot of personal support and encouragement to do well in this course.
40. I assume the role of a resource person who is available to students whenever they need help.

Box 2.4: Grasha's Five Teaching Styles

Anthony Grasha identified the following five teaching styles as description of prevalent aspects of faculty presence in the classroom.

1. Expert

Possesses knowledge and expertise that students need. Strives to maintain status as an expert among students by displaying detailed knowledge and by challenging students to enhance their competence. Concerned with transmitting information and insuring that students are well prepared.

Advantage: The information, knowledge, and skills such individuals possess.

Disadvantage: If overused, the display of knowledge can be intimidating to less experienced students. May not always show the underlying thought processes that produced answers.

2. Formal Authority

Possesses status among students because of knowledge and role as a faculty member. Concerned with providing positive and negative feedback, establishing learning goals, expectations, and rules of conduct for students. Concerned with the correct, acceptable, and standard ways to do things and with providing students with the structure they need to learn.

Advantage: The focus on clear expectations and acceptable ways of doing things.

Disadvantage: A strong investment in this style can lead to rigid, standardized, and less flexible ways of managing students and their concerns.

3. Personal Model

Believes in "teaching by personal example" and establishes a prototype for how to think and behave. Oversees, guides, and directs by showing how to do things, and encouraging students to observe and then to emulate the instructor's approach.

Advantage: An emphasis on direct observation and following a role model.

Disadvantage: Some teachers may believe their approach is the best way, leading some students to feel inadequate if they cannot live up to such expectations and standards.

4. Facilitator

Emphasizes the personal nature of teacher-student interactions. Guides and directs students by asking questions, exploring options, suggesting alternatives, and encouraging them to develop criteria to make informed choices. Overall

Continued

goal is to develop in students the capacity for independent action, initiative, and responsibility. Works with students on projects in a consultative fashion and tries to provide as much support and encouragement as possible.

Advantage: The personal flexibility, the focus on students' needs and goals, and the willingness to explore options and alternative courses of action.

Disadvantage: Style is often time consuming and is sometimes employed when a more direct approach is needed. Can make students uncomfortable if it is not employed in a positive and affirming manner.

5. Delegator
Concerned with developing students' capacity to function in an autonomous fashion. Students work independently on projects or as part of autonomous teams. The teacher is available at the request of students as a resource person.

Advantage: Helps students to perceive themselves as independent learners.

Disadvantage: May misread students' readiness for independent work. Some students may become anxious when given autonomy.

Source: Grasha, 1996.

depending upon the level of class we are teaching. Grasha (1996) provides the advantages and disadvantages of each style of teaching, as well ideas on how to choose instructional strategies and make instructional changes. Interestingly, each teaching style is associated with specific instructional behaviors such as how one speaks, listens, and responds to students.

Determining Your Teaching Goals

In addition to understanding your teaching style, there are also advantages to determining your teaching goals. In order to provide a valid assessment of our teaching, it is necessary to determine what exactly we want our students to learn. The most effective teachers are those who determine what exactly they want their students to know (Bain, 2004). Usually our goals are written on the syllabus for the class and titled "course goals." However, these goals are often more general in nature, stating the learning goals for the semester as a whole. Throughout the semester, we also have instructional goals specific for each class meeting, each week of the semester, or each topic we cover. We must first determine those specific goals in order to assess whether our students have reached those goals. If you need assistance developing your own learning goals, we recommend using the Teaching Goals Inventory (TGI) and self-scoring worksheet developed by Angelo and Cross (1993) (see boxes 2.5 and 2.6). This is a well-researched tool and

---

Box 2.5: Teaching Goals Inventory and Self-Scorable Worksheet

Purpose: The Teaching Goals Inventory (TGI) is a self-assessment of instructional goals. Its purpose is threefold: 1) to help college teachers become more aware of what they want to accomplish in individual courses; 2) to help faculty locate Classroom Assessment Techniques they can adapt and use to assess how well they are achieving their teaching and learning goals; 3) to provide a starting point for discussions of teaching and learning goals among colleagues.

Direction: Please select *one* course you are currently teaching. Respond to each item on the Inventory in relation to that particular course. (Your responses might be quite different if you were asked about your overall teaching and learning goals, for example, or the appropriate instructional goals for your discipline.)

Please print the title of the specific course you are focusing on:

_____

Please rate the importance of each of the 52 goals listed below to the specific course you have selected. Assess each goal's importance to what you deliberately aim to have your students accomplish, rather than the goal's general worthiness or overall importance to your instruction's mission. There are no "right" or "wrong" answers, only personally more or less accurate ones.

For each goal, circle only one response of the 1-to-5 rating scale. You may want to read quickly through all 52 goals before rating their relative importance.

In relation to the course you are focusing on, indicate whether each goal you rate is:

(5)	Essential	a goal you always/nearly always try to achieve
(4)	Very important	a goal you often try to achieve
(3)	Important	a goal you sometimes try to achieve
(2)	Unimportant	a goal you rarely try to achieve
(1)	Not applicable	a goal you never try to achieve

Rate the importance of each goal to what you aim to have students accomplish in your course.

Continued

	Essential	Very important	Important	Unimportant	Not applicable
1. Develop ability to apply principles and generalizations already learned to new problems and situations	5	4	3	2	1
2. Develop analytic skills	5	4	3	2	1
3. Develop problem-solving skills	5	4	3	2	1
4. Develop ability to draw reasonable inferences form observations	5	4	3	2	1
5. Develop ability to synthesize and integrate information and ideas	5	4	3	2	1
6. Develop ability to think holistically: to see the whole as well as the parts	5	4	3	2	1
7. Develop ability to think creatively	5	4	3	2	1
8. Develop ability to distinguish between fact and opinion	5	4	3	2	1
9. Improve skill at paying attention	5	4	3	2	1
10. Develop ability to concentrate	5	4	3	2	1
11. Improve memory skills	5	4	3	2	1
12. Improve listening skills	5	4	3	2	1
13. Improve speaking skills	5	4	3	2	1
14. Improve reading skills	5	4	3	2	1
15. Improve writing skills	5	4	3	2	1
16. Develop appropriate study skills, strategies, and habits	5	4	3	2	1
17. Improve mathematical skills	5	4	3	2	1
18. Learn terms and facts of this subject	5	4	3	2	1
19. Learn concepts and theories in this subject	5	4	3	2	1
20. Develop skill in using materials, tools, and/or technology central to this subject	5	4	3	2	1
21. Learn to understand perspectives and values of this subject	5	4	3	2	1
22. Prepare for transfer of graduate study	5	4	3	2	1
23. Learn techniques and methods used to gain new knowledge in this subject	5	4	3	2	1
24. Learn to evaluate methods and materials in this subject	5	4	3	2	1
25. Learn to appreciate important contributions to this subject	5	4	3	2	1
26. Develop an appreciation of the liberal arts and sciences					
27. Develop an openness to new ideas					
28. Develop an informed concern about contemporary social issues	5	4	3	2	1

	Essential	Very important	Important	Unimportant	Not applicable
29. Develop a commitment to exercise the rights and responsibilities of citizenship	5	4	3	2	1
30. Develop a lifelong love of learning	5	4	3	2	1
31. Develop aesthetic appreciations	5	4	3	2	1
32. Develop an informed historical perspective	5	4	3	2	1
33. Develop an informed understanding of the role of science and technology	5	4	3	2	1
34. Develop an informed appreciation of other cultures	5	4	3	2	1
35. Develop capacity to make informed ethical choices	5	4	3	2	1
36. Develop ability to work productively with others	5	4	3	2	1
37. Develop management skills	5	4	3	2	1
38. Develop leadership skills	5	4	3	2	1
39. Develop a commitment to accurate work	5	4	3	2	1
40. Improve ability to follow directions, instructions, and plans	5	4	3	2	1
41. Improve ability to organize and use time effectively	5	4	3	2	1
42. Develop a commitment to personal achievement	5	4	3	2	1
43. Develop ability to perform skillfully	5	4	3	2	1
44. Cultivate a sense of responsibility for one's own behavior	5	4	3	2	1
45. Improve self-esteem/self-confidence	5	4	3	2	1
46. Develop a commitment to one's own values	5	4	3	2	1
47. Develop respect for others	5	4	3	2	1
48. Cultivate emotional health and well-being	5	4	3	2	1
49. Cultivate emotional physical health and well-being	5	4	3	2	1
50. Cultivate an active commitment to honesty	5	4	3	2	1
51. Develop capacity to think for oneself	5	4	3	2	1
52. Develop capacity to make wise decisions	5	4	3	2	1

In general, how do you see your primary role as a teacher? (Although more than one statement may apply, please circle only one.)

a. Teaching students facts and principles of the subject matter
b. Providing a role model for students
c. Helping students develop higher-order thinking skills
d. Preparing students for jobs/careers
e. Fostering student development and personal growth
f. Helping students develop basic learning skills

Source: Angelo & Cross, 1993.

Box 2.6: Teaching Goals Inventory, Self-Scoring Worksheet

1. In all, how many of the 52 goals did you rate as "essential"?
2. How many "essential" goals did you have in each to the six clusters listed below?

Cluster Number and Name	Goals Included in Cluster	Total Number of "Essential" Goals in Each Cluster	Clusters Ranked- From First to Sixth by Number of "Essential" Goals
I. Higher-Order Thinking Skills	1–8	_____	_____
II. Basic Academic Success Skills	9–17	_____	_____
III. Discipline-Specific knowledge and Skills	18–25	_____	_____
IV. Liberal Arts and Academic Values	26–35	_____	_____
V. Work and Career Preparation	36–43	_____	_____
VI. Personal Development	44–52	_____	_____

will allow you determine what you think students should learn in your classroom. The inventory helps you to determine what you consider to be essential goals versus those that are less of a priority. Two other very useful resources in this regard are Laurie Richlin' s *Blueprints for Learning* (2007), and Wiggins and McTighe's (2005), *Understanding by Design*. Once you have identified your teaching goals you are then better prepared to choose the classroom assessments that are linked to those goals. Remember, by connecting your assessments to your goals, the process is much more customized to your teaching needs because you are assessing what is most important to you, which in the end makes the assessment process more meaningful to you as an instructor.

Now that you have identified your teaching goal priorities, it is time to choose assessment tools that match those priorities. So, for example, in a political science course on the "Global Issues at the United Nations" a colleague would like her students to learn how to write a UN-style position paper. That is one of her goals for the course. To assess this goal, she requires that students submit three successive drafts to determine how their learning progresses from early in the semester to the final draft at the end of the semester. With each draft, learning is measured according to successive levels of difficulty and guided by targeted instructions. Here, the assessment tool is directly tied to the goal.

Assessment Tools

Probably one of the most daunting tasks one faces when beginning a pedagogical research program is attempting to figure out how one will collect data in response to the research question posed. How exactly do you fit this additional assessment into a time that is already filled to the brim? Fortunately, once classroom assessment is included regularly in your classroom, it becomes more routine. You learn how to be efficient, which in turn allows you to collect the data needed for a systematic examination of teaching practices and student learning. In addition, there are a variety of Classroom Assessment Tools, or CATs (Angelo & Cross, 1993). Think about the number of classes you teach in just one semester and in turn the number of classroom assessments that are possible in just that short period of time. Of course you want to be sure you are collecting valid data for your pedagogical research.

One important component of assessment is that you include your students in a discussion about the process itself, which we mentioned briefly earlier. This means explaining to your students the purpose of including these assessment tools, how they are going to be involved, how they will not be graded or assessed individually (unless you use a test or assignment from the syllabus), and that the process and outcome can have very positive benefits for them as well. You can explain to students that not only will you determine what teaching technique is most effective, the process also allows students to identify for themselves what material they did not understand. Finally, including your students also means communicating your results to them. After you determine the effectiveness of a particular teaching approach for a particular topic, you should inform your students of these findings. You'll be surprised that they too will be interested in what changes you are making to the classroom environment to improve the effectiveness of your teaching and in turn your ability to achieve the student learning goals. We include more details about choosing classroom assessment techniques below as well as information on a number of specific types of techniques available.

Using Student Evaluations

Most of the information we obtain about our own teaching comes from the teaching evaluations our students fill out at the end of the semester. These evaluation forms come in many shapes and sizes, with some including a small number of open-ended questions, some a relatively small number of questions with which students are asked to rate different aspects of the course on a rating scale, and still others that include a relatively large number of questions again using a rating scale. All have the same goal; to provide us with information about student learning and about our teaching. Just mention teaching evaluations and you're likely to receive an interesting variety of responses from your colleagues. While some colleagues find information provided by students on these evaluations to be informative for the development of their teaching, you might hear from other colleagues who question whether these evaluation tools really do what they are intended to do. In other words are they valid instruments? Over the last few decades, the validity of using student ratings to measure the quality of instruction has been raised over and over again. If they are valid, do they really correlate with other measures of teaching quality? What exactly do the ratings mean? Are they measuring a single factor or multiple dimensions about our teaching? If they measure factors other than our teaching, what else influences the scores?

There is no agreement on the answer to these questions. Some in this field of research claim that student ratings are not influenced by factors other than teaching effectiveness but are in fact multidimensional in nature (Marsh & Roche, 1997). In other words, when interpreting the evaluations, one could understand the different aspects of teaching that are evaluated and in turn know how to interpret the feedback accordingly and make changes to particular areas of teaching based on that feedback. Others believe factors beyond teaching influence these scores. For example, Greenwald and Gillmore (1997) state that both a grading bias exists in which higher ratings are received when higher grades are given, and a class size bias exists with smaller classes creating higher scores on course evaluations. Interestingly, others believe that what has been labeled as biases are actually factors directly related to the effectiveness of teaching. One research team closely examined the influence of what others believed biased student evaluation results. They found that factors such as interest in the topic and/or liking the teacher, which are often cited as biases in this literature, are significantly correlated with teaching behavior and therefore directly affected by teaching effectiveness (Greimel-Fuhrmann & Geyer, 2003) rather than intruding as biasing variables (see also Gurung & Vespia, 2007 for a review).

Importantly, for those who believe student evaluations are a valid measure of teaching effectiveness, many also state the importance of using additional sources for personnel decisions as well as the need to continuously improve the rating forms used (McKeachie, 1997). For a complete review of this literature, we refer you to a special issue of the *American Psychologist*, (1997) in which research findings and opinions from both sides of the argument are presented, as well as an article by Marsh and Roche (2000), in which they explain the relationship of a number of classroom variables with teaching evaluation results they found in a more recent examination. Importantly, McKeachie (1997) points out that feedback from student evaluations can be used to improve one's teaching if the results are correctly interpreted.

Our aim here is to examine how to we can use student evaluations of teaching for pedagogical research purposes. What information can we gather using this type of assessment that would provide us with feedback that would lead to more effective teaching? Fortunately, most standardized evaluation forms include questions that were included to assess specific teaching dimensions such as course organization or usefulness of homework assignments. These forms are consistent with the notion that student evaluations are multidimensional. This is particularly helpful to an instructor who is interested in one particular aspect of his or her teaching and who in turn can choose a set of evaluation questions that pertains to that dimension of teaching. For example, if you are interested in assessing your approachability and/or availability to students you could pose questions such as whether you encourage students to meet with you outside of class; whether students are able to find you during your posted office hours; how attentive you are to students during these interactions. You'll notice that responses to these questions will provide specific feedback for the particular dimension of your teaching in which you are interested. In their research examining students' evaluation of teachers, Greimel-Fuhrmann and Geyer (2003) discovered three underlying factors that accounted for a significant portion of the variability of student responses: subject-oriented teaching behaviors (e.g., provides explanations that are easy to understand), student-oriented teaching behaviors (e.g., treats all students fairly), and classroom management behaviors (e.g., most of the time is dedicated to teaching and learning). Not surprisingly, overall student evaluations were most strongly correlated with the subject-oriented behaviors. We bring this up because you might be interested in assessing specific dimensions of your teaching, and focusing improvement on the dimension or dimensions that you feel need particular attention. Perhaps you only want to assess your subject-oriented behaviors.

Developing Your Own Evaluation Forms

The fact that you might be interested in particular aspects of your teaching more than others brings us to the development of your own teaching evaluation forms. In addition to the student evaluation forms that are required by your institution, you can also consider developing an evaluation form that includes questions focused on what you identify as key components of the course with regard to the effectiveness of your teaching. This is encouraged not only at the end of the semester, but also at mid-semester, when you still have the opportunity to make changes in the course that is ongoing. Although most institutions have a required instrument to use at the end of the semester, you should keep in mind that at many institutions you are allowed or even encouraged to create an additional separate evaluation form specific to your own questions about your teaching. In this case you don't have a comparison group with which to compare the results of your evaluations, but more importantly you will receive feedback about the particular dimension of your teaching in which you have interest. This is particularly relevant if you made specific changes to your class and have an interest in determining whether this change made a difference in student learning or student perceptions of the classroom.

When creating your own evaluation questions you'll need to keep in mind that the way you pose the question influences the type of response and detail of response. If you want to avoid a simple yes or no response, be sure to use an open-ended question that is worded appropriately. Of course, some questions will simply require a yes or no to provide helpful feedback (e.g., Do I encourage students to meet with me outside of class?), while others will lead to greater detail (e.g., How do I encourage students to meet with me outside of class? Do I encourage students to meet with me outside of class, and how?). You can also use a Likert scale response form, which typically asks students to rate a certain aspect of your teaching on a five-point or seven-point scale. A scale using an odd number provides a neutral response point or mid-point, which creates a more user-friendly set of responses. So often when responding to a Likert scale, most responders are more comfortable when a mid-point option is included. More importantly, the number of choices is critical. Providing too many choices can overwhelm the responder and lead to inaccurate data. Including five and seven choices provides the variance needed to discriminate among responses, which is why we use this type of scale when asking one to voice opinions and attitudes. We don't just want someone to agree or disagree, but instead to provide information regarding the degree to which they agree or disagree with a particular statement.

Remember, when your goal is to obtain feedback regarding specific aspects of your teaching, you need to be very careful what questions you choose to ask. Some questions can lead to very general statements such as "You did a great job teaching this class." It is easier to make changes in response to feedback such as "I was not able to understand why certain grades were received on homework assignments," versus "I learned little in your classroom." In the former, it is clear that you can provide more written feedback on homework assignments in order to clarify grades for each assignment. However, the comment stating that little was learned does not point out what about your teaching is ineffective. This lack of behaviorally oriented information makes it more difficult to know what can be changed to be more effective. The results you receive from evaluations can create feedback that requires a small change in your teaching or one that requires a more widespread change that means a time investment on your part. For more detail on how to write teaching assessment questions, consider Lewis' (2001) book, which provides details not only on writing questions for your own self-generated evaluation form, but also on how to understand the comments you receive from your students. Your interpretation of the summaries and comments generated from student evaluations is a very important component. Understanding what those results really mean will be the only way to use that data to improve your teaching.

If you are sticking to the form provided by your institution, you might find that results from the form in place generate a summary of responses that an instructor receives for each course. The summary usually breaks down student responses according to specific dimensions of teaching. Looking at any evaluation form, it is clear that some questions address the clarity of instruction while others pertain to the enthusiasm of the instructor, and still other questions focus on the accessibility of the faculty member. So many evaluation forms identify for those using the forms for evaluation purposes which questions pertain to which aspect of teaching. Feedback focused on each dimension could potentially provide specific guidance on different aspects of our pedagogical choices and how we can improve the effectiveness of our overall teaching strategy.

One well-known form is the IDEA Student Ratings of Instruction, which is focused on student learning (see http://www.idea.ksu.edu/StudentRatings/index.html). In addition, you should consider creating your own form. However, if you do so, make sure you are careful when developing the questions to avoid biasing/leading language (e.g., On a scale of 1 to 5 rate your dislike for the textbook used in this class). In addition, be sure to include questions that avoid ambiguity. For instance, many instructors are interested in the level of challenge students perceive for a particular course. But we need to keep in mind that the term "challenge" to students might be very different from what we are attempting to measure. When answering this question on an evaluation form, students are likely to be thinking of the difficulty level of the course even though you were interested in the intellectual challenges in the course. Consider taking a look at the online resources that allow you to create your own evaluation form that asks questions directly related to the goals you identified for your class. These online resources will also present the idea of conducting your evaluations online rather than using the traditional pen and paper method. Keep in mind that most evaluation forms assess three distinct aspects of your course. Some questions pertain to student satisfaction of your course (e.g., On a scale of 1 to 5, please rate whether you would recommend this course to a friend), and other questions pertain to student learning in your course (e.g., I learned to apply the theories and principles taught in this class to different problems or examples) or teacher behaviors (e.g., On a scale of 1 to 5 please rate the degree to which the instructor encouraged students to participate in class). While all aspects might be important, be sure that questions included on your evaluation form will provide information that is relevant to your needs.

Direct feedback from students can be particularly useful when determining whether changes in your teaching method led to an overall increase in the effectiveness of your teaching or in the effectiveness of teaching a particular component of a course. As discussed earlier, results provided by your students using the student teaching evaluation can be informative with regard to your overall teaching methods and choices you make in the classroom. When used for pedagogical research, you probably want to develop a series of questions you put together rather than an existing required institutional form. The student evaluations you develop can include questions directed toward your specific research question. For example, if you have changed your overall teaching method, you might be interested in how clearly students thought you explained material or how often you provided useful examples in the classroom.

These evaluations do not need to wait until the very end of the semester. Why not start with a mid-semester evaluation? At the half-way point in the semester, your students have been in your classroom long enough to provide for you some feedback on a number of aspects of your teaching and classroom behaviors. The easiest way to create a mid-semester evaluation is to use questions similar to those included on the end-of-course evaluation. Wouldn't it be helpful to find out before the end of the semester that your students do not understand why they are asked to complete certain assignments for class, or that they don't know why you have them generate examples in class rather than you providing those examples? If you ask these questions at mid-semester, you are given the opportunity to make changes to the semester at hand.

Importantly, you can respond to student concerns voiced on the mid-semester evaluation form and you'd be surprised at how influential this response to concerns can be when students fill out the end-of-course evaluation forms. When students are given the opportunity to make known their concerns or ask questions pertaining to your course, and you are then given the opportunity to respond to those concerns or to answer those questions, your students know that you are interested in their thoughts. Keep in mind that, when you ask students for feedback or hear their concerns about the course at mid-semester, you do need to respond to what you hear. Often you'll need to provide an explanation for assignments students are given or why you've chosen a particular teaching approach in the classroom. No response to their feedback could create resentment and actually backfire. In other words, your end-of-course evaluations might include comments such as "She asked for our opinion, but didn't respond to what we said and didn't make any changes based on our comments half-way through the semester." Not only can these types of questions be asked of students at mid-semester., they can also be used as classroom assessment techniques (CATs) throughout the semester. We discuss the many CATs available next.

Using Peer Reviews

The research on student evaluations indicates that these instruments can provide information regarding certain aspects about our day-to-day teaching and in turn can be used as an assessment tool to improve our teaching. However, there are many aspects of our teaching that our colleagues are more suited to judge than our students, which is why using peer reviews of your teaching can be very valuable. In her text on the peer review of teaching, Chism (1999) lists the type of assessments for which we should rely on our peers. She includes some of the following: subject matter expertise, course goals, instructional materials, instructional methods, grading practices, and choice of assessments. Chism also emphasizes the need to develop different guidelines for formative peer reviews and summative peer reviews, with formative reviews focused on providing feedback to increase teaching effectiveness and summative reviews focused on personnel decisions.

So who is going to provide this type of review of your teaching? You certainly could ask a colleague in your department to sit in your classroom and review your course materials. This would usually provide the type of expertise in the discipline needed to assess your knowledge of the subject matter. We're not suggesting asking your colleague, who is also a close friend, to provide the review. You can imagine this might lead to a number of biases and in turn potentially an invalid assessment of your teaching. If your course covers content that is very specialized, you could consider finding a peer reviewer from outside your home institution. This avenue is often inherently more logistically complicated and more costly, but if your focus is on course content this might be the only way to proceed. Finally, you could also find out if your institution's teaching center offers this type of service. Though this usually means involving someone who is not expert in your field of study, the staff members are often expert in the processes involved with peer review of teaching, which frankly might be more valuable knowledge than subject knowledge, particular under circumstances in which you are interested in certain classroom behaviors. Often, the staff at these types of centers can offer peer teaching reviews themselves or are willing to provide the training needed for others interested in conducting this type of review, but who have had no experience of observing others in the classroom for the purpose of assessment. Be mindful of the time commitment involved for whoever provides you with a thorough evaluation of your teaching using this method of assessment. Most advise that a peer reviewer provide multiple observations of your teaching in order to make it as valid an assessment as possible. Better yet, a peer review should include a review of not only the classroom itself but also the materials associated with the class in order to provide a more systematic review of the course structure and organization. This additional step, of putting together these materials, certainly requires an additional time commitment. Many faculty will remember the time required to put together materials for reappointment, tenure, and promotion. However, many might also remember the benefits. The process inherently makes you reflect on your teaching choices and practices. So, although time consuming, we are confident that the peer review process is a valid assessment, and the reflection that takes place during the process itself leads to positive pedagogical changes.

This brings us to the question that many raise when deciding on the type of assessment to use for both formative and summative decisions; how valid is this method of teaching assessment? When using peer review of teaching, the answer regarding validity rests a great deal on the preparation or training of the reviewer and the number of observers involved. You can imagine that simply walking into a classroom to observe someone's teaching without preparation could easily lead to feedback that is unfocused and useless. As Chism (1999) points out, the preparation to conducting a peer review is often overlooked despite the fact that this type of evaluation must be conducted systematically. Explicit directions and standards will provide the guidelines necessary to make this process as systematic as possible. These guidelines are usually provided by the teaching center on campus or by an administrator involved in personnel decisions such as your department chair or the Academic Dean/Provost. You'll find that peer reviewers who are best prepared are those who have had the time to practice. The most useful type of practice involves observing a classroom with others and then discussing the observations made by each individual. This can be more easily accomplished by viewing a videotaped class meeting. A group of reviewers could watch the tape as a group and discuss how they rated the different aspects of teaching. The same type of practice can take place for reviews of course materials. A sample set of materials can be created and reviewed by all members of the group, followed by discussion of the feedback created by each individual. Preparation for reviews should also include a meeting with the teacher who is to be observed. This meeting will not only provide necessary information to make the peer review more effective, but will also make the review process a collaborative one in which one colleague is assisting another to become a better teacher. During that pre-observation conference a discussion should take place that focuses on the purpose of the review. In some instances, this review is requested by the teacher. Knowing exactly what questions the instructor has about his or her classroom can help the reviewer focus on specific aspects of the classroom. Also helpful is an exchange of course material such as the syllabus, assignments/readings, and exams and perhaps a discussion of teaching goals and learning goals.

In the end, those conducting the peer reviews will have a greater understanding of their task and the expectations of their role as reviewer, they will be better prepared to accomplish their task, and the assessment feedback they provide should be more useful as a means of teaching assessment. This will allow the instructor to determine whether the observer should focus more on content than on technique, or whether both should be the focus. After all there are a number of aspects of our teaching on which a peer reviewer can provide valuable information. You might be interested in your mastery of the content you are covering. Or perhaps you'd like someone to provide feedback on your course objectives, or input on the methodology you have chosen to cover particular material for your class. Chism (1999) points out that we should not assume that the colleague we ask to observe our classroom is a skilled classroom observer. While most of us are practiced at teaching a class and of course at being a student in the classroom, many are not aware of what to observe when sitting in on someone else's class. Therefore, as we commented above, you should include a preobservation meeting to focus the observation on what the instructor would like feedback. You can use the form from Chism's text to collect information during that observation (see box 2.7). Once you gain experience at observing, you also become more skilled being an unobtrusive observer, where you are not interacting with others and simply making notes as needed.

What is very interesting about the classroom observation process is that it is not only the observed instructor who learns about a number of aspects

Box 2.7: Preobservation Conference Form

Prior to the scheduled observation, the peer reviewer might use the following form (or an adaptation of the form) to structure the discussion of the teaching context with the instructor to be reviewed. Information can focus on class goals, students, learning activities, and particular teaching style. The peer reviewer should request that the instructor bring a copy of the syllabus, text, and any pertinent material to help the reviewer understand the content and cognitive level of the course.

Instructor _____ Date _____ Time _____
Course Number   Course Title _____
Course Meeting Time   Level of Students _____

1) What are the goals for the class that I will observe?
2) What are your plans for achieving these goals?
3) What teaching/learning activities will take place?
4) What have students been asked to do in preparation for this class?
5) Will this class be typical of your teaching style? If not, why?
6) (For formative review) What would you like me to focus on during the observation?
7) Are there other things that I should be aware of prior to the observation?

Source: Chism, 1999.

about his or her teaching. Those making the observations often learn a great deal about their own teaching when sitting in on a colleague's class. There are a variety of ways to collect the information during a class meeting. Often the form you choose is dependent on your preobservation meeting with the instructor as well as the type of class. Is this a lecture focused course? Is the class format focused on discussion among students? Answers to these questions will allow the observer to pick and choose the form that suits each observation best. Observations can be made using checklists (see box 2.8) or Chism's appendix, pp. 87–9) or using Likert scales (see box 2.9). You can find forms for many different aspects of your course such as review of test materials, textbooks, the comments made on student work, and your course handouts in Chism's text.

Box 2.8: Checklist Forms

Checklist forms, with or without space for comments, focus on description (the presence or absence of certain characteristics) and emphasize low-inference items. Items are chosen in accordance with the instructional values of the instructor's unit. The measures can be simply "yes" or "no" or can be measures of frequency, such as "always," "often," "sometimes," "never." Comments can be used by the reviewer to explain the rationale for choosing the rating or for providing additional information. For example, the instructor states the objectives of the class.

Yes   No
Comment:

Possible items for checklist forms (lower-inference items)
Instructor organization
- The instructor arrives to class on time.
- The instructor states the relation of the class to the previous one.
- The instructor locates class materials as they are needed.
- The instructor knows how to use the educational technology needed for the class.
- The instructor posts class goals or objectives on the board or overhead.
- The instructor posts or verbally provides an outline of the organization of the class.
- The instructor makes transitional statements between class segments.
- The instructor follows the preset structure.
- The instructor conveys the purpose of each class activity.
- The instructor summarizes periodically and at the end of class.

Variety and pacing of instruction
- More than one form of instruction is used.
- During discussion, the instructor pauses after asking questions.
- The instructor accepts student responses.
- The instructor draws non-participating students into the discussion.
- The instructor prevents specific students from dominating the discussion.
- The instructor helps students extend their responses.
- The instructor maps the direction of the discussion.
- The instructor mediates conflict or differences of opinion.
- The instructor demonstrates active listening techniques.
- The instructor provides explicit directions for active learning tasks.

- The instructor allows enough time to complete active learning tasks, such as group work.
- The instructor specifies how active learning tasks will be evaluated.
- The instructor is able to complete the topics scheduled for class.
- The instructor provides time for students to practice.

Content knowledge
- The instructor's statements are accurate according to the standards of the field.
- The instructor incorporates current research in the field.
- The instructor identifies sources, perspectives, and authorities in the field.
- The instructor communicates the reasoning process behind operations or concepts.

Presentation skills
- The instructor's voice is audible.
- The instructor varies the tone and pitch of voice for emphasis and interest.
- The instructor avoids distracting mannerisms.
- The instructor maintains eye contact throughout the class.
- The instructor avoids extended reading from notes or texts.
- The instructor speaks at a pace that allows students to take notes.

Rapport with students
- The instructor addresses students by name.
- The instructor attends to student comprehension or puzzlement.
- The instructor provides feedback at given intervals.
- The instructor uses positive reinforcement.
- The instructor incorporates student ideas into the class.

Clarity
- The instructor defines new terms or concepts.
- The instructor elaborates or repeats complex information.
- The instructor uses examples to explain content.
- The instructor makes explicit statements drawing student attention to certain ideas.
- The instructor pauses during explanations to allow students to ask questions.

Source: Chism, 1999.

Box 2.9: Scaled-Rating Forms

Rating forms with scales and with or without space for comments focus on higher-inference evaluation of specific behaviors. Usually a five-point scale with specific anchor words such as "strongly agree-strongly disagree," "effective-ineffective," "excellent-poor" is used. Arreola (1995) cautions that standards of performance be identified (e.g. "The syllabus contains the following items:" etc.) so that reviewers are rating the same thing, and labels on the rating scale are related to the criteria to be evaluated. He also says that interior points of the rating scale should be labeled as well as end points.Others would argue that such precision is cumbersome and ignores the contextual differences between settings. For example, one department might expect a bibliography to be an essential part of a good syllabus, whereas less print-oriented departments might not. Within a given context, however, it is important that reviewers have some common understanding of what constitutes "excellent" as opposed to "very good," "fair," and the like.

Comments can go below each item, in spaces to the right or left of the item, or at the end of the form. When one form is used for a variety of situations, the rating N/A is being observed.

Illustration
Sometimes, such instruments give behavioral indicators of general characteristics in order to increase the likelihood that raters will be attending to the same characteristics. In the above item, for example, the following might be included:

The instructor is Well-prepared for class	Extremely	Very well	Adequately	Inconsistently	Not at all	Comment
	5	4	3	2	1	

Exceeds level of expected qualities	Meets level on all qualities	Meets level on most qualities	Meets level on some qualitities	Meets no/few expected qualities

This instructor is well prepared for class (arrives and starts promptly, has all materials ready , has an articulated class plan, shows content preparation).

Possible items for scaled ratings forms (high-inference items involving values).

Teacher organization
- The instructor is well-prepared for class.
- The objectives of the class are clearly stated.
- The instructor uses class time efficiently.
- The learning activities are well organized.
- The class remains focused on its objectives.

Instructional strategies
- The instructor's choice of teaching techniques is appropriate for the goals.
- The instructor has good questioning skills.
- The instructor raises stimulating and challenging questions.
- The instructor mediates discussion well.
- The class schedule proceeds at an appropriate pace.
- The instructor uses multimedia effectively.
- Board work is legible and organized.
- Course handouts are used effectively.
- The instructor provides clear directions for group work or other forms of active learning.
- The instructor facilitates group work well.
- The instructor helps students to learn from each other.
- The instructor helps students apply theory to solve problems.
- The instructor effectively holds class attention.
- The instructor provides an effective range of challenges.

Instruction in laboratories, studios, or field settings
- Experiments/exercises are well chosen and well organized.
- Procedures/techniques are clearly explained/demonstrated.
- The instructor is thoroughly familiar with experiments/exercises.
- The instructor is thoroughly familiar with equipment/tools used.
- Assistance is always available during experiments/exercises.
- Experiments/exercises are important supplements to course.
- Experiments/exercises develop important skills.
- Experiments/exercises are of appropriate length.
- Experiments/exercises are of appropriate level of difficulty.
- Experiments/exercises help to develop confidence in subject area.
- The instructor provides aid with interpretation of data.
- The instructor's emphasis on safety is evident.
- Criticism of procedures/techniques is constructive.
- The instructor works well with students and other parties in the setting.
- Clinical or field experiences are realistic.

Continued

Content knowledge
- The instructor is knowledgeable about the subject matter.
- The instructor is confident in explaining the subject matter.
- The instructor pitches instruction to an appropriate level.
- The instructor uses a variety of illustrations to explain content.
- The instructor provides for sufficient content detail.
- The instructor focuses on important content in the field.
- The instructor demonstrates intellectual curiosity toward new ideas or perspectives.
- The instructor incorporates views of women and minorities.
- The instructor corrects racist or sexist bias in assigned materials.

Presentation skills
- The instructor is an effective speaker.
- The instructor employs an appropriate rate of speech.
- The instructor uses classroom space well.
- The instructor is enthusiastic about the subject matter.
- The instructor makes the subject matter interesting.
- The instructor's command of English is adequate.

Rapport with students
- The instructor welcomes student participation.
- The instructor models good listening habits.
- The instructor motivates students.
- The instructor stimulates interest in the course subject(s).
- The instructor responds well to student differences.
- The instructor demonstrates a sense of humor.
- The instructor uses effective classroom management techniques.
- The instructor demonstrates flexibility in responding to student concerns or interests.
- The instructor welcomes multiple perspectives.
- The instructor anticipates student problems.
- The instructor treats students impartially.
- The instructor respects constructive criticism.
- The instructor does not express sexiest or racist attitudes.
- The instructor is able to help many kinds of students.
- The instructor is sensitive to individual interests and abilities.

Clarity
- The instructor responds to questions clearly.
- The instructor emphasizes major points in the delivery of the subject matter.

- The instructor explains the subject matter clearly.
- The instructor relates course material to practical situations.

Impact on learning
- The instructor helps develop rational thinking.
- The instructor helps develop problem solving ability.
- The instructor helps develop skills/techniques/views needed in field.
- The instructor broadens student views.
- The instructor encourages the development of students' analytic ability.
- The instructor provides a healthy challenge to former attitudes.
- The instructor helps develop students' creative capability.
- The instructor fosters respect for diverse points of view.
- The instructor sensitizes students to view or feelings of others.
- The instructor helps develop students' decision-making abilities.
- The instructor develops students' appreciation of intellectual activity.
- The instructor develops students' cultural awareness.
- The instructor helps students develop awareness of the process used to gain new knowledge.
- The instructor stimulates independent thinking.

Overall
- The overall teaching ability of the instructor is high.

Source: Chism, 1999.

One additional component of the peer observation to consider is the classroom group interview. During the interview, students can provide information about the overall quality of the course and the effectiveness of the instructor. The small group interview was first developed at the University of Washington by D. Joseph Clark, and he called it the Small Group Instructional Diagnosis (SGID) (Snooks, Neeley, and Williamson, 2004). As is true when conducting classroom observations, it is strongly advised that interviewers meet with the instructor prior to the interview to discuss the course logistics, to address any concerns of the instructor, and to determine the way in which the group interview will take place since it usually takes place during class time. Based on this discussion, the interviewer creates a set of questions. These questions should be constructed to address both the concerns of the instructor and those of the students. The questions originally developed by Clark for this type of assessment include the following: 1) What do you like about the course? 2) What do you think needs improvement? and 3) What suggestions do you have for bringing about these improvements?

The structure of the interview session is determined in part by the size of the class. If there are more than 20 students, perhaps two separate sessions would provide ample time for all students to provide feedback. If many students are present for the interview, you might also consider bringing along a second person to record responses so that the interviewer can concentrate on the interactions with the students. Importantly, all students' voices should be heard so that the feedback provided is not simply a small minority voice. Once again, the final step for this process is to provide feedback to the instructor based on the information collected. Perhaps the final step really needs to be the instructors' response to the feedback received from the students. As we stated earlier with regard to using mid-term evaluations, we strongly recommend that instructors respond to student comments collected during the semester, illustrating that these comments are worthy of response and do in fact make a difference in the teaching and learning process. In addition to a meeting time to discuss the students' comments, it is also advisable for the interviewers to provide a written document for the instructor to review following the discussion.

When choosing who aberves the classroom and who conducts the interviews, keep in mind that there are both pros and cons to having the same peer for both and to the different ways in which you can time the observation and the interviews. If the same person observes the classroom and then interviews the students, the observer could develop questions based on the observation to elicit student feedback on what he or she observed. However, this could also bias the interview to focus on aspects of the class that were observed during that single class meeting rather than the semester-long meetings that went beyond the one observation. This is just one factor to keep in mind when setting up the logistics when using group interviews. You'll find that group interviews often provide information not obtained through written student evaluations or peer observations, and the information is most often considered to be very useful by faculty members. For more specific guidelines on this process, we refer you to a chapter in Braskamp and Ory's (1994) text, which reviews ways to evaluate and assess faculty including the use of interviews, as well as the chapter by Snooks, Neeley, and Williamson (2004).

Feedback is also useful from peers on the exams and assignments used in a class to measure student achievement. Keep in mind that reviewers can also provide feedback on class material such as the syllabus, exams, and assignments in addition to the observation of a class. Importantly, all peer reviews should be followed by feedback in a timely manner with specific suggestions made to help the teacher reach his or her teaching goals. We often find it very useful to schedule not only the classes that we'll visit, but also a meeting time following the observations for the postobservation discussion. Keep in mind, if multiple observers are involved, the observers should discuss their feedback prior to meeting with the instructor.

Using the Tests and Assignments Already in Place

When we think about the assignments and tests we use in our classes, they are usually tied to a learning goal or learning outcome we hope to achieve. Therefore, why not start the assessment of your teaching with assessment tools you have created and included on your syllabus? After all, these assessments are used to determine if students have learned the material that you believe is important for that particular course. Therefore, each quiz, test or assignment should have specific performance goals that are tied to learning goals (see Fink, 2003; Wiggins & McTighe, 2005). So, for example, in a physics class one colleague includes learning to build a website as one of his learning goals. In turn, he has the students turn in lab report assignments on their own website they have developed. Part of the grade for each lab includes whether the assignment was correctly posted and therefore easily accessible on the website. Let us say you are teaching a course in research methods, and one learning outcome for the semester is for students to learn how to extract information from primary sources. If you assign students to read three journal articles and respond to a series of specific questions concerning the content of those articles, you would be assessing the skills directly tied to the learning outcome. In both cases, the assignments and assessments are directly linked to a particular learning goal for the course.

To make sure you have objective and clear measures for any assignment, as well as others, you should consider creating a grading rubric. A grading rubric will provide students with detailed information on what you are looking for when grading their assignment and how their grade will be determined; in turn, students are clearly aware of your expectations and they provide clear evidence to students about grading criteria. You could also consider allowing students to help develop the rubric, which some have found creates assignments that are more meaningful to students and uses language and examples that are easy to understand (Walvoord, 2004). Rubrics could also be particularly helpful if you include a peer-reviewed assignment, in which students review each other's work. At the same time, the rubric will help you focus on the learning goals as you grade each assignment according to the predetermined "rules." For the research methods course example above, a rubric such as the one in box 2.10 could be used. You should consider handing out the grading rubric to students as you explain the assignment. Of course, you need to create a rubric with as much objectivity as possible. In other words, in addition to stating that "The author's hypothesis was clearly stated," as shown in the example in box 2.10, you should also provide more detail as well as examples of what you mean by "clearly stated." This would provide students with a clear understanding of what it means for a hypothesis to be clearly stated. Without the examples, the term "clearly" is very subjective. Even more detail, such as including in the grading rubric that "the reader could understand the researcher's hypothesis as stated, including the independent and dependent variables and the direction of the prediction made," would provide a more detailed expectation and therefore an unambiguous way to state how that part of the assignment will be graded. In other words, you need to include qualities and descriptors for each performance standard. You would then create a point system based on the rubric, and each student would then receive a number of points based on how well their work fitted the predetermined rubric guidelines. To begin creating the scale, think of the highest level of performance for each standard and then the lowest level of performance, filling in the scores that fall in between then usually comes easy once the anchors are created.

If you have never used a grading rubric before and need some assistance on developing rubrics for different assignments, you should visit the online resource http://rubistar.4teachers.org/index.php. This site will not only walk you through the process of creating grading rubrics, creating the forms or templates needed, it will also provide information on how to enhance your rubrics and how to analyze the data you collect using the rubrics. Using this standardized form for grading has a number of positive outcomes for both you and your students. How often have you heard any of your students say, "I did not know what you wanted me to do for this assignment," "The assignment was not clearly presented?" or "I don't understand why I received this grade"? Using a rubric should eliminate all ambiguity with regard to your expectations and provide detailed feedback as to why a particular grade was achieved. All aspects of the assignment are

Box 2.10: Rubric Example

Reading-analyzing information: reading a journal article

Teacher Name: Dr. Schwartz

Student Name: _____

CATEGORY	4	3	2	1
Reference	All aspects of APA style were followed	Minor errors in APA style were made	Major APA errors were made	APA style was not followed at all
Intro research question	The research question posed was stated clearly	The research question posed was stated but needed a little clartification	The research question stated was very unclear	The research question was not stated at all
Intro hypothesis	The author's hypothesis was clearly stated	The author's hypothesis was a little unclear	The author's hypothesis was very unclear	The author's hypothesis was not stated at all
Participants content	The participant's/ subject's information was complete	A few pieces of participant information was missing	A great deal of participant information was missing	No participant information was stated.
Methods	The procedures were clearly summarized	The procedures were not clearly summarized	Very little information about the procedures was included	The procedure information was missing
Results	The results were clearly presented	The results were not clearly presented	The results were very unclear	The results were missing

clearly presented with specific grading points on your rubric. Again, how you state what each point represents becomes easier with practice. The example rubrics provided on the Rubistar website above will also help you avoid starting off with very ambiguous descriptions for each point on your rubric. Using rubrics will also make sure you are grading students on the aspects of the assignments that are directly tied to your learning outcomes. (Note: below we will be helping you identify those learning outcomes.) There should not be grades on your rubric that are not tied to what you want your students to be learning. Essentially, you determine what your learning priorities are and then include those priorities in the development of your rubric for each assignment or test. Once again, this provides you with a valid measure of your learning goals for the course, and using the same rubric from one year to the next allows you to carry out a valid comparison of student performance from one class to the next. As is true for any assessment you use, you'll find that adjustment is required after each use of the rubric, with student feedback providing direction for change. Of course, any change in your learning goals will also create the need for adjustment to your rubric as well.

Use of the grading rubric is just one way to create consistency in assessment from one class to the next using assignments and tests. You could also consider using the approach called primary trait scoring (PTS), which is similar to using a rubric. Walvoord et al. (1996) explain that PTS requires that grading criteria are explicit, systematic, and based on assessment research. If these requirements are met, many believe that it becomes much easier to compare student learning from one classroom to the next. To create a primary trait scoring for any exam or assignment, you would start with student samples from past classes that were successful when completing the task. Those papers and assignments can be used to identify components of the completed assignment that were necessary for different grades that would be assigned. These are labeled as the "traits," hence the name primary trait scoring. For each trait identified, you then use a Likert scale from 1 to 5 that would indicate the degree to which the student achieved that particular trait. For example, in an environmental studies course on "Quantitative Aspects of Global Environmental Problems" a colleague wants her students to demonstrate the quantitative skills they learned in class and at the same time contribute to the community's efforts to move towards more efficient and sustainable use of resource by applying their knowledge to some specific aspect of sustainable use of energy and resources at the College or the surrounding community. For a proposal paper she provides a list of components of the paper needed. So, students need to include in this proposal details about the chosen topic and how it relates to the use of energy and resources in the community. They also need to include a description of how they will investigate the question and the type of data required for this research and how they plan on obtaining that type of data. Each of these components will be considered a trait and will be required for the paper. Importantly, each score for each trait must be clearly defined. Those who teach others how to develop PTS for their classroom also emphasize the need to tie the traits used for exams and assignments to teaching goals.

Once you have developed your rubric or your PTS in a number of sections of the same course, you can then determine if any changes in your pedagogy influenced students' ability to receive high scores on the rubric or achieve high trait scores on the PTS. For example, did using student-generated examples create higher scores on the rubric or did instructor-generated examples lead to higher scores. You'll have the data available to assess which is more effective when using either of these techniques.

If your course is listed as a prerequisite for a course, there is certainly material or ways of thinking that students need to be learning in order to increase the likelihood of success in the classes that follow. Therefore, why not consider determining how well your students are prepared for these additional courses in which they enroll. Ask your colleagues to evaluate how well they feel these students are performing in their classes for which your class was a prerequisite. An exam during the first day of class that reviews the material would allow you to determine if you met the learning goals in your course. Of course, an open-book exam that requires application of the material would allow you to measure not just their retention of the material but instead their understanding and ability to apply the material in a later setting. How this is assessed is determined by your original learning goals. If you wanted students to remember particular material covered in your course, then that would shape the type of assessment to develop in the next courses.

Alternative Classroom Assessment Techniques

Instead of relying on the tests and quizzes you use for the summative evaluation of your students, you could consider alternative assessment techniques that you might use not to grade your students but to obtain information regarding your teaching technique and what students learned. Here, you are going beyond individual student achievement, or what is called summative evaluation, which we assess through the former tools, and instead are using tools that provide formative evaluation.

Many of us have experienced a class meeting where students did not seem to follow the material and have come away knowing that there was a need for changes. In essence, we have conducted a classroom assessment through listening to students' responses and watching student behavior in the classroom. You might walk out of the classroom and think about what you are going to do differently next time you cover the same material. However, when you return to your office there are a number of students waiting to talk to you and a pile of work waiting to be tackled. So by the time you come to address the changes to be made in order to improve that presentation you have to rely on your memory of that class meeting. As an alternative to relying on what can be an inaccurate memory of the details from the class, why not include during the class meeting an assessment that will record the information you can later use to more systematically make changes? CATs can provide this information and can be used as often as needed. The data you generate will allow you to determine what students are learning clearly and what they are not learning clearly. When students respond to the questions posed for these assessments, they too gain a greater understanding of what they are following and what they need to review. These assessment tools should provide feedback that is time efficient, which assesses an aspect of teaching that can be changed, and that provides information that is useful for determining what changes are needed.

The most widely used CATs (Angelo & Cross, 1993; Gurung, 2005), which cross disciplinary boundaries, include the following: 1) the Minute Paper; 2) the Muddiest Point; 3) the One-Sentence Summary; 4) Directed Paraphrasing; and 5) Application Cards. The type of assessment tool you choose will be dependent on your teaching goals and priorities. Because we all teach with different instructional goals in mind, it makes sense that we use different assessment techniques as well. The five techniques listed above each provide different types of information and therefore focus on different learning priorities. For instance, if your questions focus on what you were able to communicate clearly to your students and what you need to further perfect it, you might choose the Minute Paper technique, which asks students to indicate the most important thing learned during that class meeting and what questions remain about the material covered so far. Similarly, the Muddiest Point establishes what students found unclear by asking them to tell you the muddiest point in the day's class meeting. If you are more interesting in your students' abilities to summarize larger amounts of material, you might choose to use the One-Sentence Summary, where students are asked a specific content question that requires connecting a number of points made during a class meeting. There are a number of forms already developed that focus on a particular type of teaching technique. For instance, Bligh (2000) examines the use of lectures in the classroom and includes a short evaluation form for students to provide you with feedback focused on your lecture for a specific class meeting (see box 2.11).

Box 2.11: ••

What's the Use of Lectures?
Form A Preliminary Inquiry

Lecture Evaluation
In order to help me to improve my lectures, please complete the form below. Your response will be treated as strictly confidential and anonymous. Please do not put your name on the paper.

1. What is your overall opinion of this lecture compared with lectures generally?
    Place an X in the appropriate box. Please comment.

    Poor [ ][ ][ ][ ][ ] Good

2. State your objectives in attending this lecture. To what extent have they been achieved?

3. Give two things you liked about this lecture:
    A.
    B.

4. Give two things you disliked about this lecture:
    A.
    B.

5. If I were to teach this topic again, what changes would you recommend I make?

Source: Bligh, 2000.

On the other hand, if your priority for the day was to make sure students can communicate the material clearly in their own words, then you might choose the Directed Paraphrasing tool. Finally, if the learning goal for the day is focused on students' understanding of how the material applies to situations beyond the classroom, you might choose to use the Application Cards approach, which asks students to provide examples of how a concept of theory applies to a real-life situation.

Fortunately, most CATs are very adaptable to these differences and can be formatted to fit each individual's teaching and learning priorities. An important piece of advice offered by Angelo and Cross (1993) is to gain experience using these assessment tools by starting CATs in a course that you believe is going relatively well. Once you are confident in your CAT use, then you can move on to a course in which you feel change is more likely needed. Angelo and Cross' (1993) provide a step-by-step plan, and all the CATs mentioned above are described in detail in their text. We should also add (in the spirit of fostering pedagogical research) that these CATs have been subjected to empirical testing and SoTL publications validate their use. For example, Almer, Jones, and Moeckel (1998) demonstrate the utility of using the Minute paper in an accounting course (see also Chizmar and Ostrosky, 1998). Evidence provided by use of CATs will be particularly useful when creating your teaching portfolio.

Teaching Portfolios

Because many faculty members are being made accountable to provide some type of evidence of the effectiveness of their teaching, the teaching portfolio has become a well-known way in which to provide such evidence (Bernstein et al., 2006). Seldin (2004) provides an excellent resource on the teaching portfolio, explaining not only what the portfolio is, but also how to put one together, as well as examples from different disciplines. There are many different reasons to construct a teaching portfolio. The purpose for creating the portfolio will help you determine what documents to include. Although many faculty members create a teaching portfolio in preparation for an upcoming review or perhaps to organize material for a teaching award review, fewer use this tool as a resource for improving their teaching. But a teaching portfolio is an excellent way of organizing the many aspects of teaching and in turn creating a structure for assessing your teaching strengths and weaknesses. The portfolio can include information from a single course or from all of your courses over a certain period of time. Your decision on what to include will be determined by the reasons that led you to create the portfolio. Seldin (2004) includes an eight-step guide on how to create the portfolio.

If your teaching portfolio is created to provide a document for self-reflection on your teaching, this should help you shape the types of materials to include. In this case, you are usually the primary reader of the documents you include in your portfolio, although it is likely a good idea to also keep in mind that you can use the portfolio for other uses such as for reappointment, tenure, or award consideration materials. Your portfolio should begin with a statement of teaching that describes your teaching philosophy, your strategies, and your objectives. In your teaching philosophy statement you describe why you choose particular teaching techniques and how you carry that out in the classroom with specific examples. You want to be able to connect your actions in the classroom with your overall philosophy and your objectives. If you put together a portfolio at the beginning of your teaching career, it is very informative to keep the information updated with each passing semester. This will allow you more easily to understand how your teaching changes over the years and the reasons for those changes. Too often we think we'll remember the changes made to particular classes and why those changes were made, but those details fade and we are unable to recall when changes were made and why. Once again, you should connect your ongoing development as a teacher to your philosophy of teaching. You'll notice some very interesting connections between the two as you document these changes.

Once you've sat down to write down your philosophy of teaching and the pedagogical techniques you choose that fit well within that philosophy, it is time to determine what documents to include in your portfolio to provide evidence for all of the above. These documents can include examples of syllabi and how they have changed over the years, or you can include student assignments/papers that illustrate the type of learning goals you hope to achieve in your classroom. Often the documents are included as appendices and are referred to within the narrative you include. As you can imagine, the documents you choose to include will likely be very different from those chosen by your colleagues. After all, a teaching portfolio is very individually determined given that it reflects who you are as teacher. Once you've chosen what to include in your portfolio, you need to provide statements for each document. At this point you should consider again why you included each document, which will allow you to illustrate how that document provides evidence for that particular aspect of your teaching. So, for example, you might have found in a psychology senior research course that students were having trouble interpreting their results and writing a discussion section for their research paper. In response to this problem, you might have decided to include a new in-class assignment that allowed for more detailed instruction on how to write a discussion section for a research paper, as well as a homework assignment that provided an assessment of your student's ability to write a discussion section. In your teaching portfolio, you would describe these new assignments, include them with your materials, and discuss why these new assignments were necessary. This would provide the readers of your portfolio with concrete evidence that you continue to make pedagogical changes to improve the effectiveness of your teaching.

As is true for any type of portfolio, the order in which you present your documents is an important decision. It really tells a story about the history and development of your teaching. Therefore, how you organize the materials significantly changes how the story is told. The order of your documents is another decision that is dependent upon the purpose of the portfolio. If you are putting together these documents to provide evidence for you and/or others regarding the effectiveness of your teaching, you should create an organization that prioritizes the material that illustrates such evidence. If the purpose of the portfolio is to illustrate your scholarly development within your discipline, then the organization of your documents should prioritize evidence of that scholarly work.

If you are new to this process, we strongly recommend that you ask a colleague to provide a peer review of the material. This is particularly useful if the portfolio is used for evaluation purposes (e.g., tenure decision). Your colleague can tell you whether you've written a clear teaching philosophy, you've included relevant documents, and the organization of your portfolio is optimal.

Learning to Conduct Pedagogical Research: How to Get Started: Designing your Pedagogical Research Program

Now that we've reviewed the many tools available to obtain information and evaluation regarding your teaching (e.g., student evaluations, teaching portfolios), we will begin to put those tools to use to create your pedagogical research program. As is true for any research program, as you develop your research ideas keep in mind some basic questions in order to determine the viability of your project. First, how long will it take me to complete this research? Do you remember how long it took to complete your dissertation compared to how long you thought it would take to complete? You often hear you should take the amount of time you think it will take and multiple that by two to get a more realistic time frame. The same is true for pedagogical research. Do not expect quick results, particular when you are examining changes in student learning in your classroom. Another question pertains to the complexity of your project. The more complex a research design the more time commitment and participants needed to complete the project. Finally, keep in mind the cost. Are the resources available to fund the many components of any research project? Do you have the people necessary to help carry out the project? Do you have funds needed for the materials? We pose these questions not to create roadblocks just as you begin to think about pedagogical research, but instead to increase the likelihood of you successfully completing your research.

The process of designing your pedagogical research begins like any other research endeavor; you need to begin by stating the problem at hand. In the case of pedagogical research the question is often focused on determining whether a particular teaching technique you've chosen to use really works or whether the technique is as effective as you'd like it to be. Do the students understand the material more when that technique is used, or should an alternative teaching approach be considered? By identifying this question and carefully examining how you hope to use your results, you can then create a design for your research that will provide you with the answers you need. Making that connection between the use of your findings and the choice of the appropriate assessment tool is essential.

Many of the assessment tools we use are put in place to provide us with a measure of our students' understanding of the material to be learned. In many instances we are attempting to create an observable measure of the unobservable cognitive processes that go on in our students' minds as they attempt to learn new material. When we measure student learning, we are after all indirectly measuring the effectiveness of our teaching. In order to make your assessment worthwhile, you need to make sure that the observable measurement is clearly connected to the unobservable process of learning. In other words, you need to use a valid measure to assess your teaching. It certainly doesn't make sense to teach your students about

European history and then assess their knowledge of the topic with an assignment that includes only questions about the US Civil War. This would provide you with no information regarding the pedagogical technique you chose to use when teaching your students about European history. When we use valid assessment tools, only then can we use the data generated to make informed decisions about the effectiveness of our teaching.

One important component of pedagogical research that needs to be considered is the role of the Institutional Review Board, or IRB, on your campus. This committee, of at least five members, will decide if a proposed research project is ethical, including appropriate informed consent and use of necessary safeguards to ensure the safety and well-being of all those participating in the research. Although many research projects that evaluate the effectiveness of your teaching or instructional strategies are exempt from this type of review, when you plan on presenting your work at a conference or submitting your work for publication, review of your research by the IRB is a must. When an institution receives any type of federal funding, IRBs are actually required by federal regulations, in this case the Research Act of 1974. Detailed information can be found through the United States Department of Health and Human Services (http://www.hhs.gov/ohrp/). Most institutions also have detailed information about the process involved in submitting research proposals to the on-campus Institutional Review Board, with specific forms that solicit answers to questions related to treatment of all participants involved in the proposed research. We will expand on the issue of research ethics and provide more information on how IRBs work in the next chapter.

Developing Your Research Ideas and Questions

In many disciplines, research questions are developed through analysis of the literature and existing work in a particular area of inquiry. Following a thorough analysis, the researcher develops new questions that are raised from the knowledge base in place and the existing theories therein. However, when it comes to pedagogical research, our ideas often stem from experiences we have had in the classroom, and there is a body of experience-based pedagogical scholarship, or wisdom-of-practice scholarship (Weimer, 2006). As we noted above, it is possible there were instances when you were just not sure that your students understood much of what you covered that day and wondered how you could have done it differently. Those are the instances that lead to pedagogical research ideas. Of course, the ideas could simply develop from changing the way you teach different aspects of a course. Or perhaps you've watched a colleague teach and wondered whether his or her way of teaching could be used effectively in your own classroom. One excellent source of ideas is watching yourself or others teach. Why not videotape your classroom and watch the teaching and learning that takes place? You might be surprised at what you "observe." Often many faculty members who watch a recording of their teaching say, "I did not know that I did that in the classroom," or, "The students do not seem to understand a word that I am saying." We can get so caught up in the moment while teaching that we can miss some valuable information or feedback that is right in front of us and that could provide direction for change in our teaching choices.

You may be familiar with the behaviors identified by Davis (1993), who categorizes effective teaching factors. The four categories include how well information is explained and organized; the type of learning environment created; the intellectual stimulation created; and how reflective one is about teaching. You can probably come up with specific dimensions of your own teaching to evaluate within each of these categories. Perhaps you are interested in students' perceptions of your grading procedures or what students learn about the material when you instruct them using small group discussions. Within each of these categories are important components of effective teaching. Perhaps you are interested in evaluating the degree to which you achieve these characteristics in your own classroom. Whatever the source of inspiration, these ideas are the start for your pedagogical research program.

Finally, Thompson, Nelson, and Naremore (2001) have developed an extremely useful interactive web-based resource: http://www.issotl.org/ tutorial/sotltutorial/home.html. Here, you will find a section dedicated to posing questions, developing designs, and creating methods for research in SoTL. Wonderful examples of well-framed questions and methods used within teaching and learning research are included.

Asking the Right Questions

Many classroom assessment tools are put in place so that one can better understand student learning and in turn improve one's teaching by choosing the most effective approach for a particular learning goal, but not all questions focus on student learning. Other assessments focus on teaching style or content knowledge. Before choosing an assessment tool, you first need to determine what exactly you want to learn about your teaching. Would you like to determine the level of interest generated from a particular lecture? Are you interested in the level of understanding your students take away from a class meeting? Would you like to determine whether students were able to construct clear connections between the information presented in class and the reading assigned for that day? Your answer to this question will determine the type of assessment you choose and the methods you use to conduct the assessment. Are you more interested in your content knowledge or your delivery of the material to your students? In other words, you need to ask the types of questions that will give you feedback that fits with your question. As Banta et al. (1996) eloquently state: "Assessment works best when the programs it seeks to improve have clear, explicitly stated purposes" (p. 17).

The questions about your teaching that you ask should be tied to the goals you have as a teacher. As Buskist and Davis (2006) discuss in their chapter on what you need to know about teaching, there are numerous teaching goals one can have when walking into the classroom. Are your teaching priorities focused on the content? In other words, do you want your students to have clear knowledge of the facts? Or, do you want your students to catch your enthusiasm for the discipline in which you've dedicated most of your life's work? Are you focused on teaching your students the importance of content to their everyday lives? Is the course a prerequisite for another course and is your goal therefore to make sure that the students leave with the requisite knowledge or skills for future courses? Knowing your goal or goals is essential, because the only way to determine if you've reached your goal is to clearly define that goal at the start. And the only way to choose a valid assessment tool is to know exactly what you want your students' to achieve. That way, you are measuring exactly what you should be measuring.

In addition to choosing a technique that will provide you with the information you want, you should also consider asking yourself how easy the technique is to administer, or whether it will provide information about your teaching or student learning that you can actually change based on the feedback you receive. After all, you are busy enough that creating an assessment tool that is overwhelming will not be an effective use of your time inside and outside of the classroom. In addition, it doesn't make sense to assess as aspect of your teaching that you are not willing to change. Focus on aspects of your teaching that you can change and those that you are willing to change.

Focus on Student Learning: Connecting Your Learning Goals, Assessment Choice, and Teaching Technique

Once your research question is in place, you now need to determine how you are going to answer it. Here is when you need to determine your choice of assessment. As mentioned above, your choice of assessment should depend on what it is you want to measure, and what it is you want to measure should depend on what you hope your students should learn. So working backward from your learning goals will help you choose the most appropriate assessment tool. This is very similar to the procedure known as backward design. Wiggins and McTighe (2005) explain that many teachers focus on what they are teaching rather than on what students should be asked to do in order to achieve their learning goals. They contrast these two approaches using the terms content-focused and results-focused design. With the results-focused approach, you start with the learning goals for each course and determine what could provide you with evidence, or what the appropriate assessment is that would illustrate that those goals were achieved.

We begin by determining these goals based on our learning priorities for each particular class. So the first question to ask your self would be: "What do I want my students to learn?" For example, in an Introductory Physics course you might want your students to learn Newton's Force Laws. In this class, we don't just want our students to pick a random equation that contains the right variables. Instead, we would like for them to be able to understand the relationship between the variables in order to choose the correct equation. How would our students illustrate to us that they have mastered this task and in fact understand these laws? This is the step at which we decide the type of assessment that will provide evidence about the learning goals. We could decide to use the Force Concept Inventory, which is an exam developed through educational research and was designed to test students' understanding of Newton's Force Laws. Given the desired goals and way we will be assessing these goals, the next step is to determine the type of teaching techniques that would lead students to perform the learning activities needed to master the material at hand. Continuing with the physics example, we could teach using peer instructions. In this case the students would be asked to convince each other of the correct conceptual understanding of the Force Laws in their own words, which research findings indicate is a more effective way to teach this material than when students learn the same information from an authority figure (i.e., the professor). Notice that we worked backward from the learning goal, to the way to assess that goal, to how we would teach the material in order for students to be able to learn the material in a manner that is consistent with our learning goal.

You will find when using this backward design that your teaching choices are clearly connected with what you want your students to learn, which should also make the assessment process more logically tied to both how you teach and your learning objectives. We've included the template from Wiggins' and McTighe's (2005) book, which provides the steps discussed above in a visual format, perhaps easier to use when first attempting to put the backward design process in use (see box 2.12). As the authors of this

Box 2.12: The Backward Design Process

Stage 1 – Desired Results	
Established Goals: • What relevant goals (e.g., content standards, course or program objectives, learning outcomes) will this design address?	
Understandings: *Students will understand that . . .* • What are the big ideas? • What specific understandings about them are desired? • What misunderstandings are predictable?	**Essential Questions:** • What provocative questions will foster inquiry, understanding, and transfer of learning?
Students will know . . . • What key knowledge and skills will students acquire as a result of this unit? • What should they eventually be able to do as a result of such knowledge and skills?	*Students will be able to . . .*

Stage 2 – Assessment Evidence	
Performance Tasks: • Through what authentic performance tasks will students demonstrate the desired understandings? • By what criteria will performances of understanding be judged?	**Other Evidence:** • Through what other evidence (e.g., quizzes, tests, academic prompts, observations, homework, journals) will students demonstrate achievement of the desired results? • How will students reflect upon and self-assess their learning?

Stage 3 – Learning Plan
Learning Activities: What learning experiences and instruction will enable students to achieve the desired results? How will the design: W = Help the students know **W**here the unit is going and **W**hat is expected? Help the teacher know **W**here the students are coming from (prior knowledge, interests)? H = **H**ook all students and **H**old their interest? E = **E**quip students, help them **E**xperience the key ideas and **E**xplore the issues? R = Provide opportunities to **R**ethink and **R**evise their understandings and work? E = Allow students to **E**valuate their work and its implications? T = Be **T**ailored (personalized) to the different needs, interests, and abilities of learners? O = Be **O**rganized to maximize initial and sustained engagement as well as effective learning?

The previous page was taken from Wiggins and McTighe, pg. 22, Understanding by Design. Check on how to include this type of table from other books.

Source: Wiggins & McTighe, 2005.

process point out throughout their text, using this procedure might at first seem backward (as the name implies) compared to the more traditional methods we use to plan different components of our courses. However, without the connections created between learning goals, assessment, and teaching strategies, you are often just making a guess at to what type of teaching will be most effective for each particular class or course you teach.

When using the backward design, and connecting your teaching methods to learning goals and assessment, you might decide that there are number of ways to engage the students in the learning process that you believe would be effective. Perhaps you've thought of several teaching strategies that should allow your students to learn the material, but you're unsure which technique would be most effective. You could then choose to use the different teaching techniques in your classroom and then determine which was most effective in achieving your student learning goal.

As you begin to develop your pedagogical research program, it is important to keep in mind that in most cases assessment of teaching and learning will provide the most valuable information only when used as an ongoing process throughout the semester. Then and only then will the data you collect allow you to really monitor the student outcomes you hope to achieve in the classroom.

Applying the Findings of Your Pedagogical Research: Using General Principles of Learning to Making Changes to Your Teaching Strategies

After using the above methods to assess a particular teaching technique, you might find from analysis of your data (see chapter 4 for ways to do this) that the students are not attaining the learning goals you hoped for and you might find it a daunting task to figure out why your teaching technique is not working. We believe that often the answer can be determined by examining some general principals of learning. These principles identify the basic steps involved in learning and what factors can significantly influence the success of the learning process.

How you teach any particular class is a choice you make based upon the material you are teaching, the students in the class, and your experiences with how successful you believe your teaching methods were when teaching the material in the past. However, our pedagogical choices should also rely on the basic principles of learning theory that describes what influences how someone acquires new knowledge. Learning theory began with the notion that we need only focus on the external factors to explain the acquisition of new behaviors (Schwartz & Reisberg, 1991). Although we cannot ignore the surroundings in which learning takes place, when evaluating the effectiveness of our teaching we must take into consideration the mental processes that take place when our students are learning new material. This cognitive approach to learning theory provides us with important findings from the field of cognitive psychology, where researchers examine the mental processes taking place when learning and remembering new material.

How can our understanding of the processes and strategies that take place inside the mind guide our teaching strategies? Learning and remembering takes place in three stages. A student must acquire the new information (acquisition), that new information must be stored in memory for future use (storage), and finally that information must be retrieved from memory when needed (retrieval). When one of these processes fails, students' performance in your classroom will suffer. After all, a student cannot demonstrate their mastery of the material if the student never took in the information in the first place, if the information was not properly stored for later use, or if that information is not accessible. It certainly does not make much sense to teach a student something that he or she will not be able to retrieve from memory when needed. Applying your understanding of what makes a student more likely to acquire the information, store it properly, and access it will certain improve the learning process.

The ability of students to learn new material is dependent in part on the way in which the to-be-learned material is organized and connected to stored knowledge. Organization of the material can either be created by the teacher or it can be created by the learner. When created by the learner, the new information is often related to existing knowledge. This inherently creates organization for the new knowledge. This organization is believed to create a greater understanding of the material and in turn a greater likelihood of remembering the information. Therefore, if you can relate the new information to information from previous class meetings, information already read in the text, or any knowledge you know your students possess, be sure to make those connections. Prior knowledge significantly influences how the incoming information is understood and learned. Even knowing the general topic of a lesson and the direction one will take during class time can significantly influence understanding and learning of that material. What is interesting is the notion that when students cannot understand or connect new information, they likely will not recall it at a later time. This is a classic phenomenon demonstrated in the memory literature by Bartlett (1932), who demonstrates that a story will be retold with many details missing when those details do not fit the knowledge base of the listener.

Another factor that also influences student's ability to retrieve information from memory concerns testing expectations. Tversky (1973) demonstrated the connection between testing students in a manner that they expected and their test performance on that material. When expectations were not met, performance on a test was significantly lower when compared to those who had the type of test they expected. These results demonstrate that, if students expect that they will be taking a multiple choice test, they acquire and store the information for future use differently than if they are told that they will be tested using an essay test. In addition, this implies that we should make clear to our students, at the beginning of the semester, the type of testing used during the semester and we should avoid making any changes to the methods described. Whatever strategies students are choosing to use when expecting one type of test appear to be less effective when different tests are given.

An additional finding from the learning literature illustrates the impact of how a student learns new information and the relationship between that acquisition and later testing (Fisher & Craik, 1977). If the incoming information is misinterpreted or understood differently than you expected, it is very possible that, when tested with the expectation that the student's interpretation is the same as the instructor's, the student will have difficulty answering questions if they acquired the material differently. In other words, how you teach and create a particular focus should be reflected in how you test students on that material.

This is not to say you can't ask them to apply the material differently – after all, we often want students to go beyond what we teach. However, we need to keep in mind the important connection between how students learn the material (which is dependent on how we teach the material) and how we would like students to illustrate their understanding of the material in question. How often do we assume that students are focusing on the material in ways that we would expect, when in fact they went in a completely different direction. You might even hear students say, "We never covered that material," when in fact the material was the focus of one class meeting. When you later discuss this with them, you find out that students were clearly learning the material, but focused on a very different aspect of the to-be-learned information than you expected. This could easily be avoided through use of one of the classroom assessment techniques (CATs) described earlier. At the end of a class meeting, you could ask students a series of question to assess their understanding of the material. At that point, you will find out that they have focused on the material very differently than expected. Your next class meeting could start off with a review of that material to provide the refocus needed. As teachers, we need to understand that how our students perform these three memory processes is dependent on their prior knowledge. Therefore, determining what our students already know should significantly influence how we teach a particular class meeting.

Sharing Your Findings and Connecting with Others in the Field

Although it might be perfectly clear to you why pedagogical research is equivalent to other scholarly activity, this is a point you might find yourself defending to your colleagues and the administration at your institution. Therefore, creating a research program with all the components of any type of scholarship is a must to help you legitimize pedagogical research to those at your institution who might be questioning the legitimacy of research focused on teaching and learning. Just as we present our discipline-specific research at regional and national conferences, the same activity is needed for your pedagogical research. In addition, knowing how to respond to others who question how your research is different from just teaching should be considered. You might need to discuss with others on your campus how your pedagogical research does not simply address what one ordinarily carries out when teaching a course but instead is a systematic evaluation of an identified aspect of one's teaching, using methodology that provides valid measures of student learning and produces findings that are presented to a large constituency in the academic world interested in the field of teaching and learning scholarship, through peer-reviewed conference presentations and journal articles.

One critical component to any successful research program is finding a means of sharing your findings. As is true for any field of research, sharing of one's ideas and findings is one important factor for keeping the field alive and moving forward. Of course, sharing your findings is also important with regards to promotion and tenure. Often, when findings from one's research program remain "in-house," many question the acceptance of that research by your peers. As mentioned above, in terms of others identifying pedagogical research in the same category as research conducted within your discipline, sharing your findings is vital. Clearly, with peer-reviewed conferences, books, and articles, colleagues and administrators are more likely to conclude that research in the area of SoTL is similar to other types of research.

There is a variety of ways in which to get the word out about your research. You can start with a discipline-specific approach; though keep in mind that your findings are often of interest in more than just one academic arena. Conferences in your discipline might include sessions dedicated to the teaching of your discipline, though one SoTL assessment found that many faculty did not find SoTL sessions at their national disciplinary conferences (Ciccone & Meyers, 2006). If that is the case, what a perfect opportunity to start offering scholarly presentations related to teaching at your disciplinary conferences. At conferences that do include SoTL programming, you'll find both general teaching sessions as well as teaching of a very specific area in your field. For instance, in the field of physics one can attend the Physics Teacher Education Coalition conference. In English, there is the Modern Language Association, where one can find a number of sessions focused on teaching. At the annual conference of the American Psychological Association and at the American Psychological Sciences conference, there are many teaching-focused sessions. The American Political Science Association recognizes that teaching is an integral part of the discipline and states that part of their mission is to support political science education and research examining methodologies used in the political science classroom. There are many other organizations that support scholarship on teaching of the discipline and provide an opportunity for sharing the results from one's pedagogical research program. Others in your field would be very interested in hearing about teaching techniques that you found to be successful for teaching particular subject matter in your field.

In addition to your own field of research, there are many conferences focused solely on the scholarship of teaching and learning. Organizations such as the International Society for the Scholarship of Teaching and Learning (ISSOTL), the Collaboration for the Advancement of College Teaching and Learning, as well as the International Alliance of Teacher Scholars all offer annual SoTL conferences. The National CASTL (Carnegie Academy for SoTL) Institute provides faculty just starting out in the field with mentoring and learning opportunities from leading scholars in the field. Also available for new faculty developers is the Institute for New Faculty Developers, which holds an annual conference on learning to establish and manage faculty development programs (http://www.iinfd. org/). ISELT (International Society for Exploring Teaching and Learning) holds a conference as well, again providing presentations from leaders in the field and allowing one to connect with those who share interests in the area of pedagogical research. Many SoTL conferences are also sponsored through academic institutions all over the country. On the website http://www.iathe.org/, run by the Institute for the Advancement of Teaching in Higher Education, you can find a list of conferences, worldwide, for upcoming years. With this conference database you can enter the theme for a conference or the organization in which you are interested, or you can simply describe the type of conference you would like to attend. For those of you just starting a pedagogical research program, attendance at one of these conferences will provide wonderful ideas on the different directions you can take given the research base to date and provide many opportunities to meet colleagues from other institutions with similar interests.

Of course, ultimately many of us would like to share our results in a peer-reviewed journal. Once again, the publications could be within your field of study. There are a number of disciplines with journals devoted solely on pedagogical research (see appendix). Examples include *Teaching Mathematics and Its Applications, Journal of Teaching Writing, Teaching Philosophy*, and the *Journal on the Teaching of Psychology*. For those who teach physics there is the online resource titled *The Physics Teacher*, and those in communication studies have *Communication Education*. On the other hand, a simple web search with the key words "SoTL journals" will turn up a long list of journals that publish SoTL research. To give you an idea of these journals, we have included a list in the appendix. Many of these journals have websites that provide detailed descriptions of the type of articles included in each journal, and some journals in this area can also be found in electronic form, such as *The Journal of Effective Teaching.*

Conclusion

The tools summarized above allow you to get started whether you are interested in using assessment tools simply to go beyond the teaching evaluations you use at the end of the semester to obtain additional measures in your classroom, or whether you simply are in need of ways to illustrate the effectiveness of your teaching for evaluative purposes (e.g., tenure, reappointment), or whether you are interested in starting a more systematic pedagogical research program of your own. Perhaps you are simply in need of ways to illustrate the effectiveness of your teaching. You might start off with the notion that you are going to use a few assessment tools to determine the effectiveness of a particular teaching technique and soon realize that this type of scholarly activity can be not only helpful in achieving greater effectiveness in the classroom, but also an exciting area of inquiry and a whole new focus for one's scholarship. Of course, pedagogical research needs to focus not only on how we teach, but also on how students learn. What follows in the next chapter is exactly that: how to take your pedagogical research program and focus on student learning.

Appendix: Examples of Discipline-Specific SoTL Journals

International Journal of Web-Based Learning and Teaching Technologies
Journal of College Science Teaching
Journal of Computers in Mathematics and Science Teaching
Journal of Teaching in International Business
Journal of Research in Science Teaching
Journal of Teaching in Social Work
Journal of Teaching Writing
Pedagogy : Critical Approaches to Teaching Literature, Language, Culture, and Composition
Teaching Anthropology
Teaching Children Mathematics
Teaching History
Teaching Mathematics and its Applications
Teaching Music
Teaching Philosophy
Teaching of Psychology
Teaching Sociology
Teaching Statistics
Teaching Theology and Religion

SoTL Journals

Academic Commons
Academic Exchange
Active Learning in Higher Education
Assessment Update
Change: The Magazine of Higher Learning
College Teaching
Creative College Teaching Journal
Deliberation
F-LIGHT
Higher Education Research and Development
Innovative Higher Education
Interdisciplinary Journal of Problem
International Journal of the Scholarship of Teaching and Learning
International Journal Teaching and Learning in Higher Education
Inventio: Creative Thinking About Teaching and Learning
Journal for the Art of Teaching

Journal of Cognitive and Effective Learning
Journal of Effective Teaching
Journal of Faculty Development
Journal of Graduate and Professional Student Development
Journal of Scholarship of Teaching and Learning
Journal of Student Center Learning
Journal of University Teaching and Learning Practice
Journal of the Scholarship of Teaching and Learning
Journal on Excellence in College Teaching
Learning and Teaching in the Social Sciences
Learning and Instruction
Learning and Teaching in Higher Education
Learning Inquiry
Michigan Journal of Community Service Learning
National Teaching and Learning Forum
Reaching Through Teaching
Teaching in Higher Education
Teaching Professor
What Works in Teaching and Learning

3

Pedagogical Research

Focusing on Learning

Will providing students with copies of my PowerPoint slides help them learn? Will students learn better if I assign them to groups for group work or if I let them form their own groups? Do those clickers actually do anything for learning? Can students increase retention without increasing study time?

Perhaps you too have asked questions such as these. We both did. Using the methods of pedagogical research, finding the answers are not that difficult. Thanks to SoTL, the answers to the four questions above are already known, and we can all use and build on the results. For example, Chapman et al. (2006) tested whether the method of group member assignment makes a difference. Using a large sample of marketing students, they found that, compared to students who were randomly assigned to groups, students in self-selected groups reported significantly better learning experiences than students in randomly assigned groups. Brewer (2004) tested the effectiveness of clickers – personal response systems (PRS), or classroom performance systems (CPS) in biology classes – and found that the systems improved student attitudes towards the material and improved study time outside of class (see also Brezis & Cohen, 2004, for work with medical students, and Hines, 2005, for similar results in math and science classes). We'll get to whether handing out your slides aids learning later in this chapter. Finally, Rohrer and Pasher (2007) showed that you can increase retention without increasing study time. News you can use.

Teaching goals and learning goals are not the same thing. Learning goals specify student habits of mind, intellectual capacities, personal qualities – in essence what we hope students will know, what they can do, and strive for. Teaching goals focus on what teachers do (e.g., explaining specific content to students). It is important to shift from teaching goals to learning goals – from thinking about what one does as a teacher to how students interpret the subject and how they will respond to teaching. Whereas the previous chapter focused primarily on teaching, this chapter will focus on the "learning" component of SoTL and discuss pedagogical research focused on the learner. How do you know when your students are learning? In essence the proof of enhancing teaching is seen in enhanced learning. Correspondingly, the study of learning is critical in its own right. It is easy to blend research on teaching with research on learning, but we believe it advances personal pedagogical research and the field of SoTL to concentrate on each separately.

There are many key components to understanding how students learn and consequently a number of methods and tools for doing research in this area. The steps in conducting research on learning mirror the steps used to research teaching:

What are the learning outcomes you really care about?
What has been published on this topic?
What is left to be discovered or needed to be done?
How do you do it?

This last question (How do you do it?) has three main steps. First, you measure how your students are learning, then you try to optimize their learning, following which you test to see whether your efforts have paid off. The basic process is represented in box 3.1. The bulk of this chapter will provide a summary of much of what is known about how students learn to serve as a springboard for your own explorations of your students' learning. Then, we present examples of many of the measures used in studies of student learning to guide you in the design of studies of your own students. Our focus will be exclusively on the study of learning in individual classes and pedagogical research conducted by faculty on their own classes. For a broader discussion on research on learning from an institutional perspective, see Maki (2004) or for curricular assessment at the department, college, or university level, see Diamond (1998). There are many resources that provide case studies from a variety of disciplines, each describing specific classroom research projects in detail. Good resources with extensive case studies include Savory, Burnett, and Goodburn (2007) and Hutchins (2000). For examples of specific procedures see Angelo and Cross (1993) and Richlin (2006). For other general guides see Fink (2003), McKinney (2007), and Weimer (2006).

Box 3.1: Studying Student Learning

A. What do I *want* my students to learn?
    Mandates from:
    State
    University
    Department
    Discipline

B. How *are* my students Learning?
    Survey
    Focus group
    Assignment scores
        Papers
        Exams
        Multiple choice
        Short answer
        Essay
        Matching
        Fill-in-the-blanks
    Presentations

C. What can I do to get A closer to B?
    Review literature on what has been done.
    Curricular redesign
    Modification of:
        Lectures
        Assignments
        Assessments

D. How do I know if what I did *worked*?
    See B.
    Pick a pedagogical research design
    Analyze changes

Studying how students learn in general is difficult as the outcomes and means of assessments vary across disciplines. As pointed out by Bain (2004), some remarkable teachers develop highly valuable learning objectives that ignore disciplinary boundaries. Correspondingly, there is much to learn by looking at models of studying learning from a cross-disciplinary perspective. By having these different perspectives in one chapter, we hope to expose you to new ideas from a discipline other than your own that you may not have otherwise considered. You can modify the methods to fit your disciplinary needs. We hope the menu of commonly asked questions about learning and prototypical designs and measures to study such questions that we provide will galvanize your own pedagogical research.

What Do You Want to Find Out?

In the previous chapter we scrutinized what you do as a teacher; it is now time to turn the spotlight in another direction and focus on the student. First, let us map out the terrain. Ask yourself the following key question: "What influences student learning?" Try to jot down as many answers as you can. Perhaps start with a blank sheet of paper and draw in all the different influences you can. Both of us did this exercise and came up with something like what you see in figure 3.1 (we cleaned it up a lot so what you see is a version without scratched-out lines).

This simple question is the key to starting pedagogical research on learning. You may be surprised by how intuitive and obvious the answers may seem. Although your jottings may be informed by information you have read or from your experiences, and indeed there is a lot written on this topic (e.g., Bransford, Brown, & Cocking, 1999), most of us can generate some good answers even if we are not aware of the research literature on this topic at all. Part of the reason is that all of us have experience with learning (i.e., our own), and anyone who has taught a single class sees the process in action. Now the challenge is to systematically examine where the process breaks down in order to rectify the situation.

Before we get to the pragmatics of conducting research on learning, we will first do what any good research endeavor should do and look at what has already been done on student learning. We would not want you to have to reinvent the wheel or build from the ground up. Instead, we will briefly review the pertinent parts of the vast literature on student learning and

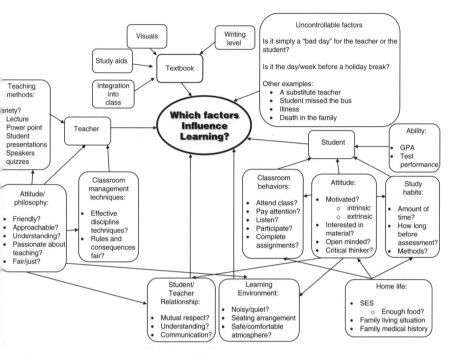

Figure 3.1: Factors influencing learning

then sketch out how you can go about conducting research in your chosen area.

What Do We Know about How Students Learn?

There has been a considerable amount written on the notion of learning styles, and many instructors and even some introductory textbooks discuss the topic. Learning styles are presumed by many educators to be very important for student success. This presumption has spawned a large body of research. Investigators use learning style inventories to explore differences among students, explore educators' opinions of learning styles, and suggest connections between learning styles and other constructs (Vasquez, in press). Should you run right out and give your students a test to see what their style is so that you can change the way you teach? In one of the most comprehensive and recent reviews on the topic, Vasquez (in press) shows that there is little empirical evidence in support of the strongest learning style claims, such as that a person with a particular learning style is unable to learn in an "incompatible" teaching style. She goes on to point out that most learning style inventories have not published validation data (Harrison, Andrews, & Saklofske, 2003), and several recent empirical studies show that learning style is unrelated to academic performance (e.g., Kratzig & Arbuthnott, 2006). Similarly, Rinaldi and Gurung (2005) did not find any evidence for improvements in learning when the instructor created assignments designed for different styles of learners. If your gut tells you that all this research has missed something, there is perhaps still some pedagogical research that can be done on this topic (but we suggest starting elsewhere).

Just as the influence of students' own learning style on their learning may provide one trailhead for pedagogical research, it may be prudent to take a step back and examine students' ways of knowing as well. The way a student approaches learning is a broader topic that bears a little more attention for its utility in our quest to optimize learning. Whereas a learning style may include fixed behaviors or tendencies to resonate with certain forms of instruction or text (e.g., lecture based versus discussion based), a way of knowing relates to one's mental model of how knowledge is gained. There are broad differences in the ways that people want to learn (or in their approach to knowing). Tweed and Lehman (2002) organized a wide body of findings and compared the *Socratic method* of learning, exemplified by the questioning of one's own and others' beliefs, the evaluation of others' knowledge, having high esteem for self-generated knowledge, and focusing on error to evoke doubt, with the *Confucian method* of learning, exemplified by effortful, pragmatic, and respectful learning, behavioral reform, and the acquisition of essential knowledge. The Confucian and Socratic models can easily be conceptualized as representing two ends of the learning continuum within all individuals. The consideration of individual differences in ways of knowing merging educational theory with this new cultural dichotomy in learning makes for a more powerful heuristic tool for educational reform and the scholarship of teaching.

Even a cursory look around American college classrooms will reveal that most students engage in rote memorization and feel pressured to memorize the material. Many students (especially those in community colleges and technical/vocational schools) illustrate an extremely pragmatic approach to learning. They are concerned with whether their coursework will help them get a good job, and are often turned off by courses (e.g., general education requirements) designed for the broadening of intellectual horizons (Huba & Freed, 2000). These drives to memorize for the test and to be pragmatic are both major aspects of the Confucian style. The recent initiatives to make learning more active and the established need for instructors to modify their techniques to increase student engagement with the material (Grasha, 1990; Huba & Freed, 2000) testify to a need for more Socratic learning. Pedagogical writings urging educators to utilize multiple instructional styles suggest that, more often than not, methods like the traditional lecture should be modified with other instructional styles that will engage different styles of learning and knowing (Claxton & Murrell, 1987; Grasha, 1990).

A substantial body of pedagogical writing on the ways that people learn and acquire knowledge bears on the Socratic-Confucian framework. For example, Bloom and colleagues (Bloom et al., 1956) initiated the examination of learning by proposing that optimal learning is achieved by having students analyze, evaluate, synthesize, and apply knowledge beyond just remembering and comprehending it. Anderson and Krathwohl (2001) have revised the taxonomy so that it now encompasses two dimensions: a knowledge dimension and a cognitive processing dimension. Perry (1970) discussed different types of students, distinguishing *Dualistic students*, for whom knowledge is certain, and right or wrong is acquired from authority, from students who are *Uncertain* (replacing the right or wrong dichotomy by separating knowledge into what is known versus unknown), and students who use *Relativistic Thinking*, for whom some knowledge claims are better than others, and for whom knowledge is validated by evidence relevant to context. Perry's model was adapted to better incorporate gender differences by Belenky et al. (1986). Women, for example, are more likely to read textbooks and be more accepting of the material therein (Gurung & Martin, 2007).

Similarly, Magolda (1992) proposed a model of epistemological reflection to distinguish between different ways of knowing. *Absolute Knowers* acquire information from authorities, either by listening or by actively questioning and responding to authority. *Transitional Knowers* focus on understanding knowledge, via accessing others' views regarding uncertainty or via being forced to think. *Independent Knowers* feel free to decide their own opinions, focusing either on peer views or their own views, and *Contextual Knowers* construct knowledge from judging the evidence, others' views, and own beliefs. Similarly, King and Kitchener (1994) proposed their Reflective Judgment Model with seven stages of knowing. One evolves through these stages as cognitive capacities develop, and this is closely correlated with age, although the type of instruction can certainly influence procession along the continuum. In Stage 1, knowledge is certain, and authorities' beliefs are accepted. In Stage 2, knowledge is certain but not always available. In Stage 3, knowledge is temporary and uncertain, with the hope that absolute knowledge will be possible. In Stage 4, some knowledge is permanently uncertain, accompanied by an idiosyncratic evaluation of knowledge claims. In Stage 5, rules of inquiry in particular contexts are used to justify beliefs, and in Stage 6 generalized rules of inquiry take over as knowledge is viewed as being constructed. Finally, in Stage 7, some knowledge claims are valued over others based on critical evaluation of the evidence. Such extensive frameworks of knowing/knowledge acquisition provide us with pragmatic innovations to enhancing education. As teachers we can use models such as these to modify the types of questions we raise in class and the structure of the class assignments we design. Being cognizant of these types of knowing can help us better understand why some students do better than others especially in higher-level classes, where we expect more from our students and hope to take them to higher levels of critical thinking.

Cognitive science, the interdisciplinary study of the mind, thinking processes, and intelligence, also provides some key insights into the many processes that influence learning in addition to the issues described above. Although there too many good studies to list here, the interested reader should read Bransford, Brown, and Cocking (1999) and Hacker, Dunlosky, and Graesser (1998). For example, Bransford, Brown, and Cocking (1999) report on a two-year study conducted by the Committee on Developments in the Science of Learning and a second National Research Council committee that explored how research could be linked to actual practice in the classroom. In like vein, the International Mind, Brain, and Education Society recently launched a new journal, *Mind, Brain, and Education*, to promote the integration of diverse disciplines that investigate human learning (Fischer et al., 2007).

Student Engagement: If You Engage Them, They Will Learn

Student engagement has been receiving more and more attention lately (e.g., Kuh et al., 2005). Engagement is conventionally described as holding a student's attention but in the academic context also suggests deep inter-action of the material, class, and university. Students who are engaged allow themselves to be involved and a part of the class. When a student is engaged, he or she is more apt to study and participate in class and there-fore be successful with their college careers. Correspondingly, increasing engagement is an important part of optimizing learning. You could almost exclusively focus your efforts on getting your students to be more engaged. But how do you know if your efforts are paying off? How does one assess engagement?

There are various instruments that are used to assess student engage-ment. The most popular and widely used instrument is the *National Survey of Student Engagement* (NSSE and referred to as Nessie). The survey, based on the pioneering work of Pace and the College Student Experiences Ques-tionnaire research program, was developed to directly tap into the under-graduate educational experience by the Center for Postsecondary Research at Indiana University. Administered mostly to first-year college students as well as college seniors, it is commonly used to compare the levels of engage-ment between the two. Many faculty at various institutions have found the results of NSSE to be positively related to persistence and academic per-formance (Carini, Kuh, & Klein, 2006; Kuh et al., 2005).

The NSSE can be a very useful aid in our endeavors to optimize student learning. The instrument itself consists of 29 sections, of which some sec-tions have multiple parts, making a total of 100 items. The items of the first 14 sections lie within five different domains: *supportive campus envi-ronment, enriching educational experiences, student faculty interaction, level of academic challenges,* and *active and collaborative learning.* The last 15 sections of the NSSE gather demographic information.

The domains within the NSSE attempt to cover various aspects of student engagement. The questions that pertain to the *supportive campus environ-ment* component are about how the institution assists with, and commits to, the success of its students. Some of these items may touch on helping students succeed with academics and promoting good relationships between students and their peers. The domain of *enriching educational experiences* addresses student exposure to diversity and new ideas as well as technology and work outside of the classroom. Items on the NSSE ask about how often students talk with other students who are of a different ethnicity, using technology to complete assignments, and participating in co-curricular activities and community service. *Student interaction with faculty members* is another domain that discusses student contact with faculty members outside of the classroom. Items include discussing assignments and grades with an instructor to working on a research project with an instructor. The domain of *level of academic challenges* touches on the work students are assigned and cognitive tasks that students may use to complete assigned works. The NSSE items also include how students prepare for class. The last NSSE domain, *active and collaborative learning*, assesses whether students are actively involved with their education by working with others. These items include getting involved with class discussion and tutoring other students. These domains cover the aspects that are currently thought to be the backbone of student engagement.

A great strength of the NSSE is that it has been validated in a number of ways and, given it has been used nationwide, there is a lot of comparison data. Of course, it is very general and, although useful to test engagement in your class, it does tend to lend itself to tapping into larger samples such as an entire freshman class. A good alternative, and one perhaps more likely to be used by the majority of the readers of this book, is the Classroom Survey of Student Engagement (CLSSE, or Classie) developed by Bob Smallwood and Judy Ouimet. The CLSSE is a measure that can be used by faculty to measure student involvement in a particular class (Kinzie, 2007). This measure has also been validated and is available free of charge (as compared to the NSSE). Note, however, that many schools are using the NSSE. If your school or university is using the NSSE you can use any subset of items from the scale to test engagement in your class. This information is usually available through an institutional research office. Sample items from both scales are shown in box 3.2.

How Can You Investigate Your Students' Learning?

The ways students approach learning are important to be aware of but they may not be as pragmatic as you would like. Instead of having you start with a blank slate, we have attempted to summarize the large research literature on student learning into a visual heuristic. The map in figure 3.1 (page 91) will help you embark on your pedagogical research into student learning. The figure lists the main categories of factors that influence student learning, and then lists the major components of each factor. There are additional components that fit under each factor but we wanted to not clutter up the model with superfluous details. Instead we will expand on

Box 3.2: CLASSE_{STUDENT}

Classroom Survey of Student Engagement*

This survey includes items that ask about your participation in [Course XYZ] and about educational practices that occur in this class. Your honest and straightforward responses to these questions will help us identify targets for improvements and enable us to provide an even higher quality academic experience.

PART I: ENGAGEMENT ACTIVITIES

So far this semester, how often have you done each of the following in your [Course XYZ] class	Never	1 or 2 times	3 to 5 times	More than 5 times
1. Asked questions during your [Course XYZ] class?	☐	☐	☐	☐
2. Contributed to a class discussion that occurred during your [Course XYZ] class	☐	☐	☐	☐
3. Prepared two or more drafts of a paper or assignment in your [Course XYZ] class before turning it in	☐	☐	☐	☐
4. Worked on a paper or a project in your [Course XYZ] class that required integrating ideas or information from various sources	☐	☐	☐	☐
5. Included diverse perspectives (different races, religions, genders, political beliefs, etc.) in class discussions or writing assignments in your [Course XYZ] class	☐	☐	☐	☐
6. Came to your [Course XYZ] class without having completed readings or asignments	☐	☐	☐	☐

Continued

7. Worked with other students on projects during your [Course XYZ] class ☐ ☐ ☐ ☐

8. Worked with classmates outside of your [Course XYZ] class to prepare class assignments ☐ ☐ ☐ ☐

9. Put together ideas of concepts from different courses when completing assignments or during class discussions in your [Course XYZ] class ☐ ☐ ☐ ☐

10. Tutored or taught other students in your [Course XYZ] class ☐ ☐ ☐ ☐

11. Used an electronic medium (list-serv, chat group, Internet, instant messaging, etc.) to discuss or complete an assignment in your [Course XYZ] class ☐ ☐ ☐ ☐

12. Used email to communicate with the instructor of your [Course XYZ] class ☐ ☐ ☐ ☐

13. Discussed grades or assignments with the instructor of your [Course XYZ] class ☐ ☐ ☐ ☐

14. Discussed ideas from your [Course XYZ] with others outside of class (students, family members, coworkers, etc.) ☐ ☐ ☐ ☐

15. Made a class presentation in your [Course XYZ] class
    ☐ Never   ☐ Once   ☐ 2 times   ☐ More than 2 times

16. Participated in a community-based project (e.g., service learning) as part of your [Course XYZ] class
    ☐ Never   ☐ Once   ☐ 2 times   ☐ More than 2 times

17. Discussed ideas from your readings or classes with your [Course XYZ] instructor outside of class
    ☐ Never   ☐ Once   ☐ 2 times   ☐ More than 2 times

18. Received prompt written or oral feedback on your academic performance from your [Course XYZ] instructor
    ☐ Never/Rarely   ☐ Sometimes   ☐ Often   ☐ Very Often

19. Worked harder than you thought you could to meet your [Course XYZ] instructor's standards or expectations

☐ Never/Rarely   ☐ Sometimes   ☐ Often   ☐ Very Often

PART II: COGNITIVE SKILLS

So far this semester, how much of your coursework in your [Course XYZ] class emphasized the following mental activities?

	Very Little ▼	Some ▼	Quite a Bit ▼	Very Much ▼
20. **Memorizing** facts, ideas, or methods from your courses and readings so you can repeat them in pretty much the same form	☐	☐	☐	☐
21. **Analyzing** the basic elements of an idea, experience, or theory, such as examining a particular case or situation in depth and considering its components	☐	☐	☐	☐
22. **Synthesizing** and organizing ideas, information, or experiences into new, more complex interpretations and relationships	☐	☐	☐	☐
23. **Making Judgments** about the value of information, arguments, or methods, such as examining how others gathered and interpreted data and assessing the soundness of their conclusions	☐	☐	☐	☐
24. **Applying** theories or concepts to practical problems or in new situations	☐	☐	☐	☐

PART III: OTHER EDUCATIONAL PRACTICES

So far this semester

25. How often in your [Course XYZ] class have you been required to prepare written papers or reports of more than 5 pages in length?

☐ Never   ☐ Once   ☐ 2 times   ☐ 3 or more times

Continued

26. To what extent do the examinations in your [Course XYZ] class challenge you to do your best work?
    ☐ Very little   ☐ Some   ☐ Quite a bit ☐ Very much

27. In a **typical week** in your [Course XYZ] class, how many homework assignments take you more than one hour each to complete?
    ☐ None   ☐ 1 or 2   ☐ 3 or 4   ☐ 5 or more

28. In a **typical week**, how often do you spend more than 3 hours preparing for your [Course XYZ] class (studying, reading, doing homework or lab work, analyzing data, rehearsing, and other academic matters)?
    ☐ Never/Rarely ☐ Sometimes   ☐ Often   ☐ Very Often

29. How many times have you been absent so far this semester in your [Course XYZ] class?
    ☐ None   ☐ 1–2 absences   ☐ 3–4 absences   ☐ 5 or more absences

30. How frequently do you take notes in your [Course XYZ] class?
    ☐ Never/Rarely ☐ Sometimes   ☐ Often   ☐ Very Often

31. How often do you review your notes prior to the next scheduled meeting in your [Course XYZ] class?
    ☐ Never/Rarely ☐ Sometimes   ☐ Often   ☐ Very Often

32. How often have you participated in a study partnership with a classmate in your [Course XYZ] class to prepare for a quiz or a test?
    ☐ Never   ☐ Once   ☐ 2 times   ☐ 3 or more times

33. How often have you attended a review session or help session to enhance your understanding of the content of your [Course XYZ] class?
    ☐ Never   ☐ Once   ☐ 2 times   ☐ 3 or more times

34. How interested are you in learning the [Course XYZ] courses material?
    ☐ Very   ☐ Uninterested   ☐ Interested ☐ Very Interested
    uninterested

PART IV: CLASS ATMOSPHERE
So far this semester, what are your general impressions of the [Course XYZ] class atmosphere?

35. How comfortable are you talking with the instructor of your [Course XYZ] class?
    ☐ Uncomfortable ☐ Somewhat   ☐ Comfortable   ☐ Very
                       Comfortable   Comfortable

36. How much do you enjoy group work with your classmates in your [Course XYZ] class?
    ☐ Very Little ☐ Some ☐ Quite a Bit ☐ Very Much

37. How difficult is the course material in your [Course XYZ] class?
    ☐ Easy ☐ Somewhat Difficult ☐ Difficult ☐ Very Difficult

38. How easy is it to follow the lectures in your [Course XYZ] class?
    ☐ Difficult ☐ Somewhat Easy ☐ Easy ☐ Very Easy

PART V: OPTIONAL [COURSE XYZ] ITEMS
So far this semester

39. [Course XYZ] class unique item #1
    ☐ Option 1 ☐ Option 2 ☐ Option 3 ☐ Option 4

40. [Course XYZ] class unique item #2
    ☐ Option 1 ☐ Option 2 ☐ Option 3 ☐ Option 4

41. [Course XYZ] class unique item #3
    ☐ Option 1 ☐ Option 2 ☐ Option 3 ☐ Option 4

42. [Course XYZ] class unique item #4
    ☐ Option 1 ☐ Option 2 ☐ Option 3 ☐ Option 4

43. [Course XYZ] class unique item #5
    ☐ Option 1 ☐ Option 2 ☐ Option 3 ☐ Option 4

44. [Course XYZ] class unique item #6
    ☐ Option 1 ☐ Option 2 ☐ Option 3 ☐ Option 4

45. [Course XYZ] class unique item #7
    ☐ Option 1 ☐ Option 2 ☐ Option 3 ☐ Option 4

46. [Course XYZ] class unique item #8
    ☐ Option 1 ☐ Option 2 ☐ Option 3 ☐ Option 4

PART VI: DEMOGRAPHICS

47. How many credit hours are you enrolled in this semester?
    ☐ 1–6 credit hours ☐ 7–11 credit hours
    ☐ 12–15 credit hours ☐ >15 credit hours

Continued

48. What is your classification?
   ☐ Freshman (<30 hrs)   ☐ Sophomore (30–59 hrs)
   ☐ Junior (60–89 hrs)   ☐ Senior (90+ hrs)

49. What is your academic major?

Please enter your student identification number here _____

If you do not know your ID number, please print your first and last name.

We ask you to identify yourself by student identification number in order to permit us to relate your responses to the particular educational experience you've had at the **[University of North Florida]**. Please know that your individual responses will remain confidential. No individual responses will ever be identified in any report, shared with your faculty instructor, or in any other way made available. As a student-centered university, we know we will make the best decisions to improve the educational experience when those decisions are informed by student feedback. Thank you for helping us attain this goal.

Thank you for taking the time to complete this survey

*Items #1–#28 adapted with permission from the National Survey of Student Engagement, Copyright 2001–06 The Trustees of Indiana University

---

the different areas below. It is our hope that the visual will help you pick which aspect of student learning you want to focus on and perhaps attempt to improve. For example, you could choose to focus on improving how your students read, how they study, how they take notes or tests, or even on working on some of the psychological factors associated with learning. This section provides a good global guide to research on student learning that transcends more specific interventions such as improving critical thinking or close reading skills, which we will also touch on.

Above all, study behaviors appear to be the most important component in student learning, and poor study skills are highly correlated with low grade point averages (Proctor et al., 2006). All four of these components – psychological factors, note-taking, reading, and studying – are interrelated, and each necessarily supports the other. One clear interrelated idea is the fact that students are ingenuous to their own abilities (Lynch, 2006; Winne & Jamieson-Noel, 2002). They are unable to identify strengths and weaknesses, and many times they regard their abilities more favorably than they should. Many freshmen are unable to realize that the passive learning they engaged successfully in during high school will prove itself to be unsuccessful in the college setting. Many freshmen have difficulties monitoring their studying and are unable to select the best strategies to learn the material at hand (Nist et al., 1991; Winne & Jamieson-Noel, 2002). Let us take a closer look at student study behaviors.

How Do Students Study?

Students use a variety of techniques to increase their test scores and learn material. A large body of research has attempted to identify the techniques that are optimal (e.g., Gurung, 2005; Weinstein & Palmer, 2002). Measures of study behaviors, also called study skills, study strategies, or study techniques, can serve as a diagnostic tool to help instructors identify students in need of additional help, as well as provide students with better awareness of their strengths and weaknesses and, correspondingly, ways to optimize their learning. There are many different ways to study, but not all methods may enhance learning. There is a sizeable literature on how students should study (Al-Hilawani & Sartawi, 1997; Fleming, 2002; Gettinger & Seibert, 2002; Hattie, Biggs, & Purdie, 1996) and some good measurements of how students actually do study (Weinstein & Palmer, 2002).

Study behaviors can be broadly defined as behaviors serving to acquire, organize, synthesize, evaluate, remember, and use information (e.g., Harvey, 1995). Such behaviors include time management, goal setting, selecting how, and where what to study, and self-testing, and are related to note taking and reading ability. Study skills can be divided into four main categories: repetition-based (e.g., flashcards and mnemonic devices such as HOME for the Great Lakes) and cognitively based (e.g., studying with a friend and group work) strategies, procedural (e.g., time management, organization, and scheduling study routines), and metacognitive (e.g., taking quizzes to test self-knowledge; for more details see Gettinger & Seibert, 2002) and also include knowing how to pick a good environment (e.g., not have the music playing).

Empirical tests comparing these different methods are equivocal. Some research suggests that the types of study techniques that a student uses affect exam performance (Bol et al., 1999). Other research suggests that there is no one style that is useful for everyone and that a repertoire of techniques is best (Hadwin & Winne, 1996; Nist et al., 1991). For example, repetition/rehearsal, which requires a minimal amount of processing, may be useful only in remembering small amounts of information (Gettinger & Seibert, 2002). Memorizing facts and definitions do not correlate with students' exam scores, but procedural/organizational-based skills, meta-cognitive-based skills, and skills that increase elaboration show positive correlations with test scores (Carney & Levin, 1998; Chen & Daelhler, 2000; Elliot, McGregor, & Gable, 1999; Motes & Wiegmann, 1999). Dickinson and O'Connell (1990) also showed that time spent organizing course material (e.g., taking notes on the textbook) related to test scores, whereas actual hours spent studying did not. Of all the different ways students can study, arguably the most effective category is one relating to metacognitive processes.

Metacognition

How do students know if they know something and how much they know? Does studying affect this feeling of knowing and does the feeling of knowing affect studying? How should students study in order to experience success? How can teachers help students learn more effectively? Questions such as these are targeted by research on *metacognition*. Metacognition, or thinking about how you think, refers to general activities of reflecting and directing one's own thinking (Pelligrino, Chudowsky, & Glaser, 2001). The term originated in John Flavell's pioneering work, and his request for further research now serves as the basis for its study (1971, p. 273; 1977). Currently, the consensus definition of metacognition is the knowledge of one's knowledge, processes, and cognitive and affective states; and the ability to consciously and deliberately monitor and regulate these (Hacker, Dunlosky, & Graesser, 1998).

The theoretical characteristics of metacognition have dominated research since the 1960s; however, the newest area of inquiry has produced research with a focus on educational application. According to Hacker, Dunlosky, and Graesser (1998, p. 17), "many researchers [are] convinced of the edu-cational relevance that metacognitive theory has for teachers and students, [and] are shifting their attention from the theoretical to the practical, from the laboratory to the classroom." A number of lab studies have explicitly demonstrated the benefits of monitoring of one's thinking (e.g., Dun-lowsky & Nelson, 1997; Koriat & Bjork, 2005) and cognitive research on metacognition is now beginning to move into real-world settings and the classroom (e.g., Metcalfe, 2006). Metacognitive theory can help teachers create classroom environments that foster flexible and creative strategic learning (Borkowski & Muthukrishna, 1992). This culmination of research suggests students will benefit from teachers who indeed utilize the instruction of metacognitive processes to facilitate learning (see Dunlosky & Lipko, 2007; Hacker Dunlosky, & Graesser, 1998; Metcalfe & Greene, 2007, for reviews).

There are four main categories of metacognitive research.

1. *Cognitive monitoring.* Cognitive monitoring addresses individuals' knowledge and ability to monitor if they know, what they know, and their thought processes (Brown, 1978; Schneider, 1985). Individuals monitor incoming information during their own thinking and then use this information to control consequent memory processes. A goal of research is to assess if how much people know about their memory is a significant predictor of their performance on a memory task (Cavanaugh & Perlmutter, 1982). The accuracy of memory monitoring and the effect the amount of time between learning and monitoring has is discussed as a component of the way memory affects learning (Nelson & Dunlosky, 1991).

How does predicting future performance affect learning? This question is based upon research asking whether students' predictions are accurate (Maki & Berry, 1984; Glenberg & Epstein 1985). After students have read an assigned text, their ability to make predictions about their performance on future assessments is a complex process that involves different judgments. A student must first judge how well he or she understands the text and how much learning has occurred. Students who are able to read text material and consequently judge when they need to learn more will attain a life-long learning goal. Glenberg et al. (1987) and Maki and Serra (1992a) suggest familiarity with the topic domain may have an effect on the accuracy of prediction. Second, the students must take into account forgetting as a result of the retention interval and interference from learning new material. Third, the accuracy of predictions will depend on the students' knowledge about the format of the test (including types of questions and their degree of difficulty). The earliest reports concerning the accuracy of prediction influencing learning outcomes yielded mixed conclusions; however, the most recent research on test prediction accuracy uses multiple test items for each prediction (Gillstrom & Ronnberg, 1995; Magliano, Little, & Graesser, 1993; Maki, 1995; Maki & Serra, 1992a, 1992b; Weaver

& Bryant, 1995). These studies, conducted after 1990, demonstrate that greater accuracy has been observed on test prediction. Students can be trained to be better at knowing if they did well on a test. Kennedy, Lawton, and Plumlee (2002) test how accurate students' self-assessments are and observe that students cannot accurately assess their performance because they do not know what they don't know (p. 244). Furthermore, "incompetent students" overestimate by a larger margin than the "competent students" underestimate (Kennedy, Lawton & Plumlee, 2002, p. 246). Therefore, the students who need the most help are overestimating their levels of understanding and their performance levels on exams. Overall, the research offers mixed conclusions regarding prediction influencing learning outcomes.

Do students' predictions of future performance correlate with standard measures of learning (e.g., exam scores)? Students' ability to predict when they need to learn more, based upon their knowledge judgment of what they already know, is a life-long learning tool. More research with this focus should be the goal rather than finding ways to help students predict future test performance; the standard for learning and true understanding is reduced to mere window dressing if it is only measured by students achieving high scores on an exam. Schoenfeld (1987) demonstrates cognitive monitoring as the need for accurate self-assessment of what one knows or does not know. When students know the condition of their own knowledge only then can they effectively self-direct their learning of new material. Hart took this a step further by investigating individuals' accuracy in monitoring their stored knowledge (1965). Are we aware that we automatically respond to what we already know and ignore that which we are not familiar? David Ausubel (1968), an educational psychologist, states: "The most important single factor influencing learning is what the learner already knows. Ascertain this and teach him [her] accordingly." When teachers attend to what their students are thinking with what they know, it will allow better decisions to be made on how to support the development of students' understanding (Bransford, Brown, & Cocking, 1999).

2. *Evaluating thinking processes.* The second category of metacognition includes research focusing on the control of one's own thinking processes in order to deal with changing demands. Students will maintain using instructional strategies that will improve their learning, if they are taught the value behind the strategies (Lodico et al., 1983). Therefore, when teachers have students perform in class activities or complex homework assign-

ments, making them aware of why they are doing it improves learning. The increase in the complexity of tasks also increases the difficulty in monitoring the thought processes to complete them (Schneider, 1985). Fortunately, evidence suggests the human brain can be intentionally reorganized by instruction (Bach-y-Rita, 1980, 1981; Crill & Raichle, 1982, as cited in Bransford, Brown, & Cocking, 1999). For example, Neville (1984) studied the difference in the brains of deaf people who use sign language and those who do not use sign language and found clear differences in the parts of the brain that are active during language processing. These deaf individuals' different language experiences explain how types of instruction can transform the brain, making it possible to use varied sensory input to accomplish its communication functions. Guided learning and learning from individual experience also demonstrate the intentional reorganization of the brain (Jones & Schallert, 1994; Kolb, 1995).

Requiring students to give reasons for their answers is another tip from metacognitive research for you to incorporate in your classes. Discussing why an answer is correct has been shown to improve task performance (Berardi-Coletta et al., 1995; Dorner, 1978; Ericsson & Simon, 1993). The process of giving explanations requires individuals to focus their attention on the task at hand while simultaneously evaluating his or her progress. When teachers have students give reasons for their work, while doing in-class activities or homework problems, making them aware of evaluating why they are doing it improves learning (Bransford, Brown, & Cocking, 1999). This effective technique allows teachers to ask students to think aloud in order to gain information and better understand how the individual student approaches the problem solving process.

3. *Affective state(s)*. The third category of metacognition research includes the self-assessments of one's affective state as a strategy of metacognition. More simply stated, how does how one is feeling (happy, sad) influence one's thinking (Borkowski et al., 1990)? Self-efficacy encompasses self-appraisal and self-management as two features of metacognition (Paris & Winograd, 1990). Self-appraisals are individuals' reflections about their knowledge, their affective states concerning their knowledge, abilities, motivation, and characteristics as learners. Self-management involves the individuals' mental processes that help coordinate the various aspects of problem solving (Paris and Winograd, 1990). Borkowski et al. (1990, p. 54) demonstrate that these personal-motivational states frequently determine the course of knowledge acquisition, the likelihood of strategy transfer, and the quality of the individual's understanding about the function

of mental processes. This set of research concentrates on the importance of self-appraisal and -management, as tools to help individual learners become actively involved in the construction of their knowledge. The majority of this research has been lab based and more needs to be done in the environment of school classroom settings.

4. *Active metacognition.* This set of techniques involves active involvement with the course material and more explicit behaviors such as organization and one of the most critical elements to learning, self-testing. Self-testing, an important aspect of metacognition, has been found to be a significant factor in student success (Gurung, 2005). Students who take practice exams and online quizzes perform significantly better than those who do not self-test (Balch, 1998; Flora & Logan, 1996). These results notwithstanding, not every study finds quizzes to be as useful to student learning (Klass & Crothers, 2000), and the way quizzes are administered, especially if online, has to be closely monitored (Gurung & Daniel, 2005). Furthermore, student evaluation of quizzes are often quite favorable because students perceive them as helping to assess their weaknesses, motivate reading of the textbook, and provide another medium in which they can apply the material. One of my favorite student comments is along the lines of: "Boy, you make us do a lot of stuff, but I am glad you do because it makes me study." Practice exams are similarly perceived to be useful and motivating for the same reasons (Balch, 1998).

Other effective active metacognitive study strategies include elaboration, self-explanation, and generation. Students who engage in elaboration and self-explanation are making links between the material, their life, and previous knowledge Chi et al., 1994; Nist et al., 1991). Linking the material is more effective than just summarizing the main ideas (Chi et al., 1994). Students who generate questions and study materials in preparing for examinations are also very successful (Foos, Mora, & Tkacz, 1994). Students who generate their own study materials remember and learn material more effectively than students who receive study materials from others. Foos, Mora, and Tkacz found four levels of student performance: at the lowest level, the students were informed to study for an exam (control), at the low level, students were given materials, such as a study guide, and informed to use them, at the higher level, students generated their own outlines of the material; and at the highest level, students generated their own questions or questions and answers to study the material. They found the students at the highest level were the most effective learners.

Organization is also a key aspect of metacognition and can entail many different meanings. It can include organization of a space or organization of time, but the construct of organization as a study strategy embodies integrating the material with prior knowledge, finding meaning in the material, answering objectives, combining lecture and reading notes, and finding a structure to the material (Dickinson & O'Connell, 1990). Organization is a more effective study strategy than purely reading and reviewing. Students who are unsuccessful may be naïve to the fact that organization is effective. They may believe reading/reviewing is an effective enough strategy when it is not, as evidenced by their low scores. It may be that these students are unable to use metacognition and correct their studying habit mistakes.

Future directions. Although researchers have started laying the groundwork for the positive implications of metacognition for learners and taking cognitive science into the classroom (e.g., McDaniel & Einstein, 2005; Metcalfe, 2006; Roediger & Karpicke, 2006), the theory and practice suggested by research has not yet been made fully applicable to teachers and learners.

Pedagogical research on learning provides the perfect venue to take the results of cognitive lab studies and apply and test them in the classroom. Take student use of pedagogical aids, for example. Gurung (2003; 2004) showed that student use of pedagogical aids in textbooks (e.g., summaries, review questions) shows little to no relationship to their grades. In fact, use of some aids such as key terms was related to worse exam scores. Furthermore, students who did not score well did not utilize pedagogical aids to significantly change performance on later exams. Is this because students do not know what they are doing wrong and therefore do not know how to improve future performance? Do students need to be taught strategies to assess their "feelings of knowing" successfully in order to improve performance? As noted earlier, Kennedy et al. (2000) observed that students cannot accurately assess their performance (p. 244) because "incompetent students" overestimate their performance while "competent students" underestimate their performance (p. 246). To jumpstart your literature review and help you decide on a question for your own research, we provide a more detailed summary of some of the major research questions in metacognition with relevant resources in the appendix at the end of this chapter.

This literature review highlights some valuable implications for teachers and students in the area of metacognition and provides you with some key directions for your pedagogical research on student learning:

1) Students need instruction on how better to evaluate what they know in order to predict what they need to study for enhanced understanding and performance. The more complex the material is the more difficulty students will have in monitoring their thought processes. Further research in this area is needed.

2) It is important for teachers to make students aware of why they are doing certain instructional activities because it will improve their learning. Furthermore, students' learning should be improved when they have to give reasons for their work to make them aware of evaluating why they are doing it. When students give reasons for doing work, it serves a dual benefit of allowing teachers to gain insight and assess where the student is at in terms of how he or she approaches problem solving.

3) Instruction does affect the kinds of information our brains store. Therefore, sensory learning and learning from individual experience are the most powerful learning tools because they stimulate a reorganization of the stored information. Moreover, students' personal-motivational states frequently determine the course of knowledge acquisition and quality of understanding for the material being learned.

4) Students' prior knowledge affects what and how they will learn in the future. Therefore, it is imperative for instructors to assess and attend to what students know as a basis for forming further student instruction and enhancing students' development of understanding. This is obviously the most effective use of both the student's and the teacher's time in promoting a successful learning environment.

Measuring Study Behaviors

The existing literature does not include a comprehensive assessment of a wide variety of studying techniques, nor does it provide studies that both assess techniques and measure learning outcomes. Furthermore, students are often unaware that some of their habits, such as having music on while studying, may hurt their learning. Early attempts to assess study behaviors go back to Wrenn's *Study-Habits Inventory* (1933) and *The Student Skills Inventory* (Locke, 1940), and a *Survey of Study Habits and Attitudes* (Brown & Holtzman, 1955). More recently, many researchers have used scales such as the *Learning and Study Strategies Inventory* (LASSI; Weinstein & Palmer, 2002). The LASSI has seen more extensive use, 2,274 schools use it (www. hhpublishing.com/_assessments/LASSI/index.html) and it has 10 subscales and 80 items (see box 3.3).

Box 3.3: Subscales and sample items from the LASSI W and P (2002)

Scale: ATT: The *Attitude Scale* assesses students' attitudes and interest in college and academic success. It examines how facilitative or debilitative their approach to college and academics is for helping them get their work done and succeeding in college (sample item: I feel confused and undecided as to what my educational goals should be). Students who score low on this scale may not believe college is relevant or important to them and may need to develop a better understanding of how college and their academic performance relates to their future life goals.

Scale: MOT: The *Motivation Scale* assesses students' diligence, self-discipline, and willingness to exert the effort necessary to successfully complete academic requirements (sample item: When work is difficult I either give up or study only the easy parts). Students who score low on this scale need to accept more responsibility for their academic outcomes and learn how to set and use goals to help accomplish specific tasks.

Scale: TMT: The *Time Management Scale* assesses students' application of time management principles to academic situations (sample item: I only study when there is the pressure of a test). Students who score low on this scale may need to develop effective scheduling and monitoring techniques in order to assure timely completion of academic tasks and to avoid procrastination while realistically including non-academic activities in their schedule.

Scale: ANX: The *Anxiety Scale* assesses the degree to which students worry about school and their academic performance. Students who score low on this scale are experiencing high levels of anxiety associated with school (note that this scale is reverse scored). High levels of anxiety can help direct attention away from completing academic tasks (sample item: Worrying about doing poorly interferes with my concentration on tests). Students who score low on this scale may need to develop techniques for coping with anxiety and reducing worry so that attention can be focused on the task at hand.

Continued

Scale: CON: The Concentration Scale assesses students' ability to direct and maintain attention on academic tasks (sample item: I find that during lectures I think of other things and don't really listen to what is being said). Low-scoring students may need to learn to monitor their level of concentration and develop techniques to redirect attention and eliminate interfering thoughts or feelings so that they can be more effective and efficient learners.

Scale: INP: The *Information Processing Scale* assesses how well students can use imagery, verbal elaboration, organization strategies, and reasoning skills as learning strategies to help build bridges between what they already know and what they are trying to learn and remember, i.e., knowledge acquisition, retention and future application (sample item: I translate what I am studying into my own words). Students who score low on this scale may have difficulty making information meaningful and storing it in memory in a way that will help them recall it in the future.

Scale: SMI: The *Selecting Main Ideas Scale* assesses students' skill at identifying important information for further study from among less-important information and supporting details (sample item: Often when studying I seem to get lost in details and can't see the forest for the trees). Students who score low on this scale may need to develop their skill at separating out critical information on which to focus their attention. Tasks such as reading a textbook can be overwhelming if students focus on every detail presented.

Scale: STA: The *Study Aids Scale* assesses students' use of supports or resources to help them learn or retain information (sample item: I use special helps, such as italics and headings, that are in my textbooks). Students with low scores may need to develop a better understanding of the resources available to them and how to use these resources to help them be more effective and efficient learners.

Scale: SFT: The *Self-Testing Scale* assesses students' use of reviewing and comprehension-monitoring techniques to determine their level of understanding of the information to be learned (sample item: I stop periodically while reading and mentally go over or review what was said). Low-scoring students may need to develop an appreciation for the importance of self-testing, and learn effective techniques for reviewing information and monitoring their level of understanding or ability to apply what they are learning.

Scale: TST: The *Test Strategies Scale* assesses students' use of test-preparation and test-taking strategies (sample item: In taking tests, writing themes, etc., I find I have misunderstood what is wanted and lose points because of it). Low-scoring students may need to learn more effective techniques for preparing for and taking tests so that they are able to effectively demonstrate their knowledge of the subject matter.

The LASSI taps into many of the aspects of student behaviors that can influence learning. The authors designed the scale and its subscales to cover three broad domains: *skill, will,* and *self-regulation*. The *skill* subscales assess a student's information processing, selection of "main ideas," and testing strategies, and scales examining behaviors and thought processes related to identifying, acquiring, and constructing meaning for important new information, ideas and procedures, and how they prepare for and demonstrate their new knowledge in tests or other evaluative procedures. The *will* subscales assess student attitude, motivation, and anxiety, measuring students' receptivity to learning new information, their attitudes and interest in college, their willingness to exert the effort necessary to successfully complete academic requirements, and the degree to which they worry about their academic performance. The *self-regulation* subscales assess concentration, time management, self-testing, and use of study aids, measuring how students manage their learning process through using their time effectively, focusing their attention and maintaining their concentration over time, checking to see whether they have met the learning demands for a class, an assignment or a test, and using study supports such as review sessions, tutors, or special features of a textbook (Weinstein & Palmer, 2002). The LASSI has not been without criticism but it seems to stand up well to those who question its validity, reliability, and factor structure (Cano, 2006).

If you do not want to pay for the permission to use a scale such as the LASSI you can design your own. Although it is difficult to create valid and reliable scales you can use some of the basic guidelines discussed in this book to give you a good measure of what you want. If your main goal is primarily to better understand how your students learn and you are not as concerned about getting your results published, elaborate demonstrations of validity and reliability are not as important. A number of home-grown measures have been developed and used (and published). For example, the *Study Habits Inventory* (SHI; Jones & Slate, 1992) is a 63-item questionnaire designed to assess typical college student study behaviors. Research using the SHI shows that students have trouble with time management, note taking, and understanding how to prepare for different tests (Kuhn, 1988). Scales such as the SHI are developed using a common methodology that provides a good heuristic for pedagogical research: Past research is used to inform the writing of new items or questions (e.g., Gurung, 2005) and/or students themselves are asked to generate items (e.g. Carrell & Menzel, 1997).

In an attempt to create a shorter, more specific assessment tool, Gurung (2005) assessed how students actually study and tested whether certain study habits were more conducive to learning than others. This study provides you with a concrete example of how you can take the information in box 3.1 and use it to generate your own pedagogical research. Gurung assessed 229 introductory psychology students' use of 11 different study techniques and then correlated their responses with their exam scores. The results of this study provide a detailed picture of what students spent time on and how effective the different methods were. Interestingly, not all techniques were effective – the most effective techniques were often not the ones used the most. For example, although the three most frequently used techniques (reading notes and the text, using mnemonics) significantly correlated with exam scores, one of the strongest predictors of exam scores, testing knowledge, was one of the least-used techniques. Other techniques commonly used by students (rewriting notes, reviewing highlighted material and figures and tables in the text) did not relate to exam scores. Perhaps most importantly, the number of hours studied was only weakly associated with exam score. This finding suggests that how students study may be even more important than how long they study and provides a strong rationale for the use of this measure. The effectiveness of many common study suggestions such as using flashcards did not receive empirical support. The study also found detriments to studying. Students who skipped class, listened to music, watched television, or used the Internet while studying performed worse on the exam.

Carrell and Menzel (1997) used a different approach to asking the same question (i.e., How do students study?). Three hundred and three students in a basic speech class at a mid-sized midwestern university were asked to brainstorm a list of general and specific preparation processes they used to study for the final exam in their basic speech communication course. The responses were used to create a list of 16 preparation strategies. This list was administered to 500 students in basic speech communication classes. Students reported how long they spent on each of the strategies. Carrell and Menzel found that students who reviewed the study guides and who read class notes scored significantly higher on the final exam than those who did not. Similar to the findings of Gurung (2005) described above and other reviews (e.g., Hadwin & Winne, 1996; Hattie, Biggs, & Purdie, 1996), there were no significant differences on exam score as a function of the use of many of the study strategies. This prompts the question of whether a lack of study skills truly explains poor scores or some other factor such as student motivation.

Finding out how your students study and identifying what makes students who do better on your tests succeed, may provide you with the tips needed to help other students who do not do as well. Studies such as Gurung (2005) and Carrell and Menzel (1997) provide a good starting point for the assessment of how students study. One of the scales used is shown in table 3.1. Modify it to better fit your class.

Whereas scales such as the two just described assess a realm of study behaviors, it is also prudent to focus on the behaviors related to studying such as note-taking.

Note-Taking

Every one of us has probably experienced a student sitting in our classes with nary a notebook, pencil, or pen. When asked how they capture the main points of the lecture and discussions, they reply "I have a good memory." This may be true for some students, but good note-taking is a critical component of the learning process for the majority of students. First off, students who take and use notes benefit from doing so (Kiewra et al., 2006; Strage et al., 2002). Mastery-oriented students, who wish to become proficient in a topic, in particular take excellent notes during lectures and while reading (Strage et al., 2002). While reading, these students avoid the use of highlighting and will use deeper processing methods to understand the material (i.e., writing notes out, Nesbit et al., 2006). Successful students will recopy, correct, and integrate lecture notes with reading notes to gain a complete understanding of the material (Dickinson, & O'Connell, 1990; Onwuegbuzie, Slate, & Schwartz, 2001), but not all studies have found positive effects for rewriting notes (Gurung, 2005). The types of notes students use will also have an effect on their quality of learning. Students who used matrix and outline notes performed better than students using text-only notes, and the matrix notes afforded students a greater assimilation of the material and the ability to make connections between what they learned and their life (Kiewra et al., 1988). Being able to connect material learned with one's own life is an effective learning strategy (Chi et al., 1994). An effective component related to note-taking is having a process for learning new words (Onwuegbuzie, Slate, & Schwartz,

Table 3.1: Frequency and Duration of Use of the Main Study Techniques

Hours spent					How often	Study technique (listed in order of use)
0	1	1–2	2–3	>3		
1	18	32	26	16	4.01	Read your notes
4	23	34	20	11	3.37	Read the text
13	41	23	10	3	3.33	Think of mnemonic devises (e.g., CANOE for personality traits)
10	28	32	14	8	3.25	Rewrite notes and/or skim notes
8	34	35	11	2	3.15	Review highlighted information from text
9	36	31	13	4	3.11	Memorize definitions through repetition (e.g., flashcards)
8	51	24	7	1	2.96	Review figures and tables in text
16	43	23	9	2	2.89	Make up examples to understand material/incorporate into everyday life
23	42	19	6	2	2.62	Use concept checks, chapter-end questions to test knowledge
39	38	14	8	1	2.18	Take notes from the book
43	29	18	8	2	2.07	Study with a friend

						Distracters
					4.00	Have the television on
					3.78	Have music on
					3.02	Have roommates/friends/family around
					3.75	Respond to instant messaging/email on the Internet

					Level	Self-Reports
					3.43	Knowledge
					3.66	Understanding
					3.44	Confidence

Note: Hours spent represents the percentage of the class who reported using each option. How often each technique was used or each distraction was present is measured on a five-point scale (1 = *never*, 5 = *all the time*). Knowledge, understanding, and confidence was measured on a five-point scale (1 = *not at all*, 5 = *extremely*).
Source: Gurung, 2005.Table 3.2: Item-Analysis Example.

2001; Stanley, Slate, & Jones, 1999). Many students lack this important skill that would be beneficial across many disciplines.

Reading

The common way for a student to gain information is to read the materials assigned for the class. Most classes entail reading and some classes, disciplines, and instructors rely on reading more than others. Lower-level general education classes in the humanities, social sciences, and natural sciences all often require that students read a textbook that surveys a broad swatch of material ranging from thousands of years of history to centuries worth of theories and facts. Upper-level classes tend to require more close reading, and some disciplines such as English and history may have students tackle classic writings. Effective reading is integral to optimal learning, and examining how your students read and trying to improve it provides fertile ground for pedagogical research.

We know a fair amount about what constitutes useful reading. The most essential aspect of effective reading is to actively read the textbook (Onwuegbuzie, Slate, and Schwartz, 2001; Stanley, Slate, & Jones, 1999). Highlighting while reading is an insufficient learning technique, and reviewing highlighted material is also a less effective study technique (Gurung, 2005; Nesbit et al., 2006). Students who actively take notes while reading and are able to select the main ideas from the readings learn more effectively (Foos, Mora, & Tkacz, 1994; Mohamed, 1997; Onwuegbuzie, Slate, & Schwartz, 2001; Proctor et al., 2006; Stanley, Slate, & Jones, 1999).

Past research has used a methodology called *verbal protocol analysis* to understand what works well. For example, Wyatt et al. (1993) had college professors talk aloud while reading articles in their disciplines. Apparently, faculty do a lot while they read that students do not. Faculty anticipated and predicted information in the test, tested predictions as they read, actively scanned for information related to their reading goals, moved forward and back between pages to find information, varied their reading style as a factor of how relevant the text was to their reading goals, paraphrased what they were reading, and summarized what they were reading (Wyatt et al., 1993). These same reading strategies were also found to be important to understanding in a survey of over 40 verbal protocol studies (Pressley & Afflerbach, 1995). No study of student reading has shown evidence of these strategies (Pressley, Yokoi, Meter, Etten, & Freebern, 1997).

When students read is also important. Reading before the class lecture may also help students to gain the initial knowledge base needed to ask questions and make connections while the professor is presenting the aspects of the material they find most important (Strage et al., 2002). However, this efficacious strategy is rarely used by the majority of students.

Can You Improve Study Skills?

The research clearly identifies the skills and strategies needed to set the stage for optimal learning. But how do we get our students to use these strategies? Knowing about them (and if you have read the previous sections you have a solid sense of them) is a critical first step, but getting them across to our students is not as easy. Interventions are a necessary step in maximizing student learning, but what exactly is the best way to intervene? Many instructors focus solely on the content of their courses and pay little attention to training their students in how to learn. Sometimes it is because there is no time to as in the case of a broad survey course in history or psychology where the instructor feels pressured to cover a certain amount of material or chapter in the text (or the entire text!). Sometimes it is because the instructor thinks it is not his or her job to teach skills. At other times the instructor does not know how to teach about skills. At the very minimum instructors should be able to refer students to other sources of help but even to do this, students need to know when they need help. Using some of the questionnaires in this chapter as self-assessments will be a good start. Creating online modules or sets of resources for students to gain the skills they need is another possible option. Taking some class time for the most critical skills (which ones these are may vary on your class) is perhaps optimal.

Many schools offer study skills classes and programs students can take in which they learn about different ways to take notes and read, study, and take tests. Often referred to as "University 101" courses, these classes provide students with a good way to learn the skills to be successful at college although some argue that learning how to study in college should not be separated out from the courses for which one is studying (Hattie, Biggs, & Purdie, 1996; Wingate, 2006). Each professor should be engaged in student development, whether it is psychology, chemistry, or German.

Studies show that such embedded skills training is most effective for younger students (Hattie, Biggs, & Purdie, 1996). In theory, every student can benefit from learning how to be more successful. Students who are taught how to learn before reaching college or in their very first semester of college can make the most of their college years (Fleming, 2002).

Results such as those discussed in this chapter compel a closer look at the recommendations instructors make to their students. Instructors often provide study tips and urge students to use specific techniques, but the correlation between student grades and technique usage is not always significant and is often low (Carrell & Menzel, 1997; Gurung, 2003; 2004). For example, Balch (2001) provided students with six tips (e.g., specific ways to take lecture notes and self-help quizzes) but, except for elaborative encoding, reported use and course grades were not significantly correlated. Although the data do not test the causality of the association between distractions and exam scores, making such data available to students on the first day of class may help them better to design their study habits.

Key Psychological Factors Influencing Learning

There are a number of psychological factors that could explain why your students are not doing well in class. There are the usual suspects – they are not motivated or they get anxious taking tests in college – and there are other factors such as self-efficacy, self-regulation, and their orientation to their learning (Robbins et al., 2004).

The psychological construct of self-efficacy is an important predictor of grades (Lynch, 2006). Students who believe they can be successful are motivated to be successful. Student motivation is a significant feature seen in successful students (Mohamed, 1997; Onwuegbuzie, Slate, & Schwartz, 2001; Proctor et al., 2006). Students who are willing to expend the necessary effort and discipline themselves to use their time effectively are able to obtain higher grade point averages and gain a greater understanding of the material (Mohamed, 1997; Onwuegbuzie, Slate, & Schwartz, 2001; Proctor et al., 2006; Strage et al., 2002).

Students with a high mastery orientation want to be challenged, actively engage in discussions about the material, and use deeper processing strategies for learning and therefore are skilled, flourishing students (Strage et al., 2002). In contrast, anxiety and a lack of concentration, motivation, and attention to academic tasks are clear indicators of struggling students (Mohamed, 1997; Proctor et al., 2006). These aspects hinder students' ability to learn.

Something out of a student's control is their level of cognitive ability. This is an important aspect to consider. Students with a low level of cognitive ability are found to be those studying the most and expect the lowest scores (Olivares, 2002; Plant et al., 2005). Students high in cognitive ability study the least amount of time and expect higher scores. Clearly, this has large implications as to why many studies find the time-grade association to be non-significant (Dickinson and O'Connell, 2001; Gurung, 2005; but see Strage et al., 2002, for an exception). High-cognitive-ability students may already possess the necessary skills to be successful students before entrance to college, or adapted to college better and therefore are able to utilize the necessary study strategy needed for the examination they are preparing for without even being aware of it (Dickinson & O'Connell, 1990; Nist et al., 1991; Plant et al., 2005).

Designing Your Research: How Do You Study Your Students' Learning?

The preceding review gives you a taste (and more) of what we know about student learning. Much of what we know lends itself to the design of education interventions, but if you have not critically examined your students' learning before, there are some more proximal places to start your examination. You can use figure 3.1 to provide you with many options for research:

- You can test the model or parts of it using your classroom.
- You can fine-tune the model by adding missing parts.
- You can use the model to change how your students study.
- You can use elements of the model to revise your course design.
- You can modify your assessment methods based on processes in the model.

We will provide you with a number of concrete ways to study many of the elements of the model, presenting some measures and models of research. As you can see in the figure above, the key variables in the process of learning include student variables (such as age, sex, and socioeconomic status), encoding and storage variables (such as how students study), and retrieval variables (such as how you test students). Regardless of which aspect you want to focus on, the first step of the research process is to decide on a plan of action. For the moment let us not worry about how student learning is assessed, whether by an essay, paper, or multiple-choice exam; we will get to that soon enough. What are the best ways to study student learning?

One of the more obvious places to start examining student learning is to look at how they perform on tests and assignments. If you make changes to your teaching, how you present material or your course design, you can then see if there have been any changes in scores on the tests and the assignments. There are a number of different ways of testing whether learning has improved. More specifically (if you like being technical), there are a number of different research designs to see if student learning has changed as a function of something you did.

Semester-to-Semester Comparisons

The simplest way to study changes in learning is to compare your grade distributions over semesters. Is the class average the same? Are you getting the same number of A grades as D or F grades? If your averages are different you should make sure to check whether the difference is statistically significant, methods for which are fully elucidated in the next chapter. Any changes in grades could be due to three main sources, as illustrated in table 3.1. The changes could be due to something inherent to the student (study habits, effort, ability), something inherent to you (teaching technique, grading style, course design), or could be a function of the combination of both. There are more fine-tuned distinctions, of course – things going on in the world could be influencing scores, your universities admission criteria could have changed, bringing in cohorts of significantly different abilities, or any other of a wealth of possibilities.

If you examine your grade distributions over time for the same class, you may see changes even before you change anything yourself. If you have not done anything different then finding out why learning has improved or decreased is still a worthwhile investigation and later sections of this chapter will help you do that. If you do want to change your pedagogy, whether modifying instructions for an assignment or changing the way you write your tests, you can still use the simple semester-to-semester comparison, but, given that the students in your class are not going to be the same, you should consider using a more elaborate research design.

Within-Semester Comparisons

There are a number of different ways to examine changes in learning within a semester. Within-semester comparisons can take one of three main forms. First there is the *Repeated Measure Design* (RMD). This works best when you have a number of different exams or assignments in a class each of which are similar in nature. In such designs, you look for changes in responses to the same item(s) over time. The original term RMD is used in research when the assessment is identical, such as when attitudes towards smoking are measured year after year in a college student sample or knowledge about nutrition is assessed in grades 8–12. The smoking attitude measure or the nutritional knowledge measure will consist of the same number of questions asked in the same order, and differences in the responses will be taken to indicate changes in attitudes or knowledge. In academic settings and for pedagogical research using the identical questions is not practical (though some instructors who are proponents of mastery learning will allow a student to take the same exam a number of times until the student has learned the material and does well). To assess learning, using the identical items is not always necessary, but using similar items can do the trick. For example, many large general education courses give four 75-question multiple-choice exams over the course of a semester. A literature or philosophy course may have the students complete a series of short papers. To test whether learning is changing over the course of the semester you can test whether the class mean is changing over time or even compare a single student's score and see if he or she is improving over the course of the semester.

Next up in complexity is the classic (for the scientists) *Pre-Post Design* (PPD). You give your students an assignment or test that assesses their learning. You then instruct them on the topic of choice. Finally you give them another assignment or test that is very similar in nature to the first assignment. If there is a significant difference in learning between the two assessments you can assume it is due to the instruction you provided in between. This form of within-semester assessment is best done when you have a number of separate topics to cover, each of which can be cleanly delineated from each other. This form of assessment works particular well for concepts or topics that you know are problematic for students to grasp and for topics for which previous exposure has been minimal.

The most involved within-semester design is the Experimental Design (ED). Although the most rigorous research design, this method is not the best suited for pedagogical research because of the need for, and use of, comparison groups. With this method you are essentially comparing students who got something from you – special instructions, more movie clips, or extra readings – with students who did not get those same things. The basic idea is that, if the students who got the special goodies do better than the students who did not get the goodies, then the goodies enhance learning. This form of design is easier if you teach two or more sections of a course or, in the case of different instructors teaching different sections, where your class gets the goodies and the other class does not. Again, you will have different comparison groups across which you can compare scores. As long as the two groups are selected or assigned in a random manner such that the ages, educational backgrounds, effort and ability levels, and sex are similar across groups, any changes in learning between groups will be due to the differences in instruction. The wonderful thing about experimental designs is that it allows you to test for cause-and-effect relationships. If there are differences in test scores between your two groups that received different instruction but are similar in all other aspects, you can be confident the instructional differences caused the test score differences. No other research design affords you the confidence to make causal statements.

Of course, giving some students in your class special instruction that may help them, and keeping that instruction from the other students just to test the efficacy of the instruction does not sound like the most ethical thing. What may work well for placebo clinical studies does not exactly transfer well to the classroom, but we can borrow from drug trial methodology to use the experimental design in the classroom. In clinical drug trials, researchers get beyond the ethical problem of keeping a potentially helpful drug from patients (i.e., those in the control group) by giving the drug to all patients in the study after the end of the study if the drug has been found to be useful. Similarly, if patients getting an experimental drug show negative side effects the drug trial is stopped immediately. It is easy to modify this approach to test whether your students are learning better as a result of something you are doing. As mapped out in figure 3.2, you essentially split your class into two and first give half the class your special instruction. After the first exam, you give the other half of class the special instruction as well so all the students will have the special instruction and you have used the most robust test of your instructional innovations.

An example will make this easier to understand. A colleague of ours wanted to know if she should hand out copies of her PowerPoint slides to students before she lectured. Students often complained that they were too busy copying things down and were not able to focus on what she was saying enough. She knew that if she did hand out her slides some students would not come to class, but she felt it would be a worthwhile trade-off if the students who were there did pay more attention because they did not have to write as much. Nice research question: Does handing out your lecture notes in advance optimize student learning? She used the modified experimental design described above. For the first half of the semester she gave print-outs of the lecture notes to half the class and not the others (students getting the notes were randomly selected and instructed to not share these with other classmates or discuss having them). After the first exam, she gave pre-lecture notes to those who did not get them the first half of the semester. She compared scores between those who had notes and those who did not. There were no significant differences and in fact she noticed that those who got the notes beforehand actually did a little worse on the exams. On follow-up interviews the students who received the printouts reported having trouble paying attention because they no longer had to copy things down (Noppe et al., 2007).

An aside: the preceding example may make you wonder if using Power-Point or similar software in class is really helping learning. DeBord, Aru-guete, and Muhlig (2004) tested whether using computer slides had any better effect on learning and performance than using an overhead projec-tor. Two classes got exactly the same content, but one class had to read off overhead transparencies. Although students preferred the computer slides, there was no difference in student learning. Don't ditch PowerPoint yet. A growing amount of research does show that multimedia presentations can increase learning and satisfaction (e.g., Fletcher, 2003; Mayer, 2001). The key is how you use PowerPoint. As a colleague once said, "Even a black-board can be used badly." For great suggestions on how to use multimedia to optimize learning and a additional research findings on this point, see Daniel (2005).

These different research methods are summarized in figure 3.2. All of them rely on the comparisons of scores on the assessments used. The basic idea is, of course, to measure student learning and then see how you can

Basic: ←Assess some point during semester →

Post-Only: Activity/Special Assignment -→ Assess

Pre-Post :   Assess 1 (baseline measure)→ Activity/assignment→ Assessment 2

Experiment: **Alternate 1**

Group 1 Assess 1-→Activity/Assignment---→ Assessment 2

Group 2 Assess 1-→No Activity /Assignment (control) OR alternate assignment-→ Assessment 2

Experiment: **Alternate 2**

Group 1 Assess 1-→Activity/Assignment→ Assessment 2→ No Activity   → Assessment 3

Group 2 Assess 1-→No Activity   → Assessment 2→ Activity/Assignment→ Assessment 3

Figure 3.2: An overview of different research designs: most basic model (assessment only) at the bottom with group experiments at the top

get it to improve. Will student learning improve after you try something new? Will a new technique/pedagogical strategy increase learning? Very often we rely on anecdotal evidence to measure student learning. Anecdotes are not all bad: The student evaluation singing your praises and proclaiming that "Even though I got a D I still learned a lot in your class" is nice to behold, but what does it really say about how your students learn in your class? Using one of the research designs described above will ensure that you have a true measure of how learning in your classroom is changing. To optimize the measurement of change you have to be sure that your assessments are valid and reliable whether they are essays you grade or multiple-choice exams that you grade. The key testable question then becomes: How does performance vary? The valid and reliable measurement of performance then becomes the first critical step in your research endeavor.

Measuring How Performance on Your Assessments Vary

When it comes down to it, most of us know if our students have learned based on their final grades in our class. This said, most of us are also cognizant of the fact that grades are not a perfect representation of learning.

Likewise, although written assignments, papers, and essays provide students with a good way to demonstrate their learning, each of these methods can be hindered by students' writing skill level and consequently may not adequately allow them to demonstrate their learning. Some students do not do well on multiple-choice exams. Some forms of examinations (such as multiple-choice) are not optimal for testing different levels and types of learning. In short, although we rely on grades to map students' learning there could be many reasons why the exam or paper score does not adequately reflect what the student has learned. For this reason, one of the most important areas of pedagogical research pertains to assessment. Some key research questions to consider:

What are the pros and cons of different measures you use to assess learning?

How can your assignments be changed to increase learning?

How do you know if assignment modifications have increased learning?

Can another assignment/assessment better assess student learning in your class?

Assessing Learning

There are many different forms of assessing learning and there are best practices for using each one. One nice distinction to keep in mind is the difference between formative and summative assessment, a distinction we also used when talking about teaching. In the context of learning, seeking evidence of learning as the learning is taking place, a formative assessment can sometimes be even more valuable than a summative assessment that records students' progress towards course or institutional goals (Maki, 2004). A formative assessment can instigate immediate change in pedagogy. Why wait until the next semester when you can improve the learning of your students in your class the same semester? Formative assessments are more time intensive, but well worth the effort as, together with helping students learn, the assessments can help you learn about how well you are doing. Using either formative or summative assessments helps you get at one of four major goals. You can identify students who need extra help, you can determine if your class goals are being met, you can assess your students' attitudes towards the class and material, and you can assess whether your course design is effective and efficient (Diamond, 1998).

When conducting scholarship research on learning, modifying your method of assessment provides you with an easy way to see how learning changes the scores on those same assessments. Changing 1) your classroom instruction, or 2) the instructions you give a student before an exam (e.g., on how to study), or 3) during an exam (e.g., in asking the question) are three areas where you can change your pedagogy and measure the results of your change. If you write better questions for an essay exam and the answers get better (as determined by your rubric), or if your multiple-choice options improve and more students get the multiple-choice question correct, you have empirical evidence that learning has changed. What changes do you make and what exactly do you look for to assess whether the changes work? The answer varies with types of assessment used.

Multiple-Choice Exams

It seems as if there would be little to be done to improve student learning when using multiple-choice exams, but this is not the case. Although many of us who teach small classes would love to have the luxury of just using multiple-choice exams to avoid the mountains of grading that a paper assignment or essay exam entail, writing multiple-choice questions is not a walk in the park. There are some key tips for writing good questions (Davis, 1993) as shown in box 3.4.

How do you know if you have written good questions? Here is where you can use data generated from exam scoring software to guide your pedagogical research. The software can churn out a number of different statistics to help you get a sense of how well your questions were written. The most basic number to look at is the percentage of your class getting each answer correct. If less than 25–30 percent of your class is getting an answer correct, there is a problem. It could be a badly written question, it could be a concept that you did not teach adequately, a concept the students did not grasp, or something that the students just did not study. Another useful report is the number of students in the upper and lower quartiles who got the question correct. If you have a 100 students in a class there are 25 students in the highest and lowest quartiles. A good question will separate the good students from the weak ones. If 20 out of 25 of the good students get a question correct but only 4 out of 25 of the weak students get the question right, you know you have discriminated nicely. If about the same number of students in both quartiles get the question correct, the question may be too easy. You can also look for a "difficulty

---

Box 3.4: Tips to Writing Good Multiple-Choice Questions

1. Make sure that the questions span the different levels of learning, and are a good blend of factual questions and questions testing understanding, synthesis, and evaluation.
2. Write questions throughout the semester and not just before the exam.
   - Identify key learning goals/facts for chapter/section.
   - Write questions for each learning goal/fact.
   - Write a few before/after every lecture.
3. Have the bulk of the question in the "stem."
   The main facts should be present before the answers are read.
   - All relevant material should be in the stem (do not repeat phrases in the alternatives).
4. Limit the number of alternatives.
   - Even threee choices have been shown to be effective tests.
5. Make the distracters appealing and (mostly) plausible.
   - Distracters should represent common mistakes made by students.
6. Make all choices of roughly equal length and parallel in structure.
7. Do not use "all of the or none of the above" type questions.
8. Try not to use words such as "always", "never", "all", or "none."
9. Organize choices conceptually/logically.
10. Avoid negative wording or trick questions.
11. Provide approximately one minute per question.

---

factor," a number that gives you the proportion that got the question correct, and pedagogical wisdom suggests the optimal is approximately .50. For each of the choices of a multiple-choice question, you also get a "discrimination index," a number that is the correlation between that item and the total test. Correct answers with correlations that are negative or zero suggest bad questions. An example of an item analysis for a multiple-choice test is shown in table 3.2.

Many of us using multiple-choice tests may have never looked long and hard at an item analysis, essentially the process described above. When you are interested in optimizing your teaching by conducting scholarly research on your teaching and student learning, the item analyses become one of the tangible outcomes that you can work on changing. To learn more about how to conduct an item analysis consult our list of resources at the end of

Table 3.2: Item-Analysis Example

Question		Upper Quartile	Lower Quartile	Total Count	Total %	Discrimination Index	Difficulty Factor	Weight
1	1	0	1	1	3	−0.1	0.316	1
	2	0	1	2	5	−0.1		
	3*	6	2	12	32	0.4		
	4	4	6	23	61	−0.2		
	5	0	0	0	0	0.0		
	Oth	0	0	0	0	0.0		
2	1	0	0	0	0	0.0	0.816	1
	2	0	2	2	5	−0.2		
	3	1	1	5	13	0.0		
	4*	9	7	31	82	0.2		
	5	0	0	0	0	0.0		
	Oth	0	0	0	0	0.0		
3	1	0	1	4	11	−0.1	0.816	1
	2	0	0	0	0	0.0		
	3	0	2	3	8	−0.2		
	4*	10	7	31	82	0.3		
	5	0	0	0	0	0.0		
	Oth	0	0	0	0	0.0		
4	1	0	1	1	3	−0.1	0.868	1
	2	0	1	3	8	−0.1		
	3*	10	7	33	87	0.3		
	4	0	0	0	0	0.0		
	5	0	0	0	0	0.0		
	Oth	0	1	1	3	−0.1		
5	1	1	2	6	16	−0.1	0.579	1
	2	4	3	10	26	0.1		
	3	0	0	0	0	0.0		
	4*	5	5	22	58	0.0		
	5	0	0	0	0	0.0		
	Oth	0	0	0	0	0.0		
6	1	1	3	10	26	−0.2	0.474	1
	2	2	5	10	26	−0.3		
	3*	7	2	18	47	0.5		
	4	0	0	0	0	0.0		
	5	0	0	0	0	0.0		
	Oth	0	0	0	0	0.0		

Number of Respondents: 38 Number of Test Items: 60
Total in Upper Quartile: 10 Kuder Richardson 20: 0.74
Total in Lower Quartiel: 10 Kuder Richardson 21: 0.69

the book. If you have ideas of how to change your instruction and you want to test whether student learning has improved because of it, all you do is compare the item analysis statistics on the test before you made your instruction change, with the item analysis statistics on the identical test after you make the change. Significant changes signify a successful move towards optimizing your students' learning.

Written Assessments: Essays and Papers

It's all in the rubric. In the previous chapter we discussed how you can create rubrics to help you grade as part of optimizing your teaching. Rubrics are critical to measuring whether learning is demonstrated in improvements in essays and paper. Whereas a multiple-choice question has one right answer, an essay or a short answer question allows the instructor to get a better sense of what the student has learned. Whereas some short-answer question call for regurgitated facts, a good short-answer question can get the student to engage in the material. To best grade such a question a good rubric is needed. We provided examples of rubrics in the previous chapter and again refer you to sources such as the online tool Rubistar, and Stevens and Levi (2004). We have found it best to give students the rubric at the time they are given their writing assignments. Although this may seem like you are teaching to the test, it actually provides students with a clear-cut look at what they should strive for in their writing. Students vary in writing skills and first-year students in particular may not have a good sense of what makes a good college-level paper. Taking the time to make a detailed rubric for each of your writing assignments will drastically reduce the questions you get on the assignment and will also make your grading easier. Plus with a standard benchmark for grading written work, you can assess change in writing quality (and test for the significance of this change as described in the next chapter).

Assessments of Reading

Sometimes you need not rely on an exam to test what your students are learning. You can test how they read. An example from the humanities provides us with a useful model. Chick, Hassel, and Haynie (2007) challenged their students to "become eagle-eyed readers and to move toward a more sophisticated understanding of language, of relationships, and of how they approach literary texts." The instructors asked their students to read a poem at home and interpret it in writing. Students were asked to identity "patterns" seen in the poem, as well as the "elements of the poem that don't fit one or more of these patterns." Students then spent an entire class period discussing, sharing, and reflecting on each other's interpretation of the poem and finally reflected in writing on how their initial interpretations of the poem changed. In a nice addition of metacognition the students were also asked what the class activities suggest about the process of reading literature. The three instructors, all English professors, drew upon the skills of close reading and interpretation – or textual interpretation and critique – from their training as literary scholars to interpret the "data," the student responses. This is where having a rubric comes in. The responses were examined and key themes were enumerated and then summed up creating a baseline of student understanding. The instructors then gave an in-depth lecture on how to best read texts, describing skills and examples from the poetry analysis classroom exercise. They followed this lecture with another similar text analysis exercise, again enumerated and summed up the responses, and used the changes in responses from before the specialized lecture to after the lecture to indicate when learning had improved. The instructors had a clear sense of what distinguished a high-level analysis, the work of an expert, from that of a novice, and they used this to describe the student responses. The interpretations brought in by the students could be "graded" using the rubric generated from the students' own work in the previous class. This use of student work provides a nice basic model of how to assess student understanding.

Guidelines for Human Research Participants in SoTL

Both this chapter on learning and the preceding chapter on teaching provide you with a variety of ideas for conducting scholarly research on your classes, on your teaching, and on your students' learning. Whereas most basic assessments of learning and teaching can be done by the instructor without having to ask for permission from anyone else, the moment you want to move from scholarly teaching to SoTL (and consequently peer reviewed publication and dissemination of your findings) you do have to ensure that your assessment/research design is approved by your college or university's Institutional Review Board or IRB. The IRB ensures that the research follows governmentally established ethical standards and that the rights of the participants are safeguarded. This may sound like the default expectation is that you will not be ethical and hence IRB approval is needed, but this is not the case. SoTL researchers in some disciplines are unaccustomed to needing IRB approval for their disciplinary research because there has been ambiguity among these SoTL researchers regarding the IRB process, and similar ambiguity among IRB evaluators as to what review category best fits SoTL research.

To help navigate pedagogical researchers through the IRB process, Renee Meyers, the Coordinator of the University of Wisconsin System Leadership Site for the Scholarship of Teaching and Learning, created a concise guide (see McKinney, 2007, for additional information). Faculty from across the UW-System in many disciplines including Psychology, English, Education, Political Science, Biology, Information Studies, and Communication all contributed to its content (the full list of contributors and the full text is available on the companion website to this book). In the spirit of public dissemination, Meyers gave us permission to use the bulk of the document here for your benefit. We present two main subsections from the Meyers (2007) document here in the box that follows: The intersection of IRB review and SoTL research, and a set of guidelines for protecting students and their work.

A Further Note on Ethics

The guidelines for conducting ethical research demonstrate great variation at the local, national, and international levels, and, because of this, it is difficult to articulate a statement of research ethics for pedagogical research and particularly SoTL that can be applicable to all. That being said, Gurung et al. (2007) took the first step towards creating an international statement on ethics for pedagogical research. In late 2006 volunteers formed the Research Ethics IRB Subcommittee of the International Society for the Scholarship of Teaching and Learning (ISSoTL), charged with crafting a statement about research ethics and human participant use for ISSoTL that would be broadly applicable across disciplinary and national boundaries.

Every country has some form of Human Subject Protection program and guidelines. For example, in the United States, most universities have statements for their researchers mandating adherence to the requirements set forth in Title 45, Part 46 of the *Code of Federal Regulations (45 CFR 46) for the Department of Health and Human Services*. Similarly, in Canada,

Box 3.5: SoTL Research and IRB Procedures

In general, inquiry into teaching and learning questions should be exempt, an IRB category of review (in contrast to minimal risk or risk) under Title 45 Code of Federal Regulations Part 46 (aka the Common Rule). SoTL research is typically exempt as a review category because it does not disrupt or manipulate subjects' normal life experiences, incorporate any form of intrusive procedures, or identify students in such a way that it poses a risk to them. However, if you use students under 18 years of age as participants in your research project, you must move from the exempt category of review to a more extensive review. Consultation with the IRB is helpful if you are using underage participants.

The exempt review category does not mean that your research is "exempt from review by IRB." It means "exempt from full board review." All researchers who are working with human participants MUST still file a protocol and receive approval if they have plans to publish their work. If you will use the results only for the modification of your class design or teaching the pedagogical research falls under normal education assessment. This excludes funded research which should always go through IRB approval. Funders are increasingly concerned with IRB approval before funds are dispensed. In short, exempt means only that the protocol is reviewed (typically) by the IRB chair or staff, and not by the full board.

The other categories of review include expedited review and full board review. Research under the expedited review category typically is considered minimal risk, which means that the probability and magnitude of harm or discomfort anticipated in the research are not greater in and of themselves than those originally encountered in daily life or during the performance of routine physical or psychological examinations or tests (45 CFR 46, 102). Minimal risk protocols are often reviewed in an expedited manner by a subcommittee of the full board. An example of when the minimal risk category might apply to SoTL research would be if the researcher was collecting data from voice, video, digital, or image recordings for research purposes.

The risk category requires a full board review. Generally, SoTL research will not fall into this higher "risk" category. This may include research on sensitive or protected populations (e.g., minors, prisoners, fetuses, etc.), or research that results in more than minimal risks for the participants, or research that involves intentional deception of the participants. In addition, failing to fully inform subjects is deceptive, whether or not it is intentional. The federal regulations include 8 components of informed consent. See http://www.hhs.gov/ohrp/humansubjects/guidance/45cfr46.htm#46.116. Remember that students cannot give "informed" consent unless they are fully informed.

Continued

Keeping these caveats in mind, most SoTL work will fall into one (or a combination) of the following commonly recognized exempt review categories: Exemption for education. Research conducted in established or commonly accepted educational settings, involving normal educational practices, such as (a) research on regular or special education instructional strategies, or (b) research on the effectiveness of or the comparison among instructional techniques, curricula, or classroom management methods is exempted.

Exemption for research involving educational tests. Research involving the use of educational tests (cognitive, diagnostic, aptitude, achievement) is exempted, unless (a) information obtained is recorded in such a manner that human subjects can be identified directly or through identifiers linked to the subjects; and (b) any disclosure of the subjects' responses outside the research could reasonably place the subjects at risk of criminal or civil liability or be damaging to the subjects' financial standing, employability, or reputation.

Exemption for survey or interview procedures. Research involving survey or interview procedures is exempted unless (a) information obtained is recorded in such a manner that human subjects can be identified directly or through identifiers linked to the subjects; and (b) any disclosure of the subjects' responses outside the research could reasonably place the subjects at risk of criminal or civil liability or be damaging to the subjects' financial standing, employability, or reputation.

Exemption for research involving observation of public behavior. Research involving observation is exempted unless (a) information obtained is recorded in such a manner that human subjects can be identified directly or through identifiers linked to the subjects; and (b) any disclosure of the subjects' responses outside the research could reasonably place the subjects at risk of criminal or civil liability or be damaging to the subjects' financial standing, employability, or reputation.

Research for collection or study of existing data. Research involving the collection or study of existing data, documents, records, pathological specimens, or diagnostic specimens is exempted, if these sources are publicly available or if the information is recorded by the investigator in such a manner that subjects cannot be identified directly or through identifiers linked to the subjects.

As is evident from the sample of questions listed previously, and from the definition of SoTL research provided, it is likely that most SoTL research will fall into the exempt review category. Most SoTL research is conducted in "established or commonly accepted educational settings, involving normal educational practices," typically involves "research on the effectiveness of, or the comparison among, instructional techniques, curricula, or classroom management methods," and involves surveys, interviews, observations, or study of existing data.

The question of whether participants can be identified directly or through identifiers linked to the participants is sometimes a difficult call for the researcher and the IRB decision-makers alike. Meyers et al. (2007) provide a useful scenario to illustrate this issue. If a student writes about Wal-Mart in a paper, and everyone in the class knows that this student wrote about Wal-Mart, and as a researcher you want to use parts of this paper in a journal article that you are writing, is that student identifiable? The question of identification also revolves around whether this disclosure of the participants' responses outside the research could reasonably place the participants at risk of criminal or civil liability or be damaging to the participants' financial standing, employability, or reputation. In this case, it is probably unlikely that the student would be identifiable by the readership, and maybe even his/her fellow students, but more importantly, it is unlikely that making this paper public would place the student at risk unless the student works at Wal-Mart and is highly critical of Wal-Mart practices.

Certainly, it is incumbent upon the researcher to make the research participants' evidence that s/he has collected as anonymous as possible before making it public. In the above example, the researcher may well want to black out the title of the organization (i.e., Wal-Mart), or in some way make it impossible for the reader to identify the organization (if possible). In addition, it is important that the researcher explain very clearly to the participants in the Informed Consent form exactly what aspects of their research participation will potentially be made public so that when the students sign the form they understand how their work will be used. Furthermore, it is vital that the instructor very clearly delineate to the students the difference between regular assignments and those assignments that will be used for research, and to be sure that the students realize that they are consenting to the research (above and beyond just doing the assignments). Finally, it is important to remember that researchers do NOT have access to students' confidential data (e.g., overall GPA) without requesting the students' permission to use that data.

In short, if the Informed Consent form is clear and explicit, and the researcher takes every precaution to present/publish the student data in an ethical and confidential manner, then the likelihood of identification and harm are greatly reduced. The IRB decision-makers can often be helpful in guiding researchers in ways to make their data public in both confidential and ethical formats.

Guidelines for Protecting Students and Their Work
Clearly, SoTL researchers must keep student participants' information confidential. The following requirements and recommendations can be useful when preparing the IRB form:

- Instructors must ask for "informed consent" from the student research participants, and must allow any participant to withdraw from the study at

Continued

any time. Remember that only those who are 18 years of age or older can give informed consent. If you are using underage participants in your research, it would be wise to consult with your IRB. Informed consent forms are available with the campus IRB materials.

- Instructors should be careful to exclude all identifiers on student surveys or questionnaires, or other collected evidence, as much as possible.
- Student papers or assignments that are assessed for research purposes should not be analyzed until after final grades have been posted (if at all possible), and are typically rendered confidential by removing any identifiers before analysis, or having someone other than the instructor of record conduct the analysis.
- If respondents are to be tracked over time (i.e., repeated measures are needed on each student) an instructor might ask students to create an ID that only the student knows, and to use that same ID on any data that will be collected for the repeated measures analysis. The instructor would not be privy to this ID, but if s/he were afraid that the students might lose this ID or forget where they wrote it down, s/he might have another person outside the class collect the ID information on a sheet of paper, and keep it in privacy (only to be retrieved if a student forgot his/her ID).
- Sometimes (if the analysis involves student course work) it is useful for the Informed Consent forms to be collected by someone other than the instructor of record and put into a sealed envelope that is not opened until after semester grades have been filed. In this way, the instructor does not know who has (has not) consented to participate until after the class is completed.
- The instructor might not ask for consent until the end of the semester when the student can be a better judge of whether s/he wants to allow the instructor to use his/her assignments. Again, these forms are best collected by a third party, and only examined once final grades have been turned in.
- The instructor may request consent after the semester is over (although this is far more difficult to do).
- If data is collected in a D2L chat room or discussion board, get Informed Consent forms from the students, and then indicate to the students when they first sign on that all interactions in the chat room/discussion board will be used for research. Make it clear that participating implies consent. If a student does not consent to having his/her chat room comments included in the research project, make it possible for the student to complete this assignment in another way.
- Additionally, you might ask students to choose an anonymous username when participating in a chat room or D2L discussion board where interaction data is being collected.

In general, it is unlikely that disclosure of information contained in student assignments will "reasonably place the students at risk of criminal or civil liability or be damaging to the subjects' financial standing, employability, or reputation." Most student work done in the classroom is not of this nature. Additionally, much SoTL research that is quantitative in nature is published or presented in aggregate form so that individual students are not identifiable. However, SoTL research of a more qualitative nature that analyzes student papers or student discussions, and then uses excerpts or quotes from these student products in publications or public presentations, cannot present in aggregate form. But the researcher can take precautions to remove from these excerpts or quotes obvious student identifiers (name, class, year, etc.), to choose (as much as possible) excerpts or quotes that are not directly linked to students or that pose no risk to the students, and to present/publish the student evidence in the least identifiable form possible. In addition, the researcher can ask on the Informed Consent form whether the student is willing to be cited, and if so, whether they want to be identified or remain anonymous (for a sample IRB Informed Consent form compiled by Blaine Peden at the University of Wisconsin at Eau Claire, that addresses this concern, email pedenbf@uwec.edu). In the event that students are willing to allow their names to be published with their work, these issues become moot. But in these situations, the researcher must be very clear with the students in the Informed Consent process to make sure that that the students understand what aspects of their work will be made public, how it will be made public, and what that might mean for them.

Certainly, there are exceptions to all rules, but generally SoTL research fits the profile of exempt research under the Federal guidelines. The educational nature of this work, its focus on student learning, and the rare chance that its public disclosure will place the student at risk, all add up to a preferred determination of exempt status. However, it is always advisable to consult with your IRB board members in the process of preparing your application. They can be invaluable resources.

many universities subscribe to the *Tri-Council Policy Statement: Ethical Conduct for Research Involving Humans (TCPS)*, and in the United Kingdom, universities ascribe to the guidelines set forth in the *Research Governance Framework for Health and Social Care* (2005).

There is a long history of regulations for research in general (Cohen, 2006). The Nuremberg Code (1947) was the first time a court of law enumerated rules for "permissible medical experiments" and first mandated voluntary consent, giving the subject the ability to terminate participation, and ensuring that the benefits of the research outweighed the costs. Sadly, there is a long history of mistreatment of research participants including discrimination (Washington, 2007) and studies that most today would consider unethical (e.g., Milgram, 1963; Zimbardo, 1973). The US government weighed in with Kennedy Hearings on the quality of health care and human experimentation (1973) and the establishment of the National Commission for the Protection of human Subjects of Biomedical and Behavioral Research (1974). This commission yielded a set of guidelines for human research in general that is easily applied to the scholarship of teaching and learning.

The Belmont Report

The *Belmont Report* was written in 1979 after the National Research Act was signed into law in the United States. Although it was created and is applied only in the United States, it serves as a valuable starting place in this discussion for two reasons. First, its scope is sufficiently broad. It does not attempt to offer specific rules or guidelines but rather it provides a general framework for what constitutes ethical research. Thus, the general principles of the *Belmont Report* provide a foundation on which more specific guidelines may be based. Second, the report takes an interdisciplinary approach to the general principles. In other words, it was not written for a specific field of research and can be amply applied to the scholarship of teaching and learning, regardless of discipline.

We do not wish to summarize the *Belmont Report* (it is easily available online), but will only focus on those elements of the report that are most relevant to pedagogical research. Namely, we will discuss the application of three general ethical principles (respect for persons, beneficence, and justice) from the *Belmont Report* to pedagogical research.

What should be researched?

While the authors of the *Belmont Report* are clearly not referring to teaching with the statement that "practice refers to interventions that are designed solely to enhance the well-being of an individual patient or client and that have a reasonable expectation of success", this statement can clearly be applied to pedagogical research. One could reasonably replace the word "practice" with the word "teaching" and the words "individual patient or client" with the word "students." When the statement is used in this way, teaching refers to those standard practices that are expected to enhance learning.

This statement is important because it helps us articulate what needs to be researched and what does not need to be researched. The statement above that practice (i.e., teaching) should "have a reasonable expectation of success" means that those teaching practices that do not have a reasonable expectation of success (i.e., those that deviate substantially from standard approaches) should become the subject of scientific scrutiny to determine their effectiveness and their potential for harm. When applying this standard, it would not be enough for a teacher to say, "I have been trying this new technique in class and it really seems to be working well." Rather, the teacher should design and carry out a research study to determine the effectiveness of that new technique. Thus, as a profession, teachers carry the ethical obligation of exploring new or different teaching strategies and techniques.

Respect for persons

The first general ethical principle outlined in the *Belmont Report* is respect for persons, described as acknowledging that research participants should be treated with autonomy and must be free to decide whether or not to participate in a research study. This becomes specifically relevant to the scholarship of teaching and learning because there is great potential for coercion in such research.

There are two ways in which coercion can occur within the context of teaching and learning research. First, a potential participant may feel coerced to participate because of the difference in power between the instructor (i.e., researcher) and student (i.e., participant). Here, a student may participate in a research project because he or she fears a negative evaluation as a result of not participating. Second, a potential participant may feel coerced to participate because he or she appreciates or likes the professor. In this case, a student may feel uncomfortable with a particular study but decides to participate because he or she wants to do the researcher a favor. While this second type of coercion may appear on the surface to be less negative than the first type, it still infringes the participant's right to make an autonomous decision about whether or not to participate and is, therefore, potentially unethical.

To address these concerns, it is imperative that researchers take steps to minimize the degree to which potential participants feel coerced into participation. For example, strategies like utilizing another instructor's class, ensuring the person responsible for data collection is unknown to the students, and ensuring anonymity can all be used to decrease the potential for coercion.

Beneficence

The second ethical guideline addressed by the Belmont Report is beneficence or the need to "maximize possible benefits and minimize possible harm". The need to minimize possible harm is obvious within the context of the scholarship of teaching and learning. However, teaching and learning scholars have a great opportunity to maximize possible benefits as they conduct their research. This is because they can, when appropriate, use their in-class research as a means of educating students about research ethics, methods, and/or even the results of the study. In other words, an instructor could use the process of collecting data as a teaching moment to inform students about the ethics involved in data collection, the process of collecting data and how the data will be used, and, when possible, can even share with them the results of the study they participated in. Such an approach goes above the call of duty and truly maximizes the benefits to participants.

Justice

Finally, the third ethical guideline of justice argues that those people who are research participants should be the people who most benefit from the research (i.e., it would be unethical to research a particular group in excess if that group is not the group that will benefit from the knowledge generated through the research). This is an area of research ethics in which the scholarship of teaching and learning seems to truly shine. Those students who participate in such research are not only likely to benefit from the knowledge gained through the study they are participating in, but are also clearly the beneficiaries of past research on teaching and learning.

This is but the first step in the creation of an international code of ethics for pedagogical research. Given that SoTL presents some challenges more traditional research does not (e.g., course instructors doing the research themselves on students whose grades depend on the instructor), it is critical to elucidate additional protections for students. For example, pedagogical research conducted on one's own students are best administered by independent sources and the information provided to the instructor after grades are handed in. Assessments used for formative purposes (results being used to change future pedagogy within the same semester/quarter) would best be conducted anonymously. This and many other issues will be fleshed out as the subcommittee continues its work.

Conclusions

There has been a steady growth in successful research assessing the utility of teaching students specific study strategies, and a number of reviews show that interventions to improve study skills can be successful (Fleming, 2002; Hattie, Biggs, & Purdie, 1996; Kobayashi, 2006; Pressley et al., 1997). There are a small number of reviews that have not proved promising (e.g., Hadwin & Winne, 1996) although again intervening never hurts. We hope that the material in the preceding two chapters will give you many options for intervening with your students. The results of anything you do to increase learning, whether by modifying your teaching in ways suggested in chapter 2, or focusing on elements of learning described in this chapter, should be thoroughly evaluated so that you know if you have achieved anything. This in itself will ensure you are being a scholarly teacher. Publishing the fruits of your labor – the epitome of the Scholarship of Teaching and Learning – will greatly benefit your colleagues and students everywhere.

Appendix: Questions on How to Make Cognitive Research Available to Educators

How do we connect theory and practice to make research applicable?

How do we know how much we know?
○   Hart, J. T. (1965). Memory and the feeling-of-knowing experience. *Journal of Educational Psychology*, 56, 208–2146. Investigation of individuals' accuracy in monitoring their stored knowledge.

How do we know if we know?
○   Flavell, J. H. (1977). Cognitive development. Englewood Cliffs, NJ: Prentice-Hall. Discusses thinking about thinking.
○   Flavell, J. H. (1979). Metacognition and cognitive monitoring: A new area of cognitive developmental inquiry. *American Psychologist*, 34, 906–911. Discusses

thinking about one's own thoughts: tied to individuals' own internal mental representations and interactions of metacognitive knowledge, experiences, goals, and action/strategies.
○ Schoenfeld, A. H. (1987). What's all the fuss about metacognition? In A. H. Schoenfeld (Ed.), *Cognitive science and mathematics education* (pp. 189–215). Hillsdale, NJ: Lawrence Erlbaum Associates. When students know the state of their own knowledge only then can they effectively self-direct their learning of the unknown.

How does studying affect if we know or how much we know?

How does predicting future performance affect learning?
○ Berardi-Coletta, B., Buyer, L. S., Dominowski, R. L., & Rellinger, E. A. (1995). Metacognition and problem solving: A process-oriented approach. *Journal of Experimental Psychology: Learning, Memory, Cognition*, 21, 205–223.
○ Gillstrom, A., & Ronnberg, J. (1995). Comprehension calibration and recall prediction accuracy of texts: Reading skill, reading strategies, and effort. *Journal of Educational Psychology*, 87, 545–558.
○ Kennedy, E. J., Lawton, L. & Plumlee, E. L. (2002). Blissful ignorance: The problem of unrecognized incompetence and academic performance. *Journal of Marketing Education*, 24 (3), 243–252. How accurate are students' self-assessments: competent vs. incompetent students' predictions on levels of understanding and performance levels.
○ Magliano, J. P., Little, L. D., & Graesser, A. C. (1993). The impact of comprehension instruction on the calibration of comprehension. *Reading Research and Instruction*, 32, 49–63.
○ Maki, R. H. (1995). Accuracy of metacomprehension judgments for questions of varying importance levels. *American Journal of Psychology*, 108, 327–344.
○ Maki, R. H., & Berry, S (1984). Metacomprehension of text material. *Journal of Experimental Psychology: Learning, Memory, and Cognition*, 10, 663–679.

How does having students provide explanations for what they are doing when solving a problem enhance processing/performance?
○ Maki, R. H., & Serra, M. (1992a). The basis of test predictions for text material. *Journal of Experimental Psychology: Learning, Memory, and Cognition*, 18, 116–126.
○ Maki, R. H., & Serra, M. (1992b). Role of practice tests in the accuracy of test predictions on text material. *Journal of Educational Psychology*, 84, 200–210.
○ Weaver, C. A. III, & Bryant, D. S. (1995). Monitoring of comprehension: The role of text difficulty in metamemory for narrative and expository text. *Memory and Cognition*, 23, 12–22.

What roles do self-efficacy, self-appraisals, and self-management play in cognition and learning?

o Ausubel, D. P. (1968). *Educational psychology: A cognitive view.* New York: Holt, Rinehart and Winston. What students already know (prior knowledge) strongly influences what they will learn or choose to learn in the future.

o Borkowski, J. G., Carr, M., Rellinger, E., & Pressley, M. (1990). Self-regulated cognition: Interdependence of metacognition, attributions, and self esteem. In B. F. Jones & J. T. Guthrie (Eds.), *Dimensions of thinking and cognitive instruction* (pp. 53–92). Hillsdale, NJ: Lawrence Erlbaum Associates. The self-assessments of one's affective states is a strategy of metacognition.

o Brown, A. L. (1978). Knowing when, where, and how to remember: A problem of metacognition. In R. Glaser (Ed.), *Advances in instructional psychology* (Vol. 1, pp. 77–165). Hillsdale, NJ: Lawerence Erlbaum Associates. Regulation of one's own thinking processes in order to cope with changing situational demands; early research done on mentally or educably retarded children.

o Cavanaugh, J. C., & Borkowski, J. G. (1979). The metamemory-memory "connection": Effects of strategy training and maintenance. *The Journal of General Psychology, 101,* 161–174.

o Lodico, M. G., Ghatala, E. S., Levin, J. R., Pressley, M., & Bell, J. A. (1983). The effects of strategy monitoring training on children's selection of effective memory strategies. *Journal of Experimental Child Psychology, 35,* 73–277. Found that students will maintain using instructional strategies, when they learn the value of the strategy for improving their performance.

o Nelson, T. O., & Dunlosky, J. (1991). The delayed-JOL effect: When delaying your judgments of learning can improve the accuracy of your metacognition monitoring. *Psychological Science, 2,* 267–270. Discusses the accuracy of memory monitoring and the effect the amount of time between learning and monitoring.

o Paris, S. G., & Winograd, P. (1990). How metacognition can promote academic learning and instruction. In B. F. Jones & L. Idol (Eds.), *Dimensions of thinking and cognitive instruction* (pp. 15–51). Hillsdale, NJ: Lawrence Erlbaum Associates. Individuals need to be involved in the construction of their knowledge.

Are we aware that we automatically respond to what we already know and ignore that which we are not familiar (selective attention)?

How does memory affect learning?

o Schneider, W. (1985). Developmental trends in the metamemory-memory behavior relationship: An integrative review. In D. L. Forrest-Pressley, G. E. MacKinnon, & T. G. Waller (Eds.), *Metacognition, cognition, and human performance* (Vol. 1, pp. 57–109). New York: Academic. The increase in the complexity of tasks also increases the difficulty in monitoring the thought processes to complete them.

What areas of the brain are involved in learning? How does language affect learning?
Various processing areas: visual, auditory, oral.
○ Bach-y-Rita, P. (1981). Brain plasticity as a basis of the development of reha-bilitation procedures for hemiplegia. *Scandinavian Journal of Rehabilitaion Medicine*, 13, 73–83.
○ Jones, T.A., & T. Schallert. (1994). Use-dependent growth of pyramidal neurons after neocortex damage. *Journal of Neuroscience*, 14, 2140–2152.
○ Kolb, B. (1995). *Brain Plasticity and Behavior*. Hillsdale, NJ: Erlbaum.
○ Neville, H. J. (1995). Effects of experience on the development of the visual systems of the brain on the language systems of the brain. Paper presented in the series Brain Mechanisms Underlying School Subjects, Part 3. University of Oregon, Eugene.

How does instruction affect the kinds of information our brains store?
The human brain can be functionally reorganized.

Are we able to unlearn and relearn?
Is learning the act of making meaning?
Do connections bring further meaning?
What effect do the emotions/feelings have that we attach to our learning (schema process)?
What effect does reflecting have in the role of learning?
What roles do procedural and declarative knowledge play in cognition and learning?
○ Kluwe, R. H. (1982). Cognitive knowledge and executive control: Metacogni-tion. In D. R. Griffin (Ed.), *Animal mind – human mind* (pp. 201–224). New York: Springer-Verlag. Made distinctions between procedural and declarative knowledge and of what is and is not metacognitive.

4

Is It Significant?

Basic Statistics

What exactly do you do with your "data" once you collect it? Once one asks the right questions and obtains answers, the next important step is to analyze the results to see whether significant change has occurred. In this chapter we discuss the important connection between choosing research design/methods and the types of statistical analyses possible. We have to point out that research on teaching and learning is very unique. Not all the usual rules or assumptions can or do apply. If your academic background did not necessitate extensive (or any) training in statistical analyses this chapter will provide you with a treasure trove of pragmatic information. Even if you are well versed in statistics, you may not be as adept at some of the types of analyses most suitable for SoTL. Instead of having you consult additional statistical books that will rarely have relevant examples, in this chapter we review the main statistical analyses needed to conduct SoTL and also discuss the main statistical programs that can be used.

We are not going to venture into statistical theory. We are not going to demonstrate how to derive statistical formulas and then analyze classroom data by hand and slide rule. But we will give you the tools and the know-how to assess teaching and learning. We will cover both descriptive and inferential statistics and discuss pragmatic ways to conduct statistical analyzes as well as providing ways to analyze qualitative data. Figures will provide information on how to use programs such as SPSS.

Why Do We Need to Analyze Our Classroom Data?

Although this question may seem like a critical one to answer to justify a chapter on statistics, even a cursory look at the practices of most faculty in the classroom will show that it is something that is done as a part of the process of teaching. Even the instructor at the lowest level of our teaching hierarchy (see chapter 1), going through the motions, still analyzes his or her classroom data at some level. A class average of 60 is hard to ignore. A class where a third fail and a third get an A, is one that bears more attention. If you are looking at how your students do on your exams, and you have to assess students on something in order to give them a grade for a course, you are analyzing data. If you pay even scant attention to your teaching evaluations you are analyzing classroom data. Of course, that is the tip of the analysis iceberg.

Even if you do pay attention to how your students' grades change on exams semester after semester and if you monitor your own course ratings over time, this is only the beginning. One semester your class average may be an 84/100. The next it may be an 88/100. At face value there is an increase and a change, but can we pack our things and go home happy? This question cannot be answered without statistical analysis of the data. Consider the following example. You have thirty students in your class and you would really like to improve the quality of their writing. You design elaborate instructions on how to improve their writing and measure their writing before and after you deliver your special instructions. You have designed a tight rubric to grade their writing and, using this rubric, the average grade in the class moves from a 70 to a 74. Is this occasion for jumping and shouting? The grades have increased, but is the increase statistically significant? Why do we need change to be *statistically* significant? The main reason that this question is important is that it is possible that the grade increase happened purely by chance. If you had done nothing, maybe the grades would have still increased by those four points. Statistical analyses test whether this is the case. If a change is statistically significant, then you have something to be proud of.

A note of caution: Just as all change may not be statistically significant, not all statistically significant change may be *meaningful* change. Although we can launch a philosophical debate around the topic of what constitutes meaningful change in learning, there is one simple answer that is hard to negate: statistically significant changes that could not have taken place by chance are important. That said, there are some simple factors that can artificially create statistical significance. The most critical one to bear in mind is the number of students being studied (or the sample size). One of basic magic tricks that a researcher can play is to increase the number of people the research is being done on, and previously non-significant changes can then become significant. A change in class average from 70 to 74 in a class of 35 will probably not be significant. If it was a class of 1,000, that same small change may become statistically significant by virtue of the underlying assumptions and calculations involved in statistical analyses. There are some safeguards and limiting factors. For example, only pedagogical interventions that have a large *effect size* – another bit of statistical jargon – will be significant when the sample size increases. If what you did in your class is really not effectual (a simple paraphrase of effect size that adequately conveys its intended meaning), no matter how many students you have in class, the resulting change in grade will not be significant. We will discuss effect sizes again later.

So even though statistical significance can be manipulated – we have heard the adage "lies, darn lies, and statistics" – when attempting to improve your students' learning, striving for statistically significant change is the gold standard. The world of academia is filled with assessments and bean counting at various levels – departmental reviews, college program reviews, university accreditation – and having a better sense of what is statistically significant change is critical.

Qualitative or Quantitative? That Is the Question

There are a couple of easy answers to this question. One answer is: Do whatever your discipline does. The second is: Do what will best enable you to get the answers to your SoTL questions. In many situations the two answers do not point to the same research design or statistical analyses, although across the disciplines communalities arise. If you teach English and are trying to get your students to better critically evaluate a novel, one way to assess change may be assign a numerical score to how well they tackle a particular work. This may be as simple as counting up the number of unique interpretations they come up with or the number of different unique points they raise. You will essentially have numbers that can be used to understand change: Are the numbers higher after you use a special new technique than they were before? In most attempts to understand learning we assign numbers regardless of the discipline we are in. Given this common means to the ends of a letter grade (even though the numbers needed for an A or a B will vary across disciplines, and instructors), common statistical methods can be used to see if the change in student learning is significant. To determine statistical significance even qualitative research needs to be quantified. That said, it is useful to establish the differences between the two methodologies.

Quantitative analysis forms the backbone of research in the natural and social sciences though both these areas also incorporate qualitative methodologies, and qualitative methodologies are often critical to theory building and preliminary explorations. One of the main drawbacks of quantitative analysis is that it can sometimes make it easy to forget about theory. We know researchers who are so excited by having numbers to play with and fish around in that often the theory that guided the research in the first place takes second place to the emerging patterns in the numbers (there is a time and a method for letting the data shape your theory). This quest to make the world quantifiable, a hallmark of the scientific method that promotes empiricism, has been known to drive non-science discipline faculty away from pedagogical research because they baulk at the assumption that one has to be a social scientist and create numbers to better understand student learning or assess their teaching. Indeed, quantitative researchers do collect numerical information and use statistical analyses to determine whether there are relationships between the numbers, but, as you will see, this does not have to be as cold or difficult a process as it sounds. Furthermore, qualitative researchers do "process data" as well. Qualitative data processing brings order to observations and often involves coding, classifying, or categorizing the observations. In contrast to quantitative analyses, where a standardized unit (e.g., a score on a questionnaire or scale) is used, coding in qualitative analyses focuses on the concept as the organizing principle. We believe that there is a nice middle ground where one can do quantitative analyses on what starts out as a qualitative investigation.

Qualitative analyses often involve a closer connection between theory, data collection, and analyses and is most distinguishable from quantitative research by not always being driven by a formal hypothesis or ideas about how variables are related. For example, you do not have to assume that a given method of instruction is better than another or that certain classroom factors will facilitate learning more than others. Instead the main goal is to describe the situation or process in as rich detail as possible and to explore possible reasons why certain outcomes may take place. Hypotheses and theory then immerges from these observations. For example, the *Grounded Theory Method* of qualitative analysis stresses the importance of building theory using an inductive basis – using observations to reveal patterns in behavior and then constructing theory from the ground up without preconceptions.

Box 4.1: Qualitative and Quantitative Research Methods

Qualitative Methods
Focus groups
Case studies
Interviews
Text/discourse analyses
Protocol analyses
Observation

Quantitative Methods
Surveys
Content analyses
Experiments

Qualitative research is also free from one of the most stressful expectations of quantitative research – need for representativeness and generalizability. Qualitative research concentrates on explaining a given classroom or a given set of students and does not need to worry about whether that set of students is representative of the general population of students or whether the findings derived from the research carry over to other settings and classes and schools.

These two extremes of research methodology do not have to be isolated either-or propositions. In fact, in pedagogical research, it is sometimes prudent to start with a qualitative mode of investigation and use the information derived to design a quantitative study to determine the significance of the findings. The major types of qualitative and quantitative research methods are listed and annotated in box 4.1.

Setting the Stage: Important Background for Measurement and Analyses

When assessing teaching and learning the information can be in many forms. You can use the scores from exams, essays, or assignments, or you can use surveys and questionnaires (see the previous two chapters) to study your students' attitudes to learning or their impressions about your teaching. The bottom line is you need some data from your students to begin to get a sense of what is going on. The topics described in chapters 2 and 3 should give you ideas on what to test and how. In the context of statistical analyses, it is important to know something about the characteristics of the data you are collecting because different types of data need different types of analyses. Qualitative (e.g., transcript of a student focus group) and quantitative (e.g., number correct on a multiple choice exam) data or information is the first main distinction, as discussed above. When talking about quantitative data in particular, it is useful to know about the four major *scales of measurement* as each scale has appropriate statistical properties. Note: when doing pedagogical research, different situations (e.g., schools, classes, disciplines) will create natural limitations to which type of measurement scale you can use. The goal of this next section is not to blind you with jargon (and there *are* a lot of terms in the statistician's verbal tool bag) but to help you aim to collect the most robust forms of information from your students to assess their learning.

The most basic form of measurement is *nominal data*, where we are categorizing information. The sex of the student (male or female), the student's year in school (freshman, sophomore, junior, senior), or perhaps the class the student was in (e.g., section 1 or 2) are the most common categories used. They convey important information but numbers ascribed to them (e.g., female = 1, male = 2) cannot be subjected to statistical manipulation as they do not convey any information relative to each other. For example, you cannot calculate an average for nominal data as it would be meaningless. There is no average sex! Similarly, men are not necessarily twice as good (or bad) as women just because the 2 you assign them is twice 1.

Next up the ladder is *ordinal data*. As the name suggests, this scale of measurement helps us to organize data. If you give students grades on a paper or a presentation without using a number range or numerical score, you are using an ordinal scale. An "A" is better than a "B," which is better than a "C," but the difference between each grade (A and B, and B and C) cannot be assumed to be the same. Ordinal data is great to rank students, but remember that the rank cannot tell you *how different* the two students are. You know an A student did better than a B student but you cannot assume the student did twice as well or any such factor of difference.

Interval data is perhaps the most common form of measurement scale used in pedagogical research. Here the gap (or interval) between two sets of points used can be assumed to convey the same information. On an exam, the difference between a 60 and a 65 is similar to the difference between an 80 and an 85. The issue here is that there is no meaningful zero. Just because a student gets a zero on your exam does not mean they know nothing. This type of scale is easier to picture if you consider assessing a student's attitude toward your class. If you ask a student how much they liked your class and rate your class on a scale of 1 to 10 with a 1 being "not at all" and a 10 being "very much so," a score of 8 is clearly better than a score of 2 (they liked your class a good deal), and we assume the difference between a liking score of 2 and 3 is the same as the difference between a liking score of 8 and 9. What we cannot assume is that a 4 is twice the liking of a 2 or that an 8 is twice the liking of a 4. Many pedagogical researchers often forget about this limitation of interval data and draw inappropriate conclusions from such scales.

The final type of scale is rarely found in pedagogical research. *Ratio scales* are interval scales with true zero points. If you wanted to have your students do a literature search and find references to a certain topic (e.g., find academic articles critiquing the work of Andy Warhol), a simple count of the number of references they found would be a ratio scale. The student with no references would be assigned a zero with its meaning clear.

Two Main Forms of Statistical Analyses: Descriptive Analyses

Descriptive statistics are a class of procedures that allow you to easily summarize the information you have collected. The most basic descriptive statistic is the average or mean.

Averages are probably the numbers most often looked at in the assessment of learning. The average is perhaps the best way to get a good quick sense of how your students are learning. Most pedagogical research concentrates on what the average suggests. We can look at average points scored on a multiple-choice exam, on an essay exam, on a paper assignment, on an online quiz, or even the overall class average. Most quantitative research involves statistical analyses to determine if there are significant differences in the average. Does the average paper grade go up if you change the instructions for the paper? Does the average exam score change if you personally run review sessions? Does the average essay exam score increase if you provide students with a list of the potential exam essay questions beforehand? Even qualitative research can use averages once the observations are quantified. Does a student's creative use of materials in an art class increase after specific modeling from the instructor? Does the quality of close reading improve after examples of close reading are provided? Does a music student's vocal range increase after the implementation of new voice exercises? Although each of these qualitative questions can be answered without the use of quantification, using a rubric (see chapters 2 and 3) to empirically determine scores yields averages that can be analyzed for significant change. Correspondingly, knowing how to tell if the averages are significantly different is a critical part of pedagogical research.

Although the average is a useful number to look at, the average can be influenced by a number of factors that one should keep in mind. For example, averages can be influenced by *outliers*. In almost every class you will see some student who does much better or much worse than all the rest. This student is an outlier, an extreme score that can have a strong influence on the class average. This influence is even stronger in a small class. If you teach 10 students and 9 of them get scores in the range of 80 to 90 (e.g., 82, 89, 90, 81, 81, 86, and so on) and the 10th student gets a 40, the class average is a 79.9. If that 10th student got a 93 instead, the average jumps to 85.4.

As useful as a mean is, it does not always give you the best picture of how your students are doing. Other key descriptive statistics to look at are the median, the mode, the range, and standard deviations.

The median of a set of scores is the middle score. If you know the median you know that half the scores in the class fall above that number and the other half fall below it (if there is an even number of scores the median is the score halfway between the middle two scores. The nice thing about the median is that is it not influenced by outliers or extreme scores and can give you a better sense of your class. In the example above, although the mean could shift drastically between either 79.9 or 85.4 depending on the value of the 10th score, the median does not change as much, as can be seen in figure 4.1.

The mode is the most common score. If the majority of your class gets a 70, then 70 is your mode. Knowing the mode is especially important when you are using a multiple-choice test where the majority of questions are newly written (not previously tested on other classes) and where you

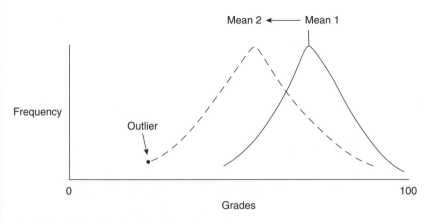

Figure 4.1: Change in Mean Due to Outlier

could get many scores clustering around a certain number. The mode is also very useful for when you use extremely subjective methods of grading or your grading rubric (for an essay, short answer, or paper assignment) does not differentiate well between students.

Watching Your Curves

The range of scores is the distance between the minimum and maximum scores and gives you are a good idea of the spread of scores. Related to the range and much more useful for assessing learning and getting a sense of your teaching is the idea of a class distribution. Mapping out a class distribution (i.e., how the grades vary or are distributed across the range) can offer some valuable insights into how your class is learning. There are two important reasons for examining your class distribution. First, it gives you a sense of the difficulty level of your grading (as you shall see below). More importantly for the purposes of this chapter, your class distribution and the shape of the curve it describes will suggest the statistics you can or cannot use to analyze your scores. Parametric statistics, for example those using t, F, or r scores, should not be calculated when your scores are skewed. Yes, if you are skewed you are skewed indeed. You have probably heard of a *normal* distribution – distribution of scores where most scores are around the mean and the others are spread symmetrically around the mean. Parametric statistics can only be used with normal distributions

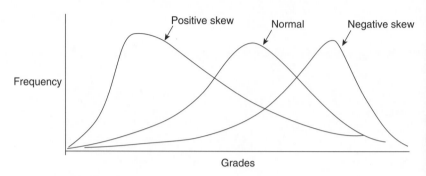

Figure 4.2: Distributions, Normal, Positive, and Negative Skew

(certain mathematical assumptions underlying a normal distribution). Most exam scores will approximate a normal distribution (see figure 4.2). If the range is large (e.g., 40 to 98) you will get a good-looking bell curve. If the range is small (e.g., 75 to 90) and most of the students cluster close on either side of the mean, you will get a tall, thinner curve. Sometimes you will not get a normal distribution at all.

Sometimes students either get what you are teaching and score high, or completely miss the point and score poorly and fail. This can happen when you are teaching a higher-level class (or perhaps any class) for the very first time and/or if you are new to a school and do not know the students well. Most new classes involve some tweaking as you go along, but if you have pitched the class too high you may see a *bi-modal* distribution. As the term suggests, there will be two modes with students clustering at a low point and a high point. This camel hump distribution is a clear sign that something is amiss, as shown in figure 4.3. If the exam or paper grading rubric was not challenging you will have students cluster around a high point, skewing your curve to the right (a negative skew). If the exam or assignment was too difficult, you will have students cluster around a low grade and the curve skewed to the left (a positive skew, though clearly not a positive situation).

Inferential Statistics

In the previous chapter we provided you with the basics of research design (see figure 3.2). Regardless of which design you use, you are going to have to be able to tell whether any differences you see are statistically significant.

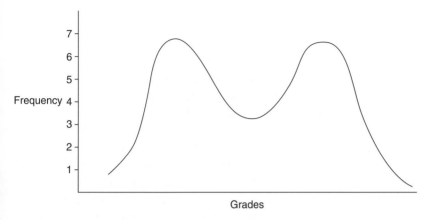

Grades

Figure 4.3: Bimodal Distribution

Did the number of "insightful comments" in a close reading exercise significantly increase after you did a two-hour discussion of how to close read? Did the number of factual questions answered go up after you instituted online quizzes? At the heart of pedagogical research is the comparison of the average score and related descriptive statistics described above.

The two most common comparisons of averages are *group comparisons* or *repeated measurement* comparisons. You use the former to compare two or more classes that may have each received different instruction, different instructors, or textbooks. You use the latter to test whether your students' learning has changed as a function of a teaching innovation or other instruction. Each of these two major comparisons entails different statistical analyses.

Comparing groups. Let us say you are teaching two sections of a class. One meets at 8 a.m. and the other meets at 3 p.m. You want to know whether the time of the class has an effect on learning. The critical test is whether exam scores (or any other assessment) varies between the two groups. Alternatively, you may want to test whether students in your section of an introductory class are learning the same as students in another section of an introductory class. You may also want to know whether students who get no instruction on how to do group work perform any differently from students who do. All these questions involve testing mean differences between two or more groups. The most common statistic used in this case is a *t-test*. Using this test allows you to calculate whether two independent groups have significantly different averages. An important assumption underlying the t-test is that the degree to which scores within each of your two samples vary is the same (homogeneous). This property referred to as *variance* is a combination of how large your range is and how many scores fall at different points of the range. Programs such as SPSS automatically test for this assumption. If it is violated you should use a class of statistics called non-parametric tests (e.g., chi-square), which we will get to soon. Another commonly used statistical test is the *analysis of variance* or *ANOVA*. The ANOVA is useful if you have more than two groups (something that would require multiple t-tests). Both statistics are extremely easy to do once your scores are entered into a statistical program. Each test makes different assumptions about the nature of the data and one (the ANOVA) is considered more robust than the other. Explicit directions on how to compute these statistics are presented later in this chapter.

Repeated measurements. Sometimes you may want to see if your students' writing is improving as the semester goes along or want to test a similar question that involves the same students doing something more than once. This could be having them retake a test and seeing if the scores improve. It could be having them take a pre-test on material they have not yet been exposed to and then testing them again after you have taught the material to see how much they have learned (i.e., Are post-test scores significantly different from pre-test scores?). For questions of this ilk, another form of t-test, the *paired samples t-test*, can be used. Similar to comparing groups, you can also use an ANOVA where, instead of two or more groups, you are testing whether the scores of the same students are changing over two or more measurements. For example, in a class with four exams, is there a significant increase or decrease in scores across exams? There is also a statistical analysis that specifically analyses repeated measures (see the General Linear Model category of analyses in SPSS described below).

But Is It Significant?

Whether you do a t-test, an ANOVA or any other statistic, you are looking to see whether the means are significantly different. The number that your eyes will gravitate to is the *p-value* or probability value. Your statistical test is significant if your p-value is less than .05. This translates into the probability that the means you are testing would have been statistically significant *purely* by chance (and not due to any real difference in your teaching, or in student learning) in less that 5 out of 100. Not bad. It gets better. Your means could be significant at the p less than .01 level. They could only have been so by a chance of 1 out of 100. Significant findings can also be possible at the p less than .001 level. The probability that the means you are testing would have been statistically significant *purely* by chance is less than 1 time out of *1,000*. Now you really do have something there. Every statistical program spits out a p-value, and you will quickly get accustomed to looking for the exact place in the output where the p-value is listed. We should point out that, although journal articles and statistical texts refer to the p-value, the actual output rarely uses the letter 'p'. For t-tests the p-value is listed under the heading 'Sig (2-tailed)'. For ANOVAs you will find the number you want under the heading 'Sig'. Examples of output with significant and non-significant differences in means are shown in table 4.1.

All Is Not as It May Seem: The Issue of Effect Size

If you have done your statistical tests and they are not significant you may conclude that indeed there were no group differences in means or that the repeated measures did not significantly vary from each other. Although

Table 4.1: ANOVA Output

ANOVA

	Sum of Squares	df	Mean Square	F	Sig.
Exam Between Groups	69.222	1	69.222	.615	**.434**
Within Groups	26092.240	232	112.467		
Total	26161.462	233			

No difference in exam scores by group (here section of course).

ANOVA

CL33

	Sum of Squares	df	Mean Square	F	Sig.
Between Groups	66.849	3	22.283	11.271	**.000**
Within Groups	245.151	124	1.977		
Total	312.000	127			

Significant difference in exam scores by group.

this conclusion may seem evident, it is not the case. Statistical significance is influenced by two major factors: sample size and effect size. If the number of students in your class is very large, this large sample size can make even small statistical differences in means significant (due to how statistical tests are calculated: see formulae in Field, 2005). By the same token, if you have a very small sample, then you may not get a statistically significant difference *even though there may be differences between groups*. This is referred to in statistical terms as making a Type II error and probably missing a true difference. Not finding statistical significance with a very small sample could just mean the research study could not detect the existing difference. There are ways to estimate whether your means *would* have been significant if you had a large sample and based on estimates of what the effect size of your effect is (a simple formula to do this is presented in Field, 2005 or most statistical texts).

Effect sizes are critical concepts for pedagogical research. Technically, the effect size is the difference between the group mean of the experimental group (the one getting special instruction) and the group mean of the comparison group divided by the control group's standard deviation. The key is that the size of the effect provides an idea of the real-world significance of the finding. Although laboratory researchers use a benchmark established by Cohen (1988), who categorized effect sizes of positive .20 as small, positive .50 as medium, and positive .80 as large, in pedagogical research, an effect size of .20 is something to be taken very seriously. Even a small effect size can have large real-world implications (the effect of aspirin reducing heart attacks has an effect size of only positive .06 (Bloom and Lipsey, 2004).

The Benefits of Control (Statistical)

If you want to increase your student learning you may devise a new method of instruction, use it, and test whether students are doing better. If students seem to have learned more (i.e., they have higher exam scores) in the new class as compared to your previous methods, how do you know it was you? What if the students the second time around were smarter?

In a robust pedagogical experiment where one group of students gets special instruction and another gets nothing, any differences in the performance of the first group of students can only be ascribed to the special instruction if there are no other differences between the two groups of students before the start of the semester or experimental period. It is very difficult to do a true experiment in a classroom and more often than not we do compare the averages of our most recent class with the average from the last time we taught it and look for changes. We have no idea whether the students are the same (a critical assumption though one that is clearly not physically possible unless your entire class retakes your class; even then they are not the same because they have been exposed to the material before). This is where controlling for some critical factors is important. Control factors range from student age and year in school to socioeconomic status (income level or education level) of the students or their parents, and even factors such as ethnicity.

The two most critical factors to control for are student *ability* and *effort*. Both are difficult concepts to hammer down, and we can probably debate what exactly a good measure of ability really is (are SAT or ACT scores really valid? What exactly does a GPA indicate?). In most pedagogical research a student's cumulative grade point average is a good stand-in for ability. If you teach primarily first-year students who do not yet have a cumulative GPA (or for second-semester students it may not mean as much) high-school GPA or even ACT scores are good controls. The only way to control for effort is to try to measure it. Some researchers ask how long students studied for the exam (total minutes being the control variable), or measure how much of a variety of different study techniques/methods (e.g., flash cards) were used. Other researchers directly ask students how much effort they put into studying for the exam. Being able to factor out such elements as ability and effort sounds nice in theory and it is actually relatively simple to do in practice, as we will show you in the nuts and bolts section below.

If the preceding sections on statistical analysis make you wish you had more data to analyze or if you have not thought of going through the trouble of gathering data on student learning or teaching (perhaps because you did not think it was quantifiable), there is something Galileo Galilei said in 1610 that is worthwhile to hang on to: "We must measure what can be measured, and make measurable what cannot be measured."

Software Options

There are a number of easily available software packages that can make qualitative analyses easier and also allow for the computation of statistical significance. Programs such as NVivo, Atlas, and Nudist are some commonly used content-analysis programs. There are also programs that make calculating statistical significance an easy proposal. Most instructors are familiar with programs such as Excel, which can get you the critical descriptions of your grades (e.g., class averages). As you ask more complex questions (e.g., What is learning related to?) and want to test differences between classes – let us say you want to see if student grades before you tried something new significantly improved after you tried an innovation – you will need some more sophisticated software. Two statistical packages available on most college campuses are SPSS (Statistical Package for the Social Sciences) and SAS (Statistical Analysis Software). Both are comparably user-friendly.

Nuts and Bolts

The key statistics that you should want to use to conduct your pedagogical research can be easily accomplished using a statistical package such as SPSS. The basic descriptive statistics described above can be also done by hand if you are so inclined (Field, 2005, provides easy references and basic formulae), and with more readily available programs such as Excel. The inferential statistics and the exciting comparison of group means in pre- and post-test designs or experiments are best accomplished with SPSS or SAS. This section will give you all you need to know to generate the main analyses you need.

If your university has a licensing agreement with SPSS (and most universities today do) you can get a CD with the program for home use for as little as $5. If you do not want to take your statistics home or on the road with you, your university machine will probably have the program loaded on already. Just load it in (or find the icon to activate it if already loaded or on a shared server) and you are ready to get a good feel for how learning is taking place in class.

When you open SPSS you will see a grid of rows and columns. Each row will come to represent each one of your students. Each column will represent a variable that you will describe. The most basic data set will include one column holding scores for an exam or paper, and as many rows as you have students. If you will be comparing more than one score or want to include all the assignment scores for your class, you will have one column for every time you give your student a grade (e.g., exam 1 score, exam 2 score, exam 3 score, paper score), plus one column that identifies the student (e.g., student ID number). The first thing to do is to click on the tab at the bottom of your screen labeled "Variable View." Type in the names of each of your assignments in the first column, with each row now representing each assignment/variable (it is a good idea to label your first box "Student Identity" and use it to ID your students). You can also have a column for first name and last names. When you are done, you can click on the tab at the bottom labeled "Data View" and you will see the grid toggle back to where each of your newly created labels will be listed across the top.

If you want to compare the scores of students across sections of your course, you will need to create a new column that identifies which section they are in. So in addition to student name, ID, and scores on different assignments, you will create a column that will signify which section the student is in (e.g., 1 for section 1, 2 for section 2 and so on). This column will be important when you compare scores across sections.

If you have a large class, you may be able to export your electronic class list into Excel and then import it directly into SPSS. Your computer help desk can walk you through the export/import process. Once you have defined your variables, you can start entering in the information. If you do this at the start of your class, you can enter in the scores as the assignments/assessments get completed. If you want to do some pedagogical calculations on your class after your class is completed and you use course-management software such as Blackboard, Angel, or Desire2Learn, you can export your class rosters (all the names and identifying material) and all your grades (quizzes, exams, paper assignments) directly into SPSS (or for some course-management programs, into Excel and then SPSS). A screen shot of a sample SPSS data file for a class is shown in figure 4.4.

Calculating Descriptive Statistics

Once you have your data entered you can use the menu across the top to calculate any of the descriptive or inferential statistics described above. To calculate the mean and get the range and the class distribution there are two options.

The quick way to get a nice feel for your scores is to click on GRAPHS from the menu on top of your screen.

SummerHealth06.sav [DataSet4] - SPSS Data Editor
File Edit View Data Transform Analyze Graphs Utilities Window Help

1 : Exam1   94

	Exam1	Exam2	q1	q2	q3	q4	q5	q6	q7	q8	q9	q10	q11	q12
1	94	90	2.00	2.00	3.00	2.00	2.00	2.00	2.00	2.00	1.00	2.00	1.00	1.00
2	92	92	7.00	7.00	7.00	7.00	7.00	7.00	7.00	7.00	7.00	7.00	7.00	7.00
3	96	96	1.00	2.00	2.00	2.00	1.00	2.00	2.00	2.00	1.00	1.00	1.00	1.00
4	94	94	6.00	4.00	4.00	3.00	6.00	4.00	7.00	3.00	3.00	4.00	6.00	7.00
5	82	70	3.00	2.00	5.00	3.00	3.00	2.00	5.00	3.00	3.00	3.00	3.00	2.00
6	84	78	5.00	2.00	6.00	2.00	4.00	1.00	7.00	3.00	1.00	1.00	4.00	4.00
7	66	70	6.00	4.00	7.00	4.00	5.00	5.00	7.00	5.00	2.00	4.00	4.00	4.00
8	98	94	1.00	1.00	5.00	4.00	2.00	3.00	4.00	2.00	2.00	3.00	2.00	6.00
9	92	96	4.00	4.00	5.00	3.00	4.00	4.00	5.00	4.00	2.00	3.00	3.00	4.00
10	92	82	2.00	2.00	2.00	2.00	2.00	1.00	4.00	2.00	4.00	2.00	2.00	1.00
11	88	90	6.00	6.00	4.00	6.00	5.00	5.00	4.00	1.00	2.00	2.00	2.00	2.00
12	90	84	4.00	4.00	4.00	4.00	4.00	4.00	4.00	4.00	4.00	3.00	4.00	4.00
13	96	94	3.00	2.00	3.00	2.00	3.00	2.00	3.00	3.00	2.00	2.00	1.00	1.00
14	96	98	3.00	2.00	3.00	2.00	2.00	2.00	2.00	2.00	2.00	2.00	3.00	3.00
15	82	90	4.00	4.00	7.00	4.00	4.00	2.00	4.00	1.00	3.00	4.00	4.00	4.00
16	86	92	1.00	1.00	4.00	2.00	1.00	2.00	4.00	1.00	1.00	1.00	1.00	1.00
17	94	96	2.00	1.00	3.00	2.00	2.00	2.00	3.00	2.00	1.00	1.00	1.00	1.00
18	94	92	4.00	2.00	6.00	2.00	3.00	2.00	6.00	2.00	1.00	2.00	2.00	3.00
19	88	88	2.00	6.00	4.00	3.00	3.00	6.00	4.00	4.00	1.00	4.00	1.00	1.00
20	88	88	2.00	2.00	1.00	2.00	2.00	2.00	1.00	2.00	1.00	2.00	4.00	4.00
21	84	80	2.00	2.00	5.00	2.00	2.00	2.00	2.00	2.00	2.00	2.00	2.00	2.00
22	94	98	2.00	2.00	3.00	2.00	2.00	2.00	3.00	2.00	2.00	2.00	2.00	2.00
23	92	92	2.00	1.00	3.00	4.00	2.00	3.00	3.00	3.00	3.00	3.00	1.00	1.00
24	82	90	1.00	1.00	3.00	2.00	2.00	1.00	3.00	2.00	1.00	1.00	2.00	2.00
25														

Figure 4.4: Screen Shot of an SPSS Data File

Scroll down the list and click on HISTOGRAM. On the left will be a box with the variables you have previously defined. Click on the variable you want descriptive statistics for, and then click on the topmost little arrow. This will put your chosen variable (e.g., Exam 1) into the little box under the label Variable.

Select DISPLAY NORMAL CURVE by checking the box next.

Click OK. The program will generate a bar graph showing the number of students who got each different level of score. It will also superimpose a normal curve on top of it and present the mean, standard deviation, and sample size (so you can check if you are missing any students).

There is a second way to get the same information with additional technical data. Click on ANALYZE and roll your cursor down to DESCRIPTIVE STATISTICS. You will now see a list to choose from.

Click on DESCRIPTIVE. You will see two boxes. On the left will be a box with the variables you have previously defined. Click on the variable you want descriptive statistics for, and then click on the arrow in between boxes. This will move your variable (say, Paper1) into the box on the right. You can select as many variables from the box on the right as you want. Remember that you can (and should) only get means on continuous interval or ratio data (see the section above).

Click on the OPTIONS button (bottom right corner) and select the descriptive statistics you want. Best bets are: mean, range, minimum, maximum, standard deviation, and skewness.

Click CONTINUE.

Click OK. The program will run the analyses for you and a new window (called the output window) will open up with the results.

Calculating Inferential Statistics

Testing whether group means are significantly different is not much more difficult than calculating a mean or descriptive statistics.

To run an independent sample t-test to compare group means, click ANALYZE from the top menu. From the dropdown menu, take your cursor to COMPARE MEANS. The cursor will now open a list of specific tests. Select and click on INDEPENDENT-SAMPLES T-TEST.

In the box on the right, click on the score you want to compare, Exam 1 score for example, and then click on the higher arrow in the center (next to the box titled "Test variable(s)"). This will move your variable, Exam 1, into the left box. Then select the variable that categorizes your groups.

Click on the variable and then on the arrow that will pop it into the box titled "Grouping Variable". Once the variable is in the box, click on the "Define Groups" box and give the two groups numbers (1 and 2 are easy).

Click CONTINUE.

Click OK. Your analysis will be calculated.

To run an ANOVA to compare group means, click ANALYZE from the top menu. From the dropdown menu, take your cursor to COMPARE MEANS. The cursor will now open a list of specific tests. Select and click on ONE-WAY ANOVA.

In the box on the right, click on the score you want to compare, Exam 1 score for example, and then click on the higher arrow in the center (next to the box titled "Dependent List"). This will move your variable, Exam 1, into the left box. The advantage of using an ANOVA is you can actually select a number of variables (e.g., comparing three assignment scores). Then select the variable that categorizes your groups.

Click on the variable and then on the arrow that will pop it into the box titled "Factor."

Click OK. Your analysis will be calculated.

Kicking It Up a Notch: Testing Multiple Factors

In pedagogical research, the most simple analysis is testing whether means differ as discussed before. You can find out whether one class is doing better than another or whether student learning changed over the course of the semester (i.e., in pre-post comparisons). Sometimes you may want to see whether such changes vary for specific groups. For example, do men do differently than women? Do students with certain learning styles do better than others? Do the upper-class students learn differently from the freshmen and sophomores? In each of these cases you will want to test additional questions together with your basic question (e.g., Did groups differ?). Each additional question is called a factor. You can test as many factors as you want, but interpreting results can get tricky. For the present purposes we shall illustrate the use of a two-factor test.

Say you want to know whether students in your morning session do better than those in your afternoon section (Factor 1: Time) *and* you want to know whether the men and women learn the same way (Factor 2: Sex). You can still use the same basic ANOVA with a twist. Part of the key is entering your scores and then creating simple codes to identify the level of each factor. If you have two sections, there are two levels of the class time factor (1 = morning; 2 = afternoon). There are two levels for sex (1 = Female; 2 = Male). A simple file for to test for differences in learning on an exam will have three main columns, one each for exam score and each of the two factors as shown in figure 4.5.

To compute your statistical analysis, click ANALYZE from the top menu. From the dropdown menu, take your cursor to General Linear Model.

Click on UNIVARIATE. Click on your main outcome measure, Exam Score in this example, and then click on the arrow at the top (next to the box titled "Dependent Variable"). This will move your variable, Exam 1, into the little box.

Click on each of your two factors, Time and Sex, and click on the second arrow to move each factor into the box titled "Fixed Factor(s)."

Click on the OPTIONS button.

Click on the variables in the box on the right (Sex, Time, and Sex x Time) and click the arrow in-between to push the variables over to the box on the right titled "Display Means for." (The Sex x Time variable is not a vari-

	Exam1	ClassTime	Sex	var	var	var	var	var	var	var	var
1	94	1.00	1.00								
2	92	1.00	1.00								
3	96	1.00	2.00								
4	94	1.00	2.00								
5	82	1.00	1.00								
6	84	1.00	1.00								
7	66	1.00	2.00								
8	98	1.00	2.00								
9	92	1.00	1.00								
10	92	1.00	1.00								
11	88	1.00	2.00								
12	90	1.00	2.00								
13	96	1.00	2.00								
14	96	2.00	2.00								
15	82	2.00	1.00								
16	86	2.00	1.00								
17	94	2.00	1.00								
18	94	2.00	1.00								
19	00	2.00	2.00								
20	88	2.00	1.00								
21	84	2.00	2.00								
22	94	2.00	2.00								
23	92	2.00	1.00								
24	82	2.00	1.00								

Figure 4.5: Three-column Layout for Exam/Class Time/Male Sex

able per se but will allow you to test whether there is an interaction between your two factors: Does exam score vary as a function of both time the class and sex of student?)

Click on Continue.

Click OK. The program will run the analysis and give you an output similar to that shown in table 4.2.

As in interpreting most output, again the key thing you want to look for is whether the test is significant or not. Although there is a lot of other interesting information presented, you want to look at the box under the heading "Tests of Between-Subjects Effects." The first column shows you the different factors. You can ignore the rows with Corrected Model, Intercept, Error, Total and Corrected Total. Your destination is the three rows with your two factors, Time and Sex, and the interaction between them, Time × Sex. Did exam scores vary by class time, sex, or an interaction between the two? If the values in the column titled 'Sig.' are less than .05, you have a statistically significant difference. If the Time row has a value less than .05 you know that the mean scores of students in one section are statistically significantly different from the mean scores of students in the other section. This is referred to as a *main effect of Time* (or of factor 1). If

Table 4.2: Two-Factor Test

Between-Subjects Factors

		Value Label	N
ClassTime	1.00	10am	13
	2.00	2pm	11
Sex	1.00	Female	13
	2.00	Male	11

Tests of Between-Subjects Effects
Dependent Variable: Exam1

Source	Type III Sum of Squares	df	Mean Square	F	Sig.
Corrected Model	14.143(a)	3	4.714	.085	.968
Intercept	182300.921	1	182300.921	3281.182	.000
ClassTime	.098	1	.098	.002	.967
Sex	9.589	1	9.589	.173	.682
ClassTime * Sex	4.785	1	4.785	.086	.772
Error	1111.190	20	55.560		
Total	192656.000	24			
Corrected Total	1125.333	23			

a R Squared = .013 (Adjusted R Squared = −.136)

Estimated Marginal Means
1. ClassTime
Dependent Variable: Exam1

ClassTime	Mean	Std. Error	95% Confidence Interval	
			Lower Bound	Upper Bound
10 a.m.	89.524	2.073	85.199	93.849
2 p.m.	89.393	2.336	84.520	94.266

Table 4.2: *Continued*

2. Sex

Dependent Variable: Exam1

Sex	Mean	Std. Error	95% Confidence Interval	
			Lower Bound	Upper Bound
Female	88.810	2.073	84.484	93.135
Male	90.107	2.336	85.234	94.980

3. ClassTime × Sex

Dependent Variable: Exam1

ClassTime	Sex	Mean	Std. Error	95% Confidence Interval	
				Lower Bound	Upper Bound
10 a.m.	Female	89.333	3.043	82.986	95.681
	Male	89.714	2.817	83.838	95.591
2 p.m.	Female	88.286	2.817	82.409	94.162
	Male	90.500	3.727	82.726	98.274

the Sex row has a value less than .05 you correspondingly know there is a sex difference in exam scores. This is known as a *main effect of Sex* (or of factor 2). Which section scores higher or which sex scores higher can be easily determined by looking at the means that will also be printed out. If the row with the interaction (Sex × Time) is significant you know that each single factor by itself is not as important as the two factors interacting. That is, scores on the exam in the class being compared do not vary just by sex or time but vary as a factor of both. One possibility is that the men in the early section do worse than the men in the later section and perhaps the women in the early section. From a statistical perspective one does not put too much effort into interpreting the significance of either one factor if the interaction of the two factors is also significant. One does not worry about main effects if the interaction is significant.

Conclusions

In this chapter we have provided details on how to conduct some critical analyses in pedagogical research. Galileo's quote notwithstanding, there are some key points to be upfront about:

- There are many questions in SoTL that may not be amenable to statistical analyses.
- There are many results that may be significant but not have a large effect size (or power).
- There may be results that are of minimal statistical significance but may have serious implications for how we teach and how students learn.

For all these reasons and those discussed in the bulk of this chapter, it is important be well aware of how to critically analyze one's "data," the evidence of our teaching and student learning.

5

Pedagogical Research as Scholarship

Resources for Success

When the campus culture includes a focus on effective teaching, this support is usually found in the form of a center called, for example, the "Center for Teaching Excellence," the "Office of Faculty Development," "The Center for Teaching and Learning," or "The Office of Professional and Instructional Development." The form that this type of center takes is depend upon a number of factors including the size of the institution, the institutional priority of this type of resource, and, of course, the financial resources available. In turn, one can find a well-staffed center with full-time faculty hired specifically to enhance teaching effectiveness across all disciplines or a single individual who is assigned to his or her part-time role as director of faculty development on campus. Of course the amount of assistance available is dependent upon the number of staff and/or faculty, though the type of assistance is usually very similar. Through these centers, a vehicle is created on campus to share SoTL experiences, providing a way to share the challenges faced when conducting this type of research. The names of the centers are diverse, and where they exist on our campuses might differ, but in most cases assistance is available for all faculty, because after all the issue of effective teaching is one that remains for faculty at all ranks. Whether a first-year assistant professor or a tenured full professor, one can always improve upon the effectiveness of teaching. So, just as students are encouraged always to take advantage of resource centers on campus, to assist with studying or writing for instance, faculty should also be encouraged to take advantage of the teaching center on campus. We often hear that those students who make use of the campus resource centers are not necessarily the ones lacking in a particular skill, but instead are interested in improving what they already do well. The same is often true of those visiting the teaching and learning centers. This chapter reviews the types of programs available at many teaching and learning centers across the country.

This chapter is twofold and will be valuable both for those of you on staff at the teaching and learning center at your institution and for those of you interested in taking advantage of the initiatives on your campus provided through such a center. Perhaps you are in the exciting position of developing a center on your campus dedicated to assisting faculty with teaching endeavors. Fortunately, many have been faced with exactly that task, with centers of teaching and learning increasing in numbers particularly over the last 10 years. So, no need to reinvent the wheel. If possible, consider attending a conference created for new faculty developers. The Institute for New Faculty Developers, which holds an annual conference, focuses on learning to establish and manage faculty development programs (http://www.iinfd.org/).

In this chapter, we describe the different types of programs that exist at a variety of institutions (from small one-person programs to large programs with many staff members) and review the factors believed to make these different types of programs successful. Also included in this chapter will be information on the types of programs developed through these centers and how these programs assist faculty at all levels, from assistant to full professor. Next, we provide guidance to those of you looking for the resources available both on your campus and beyond. We review the texts, websites, organizations, and types or programming offered to assist with developing or sustaining a teaching and learning center as well as a pedagogical research program.

Developing a Center with a Focus on SoTL

Creating the Conversations about Teaching

Are discussions about teaching a part of your campus culture? Do you and your colleagues talk about challenges and successes in your classrooms? What is very interesting is the fact that on some campuses where you would expect teaching to dominate the conversations, little discussion on the matter takes place. Here we have an instance of an institution that values good teaching but does not provide the support needed to continually nurture such a culture. At many smaller colleges, teaching is identified as the number one priority of the faculty. Although scholarship and service are evaluated and are often important components of one's responsibility, it is teaching excellence that is most prominent when questions of tenure and promotion are raised. Why then would teaching not be part of faculty discussions? Well, it is because ability to teach well is taken for granted. This assumption often presents the notion that the college only hires faculty who already teach effectively, or that it is easy to teach well and therefore there is no need to talk about it. In turn, teaching becomes a very private venture between the faculty member and the students rather than a matter of community discussion amongst faculty.

However, many faculty would in fact appreciate the opportunity to discuss openly the successes and challenges one encounters when teaching. Often, these conversations are included in the sponsored programming of a teaching and learning center or are fostered by a faculty development council or committee. The Instructional Development Council (IDC) at the University of Wisconsin, Green Bay (UWGB) jumpstarted such conversations on teaching by organizing lunchtime brown-bag sessions where an invited guest discussed a topic of interest. The IDC also started a teaching newsletter. But if such resources do not exist on your campus, simply start the conversations on your own. Invite faculty to a lunch discussion with a teaching focus and you'll likely find many of your colleagues share your desire to talk about what we are expected to do well. We preach what we practice too: we started a SoTL discussion group on campus where faculty interested in talking about pedagogical research attend monthly meetings. This is just one component of creating a campus culture that supports the continuing professional development of our teaching. You might discover that a teaching and learning center would fit well in your institutional culture and perhaps you are interested in exploring the possibility of creating such a center on your campus.

Creating a Teaching and Learning Center on Your Campus

Over the last two decades, many institutions have recognized the value of pedagogical research. The American Association of Higher Education and the Carnegie Foundation recognized the importance of SoTL programs and in turn provided the support and leadership needed to the many institutions interested in this type of initiative. Because of the leadership and resources provided by both AAHE and Carnegie, specifically CASTL, many institutions were able to establish viable SoTL campus initiatives and assist many other campuses interested in developing similar programs.

If you are interested in reading in detail how the original set of institutions set up the needed infrastructure for these programs, we recommend Cambridge (2004), which provides readers with the fine points of not only how each institution created the needed support for an SoTL program on campus, but also how they created institutional change to promote SoTL, how they used collaboration to assist with the program, and what types of data were collected to illustrate the institutional change that took place as a result of the SoTL programming.

For our purposes, we thought it would be helpful to provide a description of the different types of successful SoTL initiatives as well as a summary of the support found to be particularly important when creating such a program and the factors found to at times create roadblocks along the way. Finally, we'll provide the types of resources provided through many teaching and learning centers. The success of any teaching and learning center is dependent on a number of factors, which we'll review below. However, we feel one of the most important factors is the fit between the institution and the center itself. A center on campus for teaching and learning and/or SoTL initiatives can take many forms. Wright (2002) describes the variations with regard to the structure of a center. The two most common types of centers are the single campus center that serves as a resource for that whole campus, run as a separate center or as a component of another part of another office on campus such as the Dean's office or through a faculty committee, and the multiple campus center often located at one location of a public institution, providing services and resources for the state-wide locations. How this center is created must be guided by campus needs, and fitting the center to those needs is essential for success. In other words, the center *must* fit the culture of the institution. Clearly a center at a large research institution will differ from a center at a small liberal arts college, with different staffing requirements, different programming needs, and different resources needed.

You'll find that names chosen for these centers also provide some insight about the fit to the institution. On some campuses you'll find an "Institute for Teaching and Learning." At others the center is called "The Center for Teaching Effectiveness" or ". . . for the Enhancement of Teaching." Still others focus on the services provided, with center names such as "The Office of Instructional Services," or "The Office of Professional and Instructional Development." Finally, some centers choose a name that is more inclusive of a variety of faculty needs such as "The Center for Faculty

Development." These differences are not just in terms of name and size but also programming, as discussed below.

Where Do You Fit?

In terms of fit, there are a number of different approaches in place concerning where a teaching center and/or a center for SoTL fits, with these approaches very diverse (see Cambridge, 2004). Often, SoTL centers are created within existing faculty development centers or learning centers created initially for students, which is the case, for example, at Maricopa Community College. In this situation the center for learning that primarily served students (e.g., first-year transition to college or critical thinking seminars) became a teaching and learning center for both students and faculty. You might be in the position of becoming part of an existing center that provides programming focused on faculty development programming (e.g., teaching observations, teaching portfolios) and you are developing programming focused on SoTL/pedagogical research. On most campuses, faculty development usually refers to initiatives designed to enhance classroom teaching and student learning, while scholarly research that directly assesses the influence of specific faculty development initiatives directed at improving student learning would fall under the title of SoTL. So there is clearly a natural connection between the two types of initiatives, and including SoTL takes the work of many faculty development centers from teaching focused to both teaching and scholarship focused. There are a number of benefits provided to SoTL centers when branching off an existing teaching and learning center. For instance, many faculty development centers produce in-house publications to inform faculty of teaching programs on campus as well as teaching-focused conferences off campus and could easily provide an avenue to share scholarly results of pedagogical research as well. As we discussed earlier in the teaching chapter, this sharing of findings is a very important part of any type of scholarly work. With an existing center, there are often staff members in place to assist with the new programming, and perhaps the funding in place for the existing center can be adjusted to cover the new programming initiatives. These advantages (e.g., existing staff and budget) could be potential disadvantages as well. For instance, the staff may be dedicated to their current mission for students, with little interest to expand the mission to include faculty development. And, although having funding in place from an existing center can be an advantage, sharing funds can also be considered a disadvantage with budget lines already labeled for specific programs already in place. Obviously, a budget specific to SoTL needs would be preferable. Of course one disadvantage of coexisting with an established center is creating a new identity for that center. Clearly there are both advantages and disadvantages to this situation of creating a new part of an existing center. Whether these factors are advantages or disadvantages will be determined in part by the way the transition is handled. A smooth transition, with agreement by all to the new arrangement, can create a center of greater strength. How smooth this type of transition goes is often dependent upon the leader in place and the ability of that leader to get everyone on board for the new mission of the center.

There are instances in which no center exists and you are responsible for the center from the ground up, as was accomplished at the University of Georgia, where they started a teaching academy. When building a center from scratch with no existing structure, you have the luxury of shaping all aspects of the programming. There are no other directors with whom to discuss how to share the budget. You are the one at the wheel with few if any passengers. At the same time, finding the resources to obtain staff or funds can be more difficult because you require a whole new budget. Making the center a known entity on campus takes time. Most challenging is creating all of the programming that fits the needs of your faculty.

Determining Needs on Your Campus

The way in which a teaching and learning center is developed is very dependent on the needs and resources of each institution (Cambridge, 2004). Each institution's current needs and interests create the focus for the programming developed by the center. Therefore, regardless of the way in which the center comes about, one must keep in mind this important issue of fit. To create that appropriate fit, a director must conduct a needs assessment through interviews, focus groups, and surveys of all members of the academic community to develop goals for the center that meet these needs. You want to avoid creating programming based only on your own interests and experience. When conducting this assessment, be sure to keep in mind that different needs are likely to result for the different constituencies on campus. The needs of new faculty are often different from those of

mid-career faculty, senior faculty, department chairs, and deans. Identifying these specific needs will allow you to develop programming that will
interest each group. Importantly, this type of needs assessment will also
create what is known as faculty ownership, a factor often cited as essential
for a center to be successful. After assessing needs, one can include faculty
who are interested in being involved in the development of programs
offered, or actually doing the programs, or providing guidance for the
assistance needed for faculty who are new to the campus, or faculty who
are simply interested in learning more about teaching from their colleagues. Faculty can also be involved in the decisions required for grants
or scholarships offered through the center. This involvement is particularly
important when minimal staffing is provided to run the center. Many
centers start out as one-person centers, particularly at smaller colleges.
When resources for staff are minimal, asking for assistance from faculty on
campus known for teaching excellence is a great way to start. Why not
involve those who have received the teaching award on your campus?
Again, you create faculty ownership at the same time that you obtain the
assistance you need to provide the programming.

   If administrative support is present, often faculty who provide you with
that type of assistance can receive release time or a stipend. At many institutions teaching and learning centers fall under the auspices of the Vice
President for Academic Affairs. When the VPAA is current in the SoTL
area and aware of the advantages provided by such scholarship, this alliance
can create tremendous institutional support. Importantly, this administrative connection also illustrates to the faculty that SoTL is an institutional
priority and that pedagogical research is recognized as suitable scholarly
activity. Of course, a VPAA who truly recognizes the value of ongoing
pedagogical research on campus and would like to energize this type of
research can also create a reward system such as grant opportunities or
merit salary rewards based on SoTL initiatives.

Determining Your Goals: What Is the Purpose of the Center?

As discussed above, the assessment you conduct will provide you with the
information needed to create programming specific to your campus needs.
The assessment will also help you shape the goals of the center. Creating a
list of goals will be essential for evaluating the effectiveness of the center,

and we will discuss the importance of assessment later in this chapter. Of course, the only way to determine that your goals are achieved is to have specific goals from the start. This is not to say these goals can't change. In fact, you are likely to find that, as the center evolves, so to do the goals of the center.

Any new faculty development or teaching center on campus likely began based on an initiative identified by the administration as a priority of the institution or by a group of faculty recognizing the lack of discussion about teaching, an essential aspect of the institution. The focus of either initiative in addition to the results of your needs assessment will be great starting points for your goals. What exactly do you want to accomplish through a teaching and learning center? Many have asked this same question, and although some goals are universal, there are others that are specific to your particular academic culture. A common goal for many is to improve the effectiveness of teaching and in turn to improve the quality of the education available across all disciplines. Some directors have included in their goals that they would like to create an environment that promotes and celebrates excellence in teaching and learning that goes beyond what is typical at their institution. To achieve such change, directors often include goals that focus on administrators and wish to provide expertise and advice to the administration regarding matters of teaching and learning. These more general goals also include creating a community in which faculty regularly engage in classroom-based inquiry, in which faculty reflect on their teaching practices and share their knowledge about those findings with colleagues both at their own institution and with colleagues elsewhere, and providing resources to those interested in conducting pedagogical research. Many directors would like this renewal of teaching and learning to not just be at the level of individual faculty members, but instead at the level of departments or programs on campus.

Other objectives are determined by the specific needs of the faculty. Although many of you can conjure up long lists of faculty needs, here attention is given to needs concerning teaching and learning without an evaluative focus. Directors would like the faculty to view their center as a resource for continued development and not just one for those who need help. Many directors of SoTL centers hope, and therefore include as goal, that pedagogical research becomes part of the campus culture, which could help maintain a high profile for the center on campus. More specific goals are often set that pertain to the number of faculty using the center as a resource, with specific goals aimed at new faculty as well as more seasoned colleagues. As we've stated throughout this chapter, any SoTL center must keep in mind the institutional culture when developing goals and programming. It is these idiosyncrasies that need to be conveyed to new members of the community. Many faculty development centers include an objective focused on new faculty to ensure that new colleagues are fully aware of the academic culture in which they are entering, as well as the classroom culture specific to the campus. So often, faculty coming from other campuses are very surprised by some of the differences they encounter when starting at a new institution, particularly if they thought it would be similar to the one they have left. These differences can include classroom culture such as unproctored exams, to the number of writing assignments expected in each course, to expectations of student engagement in classroom discussions. At some institutions there are no guidelines in place while at others these types of expectations are made very clear. Knowledge on all of these issues will create a much smoother transition when first teaching at a new institution. A discussion of mentoring programs focused on these needs is included later in this chapter.

Importantly, many centers include as a goal that confidentiality is ensured when working with faculty, and would like to have the option of non-evaluative feedback separate from all tenure and promotion decisions. The staff of any center needs to focus on their role as advocates for the faculty, particularly in their role as teachers. One must develop clear policies of confidentiality so that, if a faculty member having a problem in the classroom would like to examine the cause of that problem, the details are not shared with administrators or others involved with evaluation of that faculty member. At the same time, other directors would like official recognition of scholarship focused on teaching when promotion and tenure decisions are made. This is an important distinction to make. One must ensure confidentiality when assisting faculty with teaching-related concerns, but, when faculty successfully conduct pedagogical research, this type of scholarship should be recognized when decisions of tenure and promotion are underway.

This brings us to another goal of many centers, which is the need to encourage faculty that SoTL is worthwhile. This is particularly important given the time commitment involved in pedagogical research. This brings us back to campus culture. When SoTL is recognized by the college as a valuable way to improve one's teaching *and* as a way to maintain one's scholarly endeavors, more and more faculty are likely to consider pedagogical research because the encouragement is provided from the institution. In *Scholarship Reconsidered*, Boyer (1990) provides many strong arguments for changing the way in which higher education defines scholarship. He disputes the notion that one needs to view teaching and research as two separate undertakings and provides reasons for widening the definition of scholarship to include not only what he calls the scholarship of discovery, which most in higher education would call research, but also three additional areas of scholarship – the scholarship of integration, application, and teaching. Of course, all too often many institutions of higher learning stick to the very limited definition of scholarship and follow how it is defined by other institutions. Boyer points out that it makes more sense for institutions to create a definition of scholarship that fits the institutional goals rather than attempting to define it in the way that our most prestigious universities and colleges choose. We would argue that all types of scholarship identified by Boyer have a place at all institutions of higher learning.

If you are just starting the development of a center, do not let the numerous goals discussed above stop you in your tracks. As we mentioned earlier, it is important to prioritize these goals, and, in the case of a new center, you should consider creating a time line with which to identify when you would like to attain each goal. It makes no sense to attempt each of the goals listed above in the first year. You are only asking for disappointment. Instead, take a good look at your institution, conduct a needs analysis and in turn identify what is most imperative.

Guiding Principles When Creating a New Center

As we have stated throughout this guide, it is silly to reinvent the wheel. One resource that will provide guidance based on experience of those who have come before you can be found in Gillespie (2002), in which you can find the 10 principles of good practice. We've listed the principles in box 5.1 and discuss each in detail below.

Following the previous section on goals, it makes sense to start with one particular principle identified by Sorcinelli (2002) as important to follow when creating a teaching and learning center. She states that any successful center must state clear objectives and ways to assess if those objectives are in fact being met and share both with others at your institution. Keep in mind that it is very easy to create a rather lengthy list of objectives. Therefore, as we stated above, you need to prioritize your list to avoid setting

---

Box 5.1: Sorincelli's Principles of Good Practice for Teaching and Learning Centers

1. Listen to all perspectives, increase buy-in
2. Ensure effective leadership and management
3. Emphasize faculty ownership
4. Cultivate administrative commitment
5. Develop principles, goals, and assessment procedures
6. Strategic placement of the center within the organizational structure
7. Offer a wide range of programming, but prioritize programming commitments
8. Encourage collegiality and community
9. Create collaborative systems of support
10. Provide recognition and reward

---

yourself up for disappointment. Make your goals attainable and create a time line that is feasible.

When prioritizing, keep in mind another principle that encourages directors to incorporate programming for all members of the faculty (e.g., new faculty to full professors) but also the need to prioritize your resources and not spread yourself too thin. This principle is particularly important for those who are part-time directors and, at the same time, full-time faculty members. As we hear often, it is far better to create one strong program than several mediocre programs. Also important for the success of any center is its place within the structure of the organization. Here we are really talking about the hierarchy within the organization. Do you report directly to the Dean? This direct connection provides an avenue to both the financial support needed as well as ears needed to discuss the importance of the teaching mission of the institution. Your place within the organization also pertains to your location. The physical space is important and needs to be centrally located for easy access for faculty. Easy access to the center will foster the collegiality that often results when faculty are provided an avenue to share ideas and have meaningful conversations about teaching. It creates a learning community on campus, which with time grows in size and becomes an important component of the campus culture. One can also consider collaborations with other offices or centers on campus, such as the learning center for students or the instructional technology support office. As discussed above, this is particularly useful when funding already exists at those centers and therefore could potentially assist with your programming ideas.

For a center to be successful, an individual must take charge, which requires having the time, the vision, and the skills necessary. Without this type of leader, most of the other principles are hard to manage. This leader must be willing to listen to those on campus for whom the center is designed as well as those who are providing the funding. We talked above about the importance of assessing faculty needs, but you must also keep in mind the needs to administrators as well, all of whom are also largely invested in the education of the students. Listening closely to all constituencies keeps in mind those who you would like to use the center as well as those who will provide the funding needed to make the center effective. This brings us back to the importance of faculty ownership, which listening closely will help you to achieve. Given the many roles a director needs to play, if possible, the leader's position must be full-time. Often a center begins with a director who is part-time and is also a full-time member of the faculty. We all know how time consuming the role of a full-time faculty member can be. Sometimes a course load reduction can provide a portion of the time needed, but clearly, if the development of this center is an institutional priority, a part-time position will not suffice. Then again, if a part-time position is the only option, then starting small and growing is better than no center at all. If you are in that position, you are likely to find that this is exactly how many larger centers started.

Although a strong leader is important for the success of any center, as Sorcinelli (2002) puts it, while the center must have a person in charge, the center must be faculty inspired. Making sure you are surrounded by those dedicated to the success of this type of program on campus will provide an important source of both intellectual and programming support. So, a director must identify and organize a group of faculty who are dedicated to the cause and at the same time must also keep in mind the need for continued resources. At some institutions this group, often called the Faculty Development Committee, is created through the existing committee structure on campus. As is true for most committees, a well-balanced committee across divisions of well-respected members of the community is best, taking into account gender balance as well as seniority. To ensure an effective committee, you should consider faculty development training for those assigned to the committee. The responsibilities of this committee could include, for example, program planning, evaluating grant proposals should on-campus funding be available, and acting as advocates for the center.

As a director of a teaching and learning center or the office of faculty development, one is interested in involving faculty in the development of programs offered and in making faculty input a constant. To create a campus culture in which talking about teaching is the norm and often a part of the discussions between colleagues, faculty involvement in the programming created to talk about teaching as a whole is very important. Although differences exist from one institution to the next, teaching is an important component of the reappointment, tenure, and promotion process on most campuses. As such, some faculty might not feel at ease to discuss the problems they are facing in the classroom. They might not feel comfortable seeking advice from others to help fix the problems. Of course, any faculty member can speak confidentially with the director of a teaching center who would not be involved in future evaluations. Although a great deal of mentoring can occur in that context, one would expect a larger set of ideas to solve the problem from a discussion with a group of colleagues, many of whom might have faced the same or a similar problem during their time in the classroom. By creating programs focused on teaching discussions in the form of, for instance, presentations, brown bags, or workshops, and by involving the faculty not just as members in attendance but also in development of the topics or even providing the workshops themselves, one promotes the discussion about teaching and highlights the importance of making our classrooms open rather than closed.

Keep in mind that faculty development focused on teaching can also be attractive (or made more attractive) to faculty members who are not necessarily interested in improving their teaching but instead in the scholarly activities or research endeavors/creative thinking involved in SoTL. That refocus often captures a whole different group of faculty that might not have shown interest otherwise. Some programs have recognized that for faculty in some disciplines the term SoTL is not as meaningful and in turn have used the term "teaching as research." The term itself focuses on the research component of this type of scholarship and therefore creates a greater comfort level for faculty in disciplines whose research involves analyzing evidence (or is more scientific in nature), and in this case one would be analyzing evidence of student learning. When describing the program, specific components of the research process are discussed including the use of specific questions and hypotheses about teaching and learning, collecting data as evidence to support or refute the hypothesis, and analyzing the evidence based on the data. Faculty who are involved in this type of programming would be creating a community of scholars working on SoTL projects. This cross-disciplinary dialogue could be created through scheduled discussions, seminars, and workshops that focus on common teaching and learning issues that are in their own classroom. Eventually you'll be creating a learning community for faculty, which we've heard about for students often in the last decade. Learning communities often create mentoring relationship among members, where more seasoned members can share their knowledge about the teaching culture with those new to the institution. In the former group the faculty are interested in learning to be more effective teachers through a productive line of scholarship and in the latter the faculty are more interested in creating a productive line of scholarship that leads to more effective teaching. This focus on scholarship does not change the type of scholarship itself, but instead draws in a more diverse group of faculty in the discussion of teaching and learning.

In addition to faculty support, the support needed from administrators cannot be emphasized enough. Administrators can provide the credibility needed, particularly for new centers, by attending the sponsored programs and stating the value of these programs to others on campus. Administrators are in a position on campus to make systematic analysis of teaching practices a core value at your institution. On larger campuses, one can also find administrative support through department chairs. Any buy-in provided at the administrative level provides the status needed on campus for faculty members to see that value of the center. You want to avoid having to respond to questions such as "Why do we need a center for teaching?" An administrator who sees this type of center as an important resource for faculty success should be able to provide the reasons why a teaching and learning center is vital at any institution of higher education.

An additional factor for success concerns programs that recognize faculty scholarship. A teaching and learning or faculty development center can be the perfect avenue through which to showcase faculty scholarship, both pedagogical as well as discipline-specific research programs. Too often, faculty are involved in fascinating research of which others on their own campus are not aware. We believe that providing this platform on which to present faculty scholarship and the ability to combine the discipline-based scholarship with SoTL also promote the idea that all types of scholarship are worthy of recognition. Furthermore, providing on-campus presentations of pedagogical research in this setting also provides the center an avenue through which to present the important idea of incorporating one's teaching into one's scholarship.

One last principle to guide your development of a teaching and learning center pertains to what most faculty often won't say is important to them, but can often really make a difference. We're talking here about rewards and recognition. Although many of us are intrinsically motivated to be more effective in the classroom and improve our teaching, we are also motivated by the presence of a reward system that demonstrates recognition for this type of scholarly pursuit. It is one thing to state that pedagogical research is considered appropriate scholarly work (and we'll discuss this issue later in the chapter), it is quite another to put one's merit pay/promotion/tenure where one's mouth is. At many institutions, the change in definition of scholarship to include SoTL research led to the reward system needed. A variety of rewards can be used to motivate faculty to become involved in SoTL initiatives on campus. This can come in the form of financial incentives such as stipends or grants, course release time, committee release time, or simply campus-wide recognition. The reward structure that is created must recognize those who make substantial efforts to examine the effectiveness of their teaching. The availability of such recognition is again dependent upon administrators pulling for the success of the center, which of course is dependent upon priorities that are set. If a teaching and learning center is determined to be an important resource on campus, the rewards and recognition listed above will more likely follow.

Creating Programming Initiatives to Achieve Your Goals

Once your goals and priorities are determined and you've conducted a needs assessment on your campus, the next question to ask concerns what programming should be developed to achieve your goals. Once again, do not reinvent the wheel. Instead take the wheel and shape it to fit your institution. In many instances you might find when examining programming at other institutions that the fit will be appropriate or only needs a little bit of tweaking. Some of these programs are basic in that they propose programs from which most teachers would benefit. The best resource for programming ideas is to take a look at the programming initiatives found to be successful at other centers. A better idea might be to take a look at those centers that reside at institutions of the same size or centers most similar to your own. Of course, always keep in mind your needs assessment to determine if these programs fit the needs of your faculty. If you are just starting out and have identified needs, you could consider sitting down with a group of faculty to take a look at the needs identified through your needs assessment and then have that group brainstorm the best types of programming initiatives with which to begin the center. Have them create a ranking of the top 10 programs identified on your campus. This group could provide insight about the types of programs that faculty on your campus are most likely to attend. This would help avoid what some could consider "the kiss of death," inviting a speaker to campus for a presentation with only a small audience in attendance.

Some of you might be a one-person center, while others are provided with funding for additional staffing. As many of you know, development of programming can be very time-intensive when you are just starting out. If the latter is the case and you are able to hire additional staff, be sure to find individuals with expertise in the appropriate areas. This could include expertise on pedagogical issues, learning styles, written and oral communication, assessment, disciplinary teaching techniques, or instructional technology. Your priorities should shape what type of staff expertise is most important. There are networks of individuals interested in these types of positions such as the Professional and Organization Network in Higher Education (POD). Check out their website (http://www.podnetwork.org/) for additional resources. Here you can find out about how to be added to their electronic mailing list. Making contacts would then allow you to discuss your programming needs with other directors and find out who they have invited to campus that presented an interesting program. At almost all programs, those in attendance are asked to evaluate the effectiveness of the workshop. Those assessments are often available from other directors, who are usually willing to share that information and who can tell you what their faculty liked and disliked about a particular workshop. Your needs assessment will tell you the type of programming your faculty would most appreciate. Discussing your faculty needs with other directors can be a wonderful source for finding the programs that fit your needs and that have already been tested on other campuses. A simple search on the web will illustrate the vast number of centers and the different types of websites maintained, which often include the types of programming offered at each institution.

To create a presence on campus and educate faculty quickly on what exactly is meant by faculty development, SoTL, and/or pedagogical research you could consider starting the year by featuring a nationally recognized scholar in the field as a speaker. This type of presentation can help you get the word out regarding the value of pedagogical research and the way in which it can fit within anyone's professional development. To find individuals who provide these types of presentations, consider a search on the web or even take a look at the names in our reference list. You'll be amazed at the number of individuals who are expert in the field and who regularly conduct on-site presentations and workshops. Of course, your budget will help determine who you can afford to bring to your campus. You can also continue sponsoring speakers throughout the academic year. Keep in mind these speakers don't always need to be nationally recognized. Why not have faculty from your own institution or those from neighboring colleges? This is more likely to fit your budget and it provides a natural way to continue the teaching conversations throughout the year. Many centers have created an on-campus speaking series, in which colleagues from across campus give teaching-focused presentations to other faculty. Keeping the conversation going is sometimes half the battle.

Many centers maintain a very informative website, which provides information on all regional, national, and international conferences related to the scholarship of teaching and learning. Providing funding to attend these conferences, and perhaps asking those who attend to provide a summary about the conference, could get others interested in attending similar conferences in the future. You can see that the recognition aspect of the programming once again can be very helpful to create the initial motivation and ongoing motivation for faculty to be involved in the programming offered through the center.

Some centers focus on pragmatic goals such as informing the community about SoTL. In this case, you could send representatives to the national conferences on the scholarship of teaching and learning. As mentioned in the teaching chapter, a number of organizations such as the International Society for the Scholarship of Teaching and Learning (ISSOTL), the Collaboration for the Advancement of College Teaching and Learning, and the International Alliance of Teacher Scholars all offer annual SoTL conferences. Again, by simply typing "Scholarship of Teaching and Learning conferences" into a search engine, you will see the long list of options to which you can send colleagues to become more informed about these types of scholarly endeavors. Along the same lines, you could also fund attendance at teaching-focused conferences within someone's particular discipline. As discussed in chapter 2, many discipline-focused conferences include sessions on teaching and/or SoTL.

At other centers, the director coordinates a series of scholarly conversations within and across disciplines to allow colleagues to hear each other's knowledge and questions about teaching. This can be jumpstarted by having a group of faculty reading a common set of books or articles related to SoTL. For example, you could have those interested reading this book or Boyer (1990). There are many texts available to provide interesting discussion material on pedagogy. Some concentrate on new faculty issues, while others are appropriate for faculty members at all levels of faculty rank (see the appendix at the end of this chapter). To provide additional resources, some centers use their funding to create a library of SoTL materials consisting of many of these books in addition to those listed in the appendix.

Another interesting mechanism to introduce faculty to pedagogical research is to provide competitive grants to faculty on campus. There are always faculty looking for ways to fund new and interesting research endeavors. This is a particularly inviting incentive at smaller colleges with a particular focus on teaching excellence, where combining one's teaching and research can be very rewarding. Taking a different approach, other programming initiatives focus on how to recognize those involved in SoTL work. At some institutions, awards are given to departments involved in pedagogical research. This can take on many forms such as additional funding for departmental expenses, travel funds to conferences, or release time to those involved. Some centers have created a college-wide publication on SoTL campus initiatives to provide additional recognition and inform others on campus of the findings, which can often be applied to other's courses. In addition to recognition, some centers create initiatives, which bring prestige to being involved in SoTL on campus.

Programming ideas have also explored ways to make the teaching-focused center an integral part of the campus culture. To achieve this goal at some institutions, the center has been connected with existing programs on campus such as the general education program. Every institution of higher education has a set of goals for their general education program, and perhaps research on the teaching that takes place to determine whether changes in teaching can help achieve the goals stated for general education on your campus. An SoTL center can be a particularly useful resource when an institution must provide evidence of students' learning to their accrediting agency.

Programs can also provide faculty with ways to improve teaching more directly. For example, a certain number of faculty on campus can receive financial support/release time for their SoTL work and also work as a team to create campus-wide SoTL programming initiatives. Results from these initiatives that improve teaching effectiveness are then shared with others on campus. A peer review of teaching programs can also provide information on how to improve instruction in the classroom. At some institutions, peer review is part of a scheduled process for tenure and promotion. This type of program requires the use of the best practices policies identified by the literature in the field. Of course, this is very time-intensive, and you need to be creative if you are a one-person center. What if conducting peer reviews is recognized as service to the institution? This might entice more faculty to become involved in the program. A peer-review program can be embedded within departments at larger institutions. One important component to keep in mind is the training. It is very important for those observing a classroom to know the steps to take, as discussed earlier in our teaching chapter. One resource to help with the training would be including in your center's website the important components of peer review that would provide departments with guidance on setting up their own peer-review programs.

For those of you at larger universities, your audience of interest likely includes graduate students. We include here those who are teaching assistants and teaching a course on their own for the first time. Often this includes international students whose challenges as a new teacher can include learning language and cultural norms as well as basic teaching issues. Programming for this group should also depend on needs assessment. However most of these individuals are new to teaching. Therefore many do not yet know the type of programs that would be helpful. Hearing from recent teaching assistants is particularly useful when developing the types of programs best suited for this audience since often topics that should be included in training would not be included for more seasoned faculty (e.g., how to handle cheating or other classroom problems).

Chapters 2 through 4 of this book provide some information needed to assist faculty in learning how to create their own pedagogical research program. One could use those chapters to create programming at any center for those in disciplines in which creating the methodology and conducting statistical analyses is not part of their graduate training. Going through the step-by-step procedures of the scientific method is not second nature for those in disciplines outside of the natural and social sciences, so this is likely to be very worthwhile for many colleagues interested in pedagogical research who do not have the basic skills. The programming can also include a review of the literature and publications where one would find SoTL work and where one could submit one's work once the research is complete.

Clearly the type of training offered at teaching and learning centers depends on the needs of the faculty at each institution. The diversity of programming becomes clear when searching the web and discovering that programming at one center is very different from programming at even similar institutions. To give you an idea of the diversity, we include a list of the many different types of programs found at centers across the country (see box 5.2). For instance, if an institution uses Blackboard you are likely

---

Box 5.2: Examples of Programming Titles at Teaching and Learning Centers

Professional Development Programs:
Promotion and Tenure
Publish or Perish *or* Publish and Flourish?
Successful Tenure and Promotion Techniques
Dossier Preparation
A Conversation with the Provost: The Tenure Process
A Conversation with Newly Tenured Colleagues
Teaching Portfolios – Improve Teaching and Personal Decisions
The Teaching Statement: An Integral Part of Promotion and Tenure
Taking the Mystery out of Advancement to Full
"Good Thinking, Good Funding": Supporting Faculty Scholarship

Teaching-focused Programs:
Good Course Design for New Faculty
Watching Each Other Teach
Cognitive Strategies
Course and Syllabus Design
Advising as Teaching
Gender Equity In Teaching: What Is It? Why Do We Want It? How Can We Achieve It?
Teaching Students to Ask Better Questions
Collaborative Research with Students

Engaging Students for Active Learning: Using Simulations in the Classroom
The Art of Leading Discussion
Using Humor to Enhance Traditional and Online Instruction
A Working Together: Effective Presentation and Delivery
Alternatives to Lecturing: Learning Communities
Developing Effective Syllabi: Requirements and Recommendations
Developing Learning Objectives for Your Course
Fostering Academic Honesty
Cooperative and Collaborative Learning
Cyber Plagiarism: How to Find It and How to Help Prevent It
Learner-Centered Pedagogy
Facilitating Difficult Dialogues in the Classroom
Teaching Non-Native Speakers Writing and Speaking Tips for the Classroom
Approaches for Incorporating and Appreciating Diversity in the Classroom
Can Reporting a Student for Violating the Academic Integrity Policy Be
    Educational?
Critical Thinking and Information Literacy: Using Sources to Develop Ideas
Disability Etiquette: Enhancing Interaction and Communication with Students
Copyrights and Wrongs
Academic Integrity in a Cut and Paste World: Beyond the Honor Code
Don't Infringe on My Copyright!
Citation Management with Endnotes
What is an Educated Person? Dialogue
Designing Rubrics: The Basics

Technology-focused Programs:
Teaching with Technology
Testing and Assessment in an Online Environment
Web Graphics for Online Courses
Blackboard Topics: Content and Tools
Blackboard Topics: Discussion and Quizzes
Classroom Teaching with Internet Technologies
Clickers: Student Response Systems in Action
Classroom Response Systems: Increasing Engagement and Participation
Web Grading, Anti-Plagiarism and Feedback Tools
Professional Web Pages for Faculty in One Hour – Really!
Introduction to Online Learning and Workshop
Teaching and Managing your Online Course
Revising and Improving your Online Course
Teaching and Learning with Technology
Creating Electronic Grade Books

Continued

SPSS Intermediate
Creative Uses of Blackboard
Paperless Classroom: Computer Tools for Responding to Student Writing
Online Instruction Workshop

Assessment-focused Programs:
Establishing Standards and Criteria for Grading
Classroom Assessment Techniques
Assessing Competence: Informing and Improving Student Performance
Evaluating Written Work in the Humanities and Social Sciences
How Am I Doing? Strategies for Obtaining Formative Evaluation about
  Teaching Effectiveness
Authentic Online Assessment
Outcomes Assessment Workshop
Writing Assessments: From Design to Assessment
Assignment Design: Creating Library Assignments That Support Your Course
Do They Learn What We Teach? Looking at General Education
I Video. Do You? Using Digital Video in Instruction and Assessment

to find a tutorial session provided for new faculty to familiarize them with this instructional technology tool. Along the same lines, many centers will offer instruction on teaching and learning with technology. If your institution offers online courses, you will likely come across programs specific to those courses such as managing an online course or improving your online course. For those new to the idea of using technology at all, there are also centers that offer workshops on creating electronic grade books. You often find programs related to the promotion and tenure process available, where faculty are provided with the logistics of the process, including the materials needed or how to determine students to provide letters or how to find outside evaluators for one's review. The review process might also require faculty to present their teaching accomplishments, with teaching and learning centers offering classes on how to create a teaching portfolio or perhaps how to improve teaching decisions by using the teaching portfolio and how to write a teaching philosophy statement.

Although faculty needs are different from one institution to the next, there are some types of programs needed at all colleges and universities. One such need is assisting new faculty members in making the transition to their new environment. At many institutions, these mentoring programs are provided through teaching and learning centers.

Mentoring Programs

Mentoring programs are particularly important programs that are becoming available at more and more institutions. Although we've had many years of experience as a student and an understanding of the working of an institution of higher education, that feeling of familiarity can easily disappear when we join a new institution. We often find out quickly that each institution has particularly idiosyncrasies that we need to learn rather quickly to fully understand the culture and "ways" of that institution. How can we learn the many details? Certainly, we all go through a faculty orientation and learn where classes are taught, or when grades are due, and what type of teaching evaluations are required. However, these important details don't really provide a glimpse into the culture of the institution. Researchers have identified the most common concerns of new faculty. These concerns include constraints on one's time, which of course is not a surprise since many of us ask the question "Should I focus on my teaching, my research, or my service?" A second common concern pertains to collegiality. Many new faculty members are faced with working with all new colleagues. For some this can create feelings of isolation and perhaps a lack of support. Fink (1984) points out that in fact two-thirds of new faculty recommended the need for more assistance from more experienced colleagues. By support, they most often referred to others with whom they could discuss teaching concerns. Finally, many new faculty also indicate stress about the inadequacy or lack of communication regarding expectations. Often this concern pertained to not understanding the institution's criteria when evaluating teaching.

A mentoring program often alleviates many of these concerns and in turn can create a much easier transition and a more positive first-year experience and beyond. Many new faculty members connect with a colleague who becomes his or her mentor, answering questions that range from "Where is the faculty lounge?" to "How do you teach this content in your class?" This informal set-up usually works well and often leads to a very effective mechanism to assist new faculty in learning the culture of their new institution. However, this type of informal mentoring does not ensure that all new faculty members receive the type of support needed.

Really, the amount of mentoring received is dependent whether faculty in your department are willing to provide that type of mentoring to new faculty. A more formal mentoring program eliminates the possibility that someone falls through the cracks. In most mentoring programs, faculty members who are fully aware of the academic culture are invited to be a mentor, and mentors are asked to have frequent meetings with their mentees throughout the semester.

The structure of the mentoring program is often very dependent upon the resources available to this type of initiative. In some places, mentors are selected from those faculty nominated for their teaching excellence. At some institutions, retired faculty are asked to be a part of the mentoring program. To provide very specific departmental mentoring, mentors are paired with new faculty within the same department. However, others feel that providing mentoring from someone who will not be involved in the evaluation of a new faculty member would be an excellent resource without the fear that discussing teaching problems will in no way affect promotion and tenure decisions. Mentors are often given compensation for their time through stipends or release time. Similar types of compensation are provided for the director or coordinator of the mentoring program as well.

The activities created for the mentors and the mentees are diverse as well, with most including training for all mentors, which reviews responsibilities and roles of mentors on campus, and can include how to conduct peer observations of colleagues to how to provide constructive feedback. Suggestions are made with regards to how the mentee can be most effective, including the review of syllabi, observations of each others' classes, and/or monthly meetings to discuss concerns. Most mentors are asked to meet frequently with their new faculty mentee several times during each semester and for mentors to initiate the contact because new faculty might be reluctant to ask for help when needed. Several meetings are also scheduled for the whole group to convene at teaching workshops or brown-bag discussions focused on new faculty issues. Faculty involved in these programs as mentors often comment that being a part of this type of program provides greater opportunity for collegiality, enriches their own teaching, and provides both personal and professional growth. Developers of programs often indicate that they create a mentoring program in which the institution recognizes that an invitation to a new faculty member to be a mentor is an honor and in fact recognition of the mentor's teaching excellence.

Finally, as mentioned above, a mentoring program can be created that focuses on providing assistance to faculty interested in beginning to conduct scholarship on their teaching and in need of guidance from colleagues already involved in such research. This goes beyond the typical type of mentoring found at most institutions, as described above, and instead is geared to providing a resource for all aspects of SoTL work, from generating ideas for future research, to discussing findings and where to present or publish those findings, to perhaps developing interdisciplinary research collaborations. These partnerships can also provide faculty with a better understanding of how others have incorporated their teaching scholarship and can be included as an important factor during decisions of tenure and promotion. As we discuss below, including pedagogical research within an institution's definition of scholarship can turn out to be a challenge.

SoTL and Tenure and Promotion

Tenure and promotion issues with SoTL often stem from how an institution defines scholarship. If it is more broadly defined than simply the typical discipline-specific scholarship, SoTL fits well within the definition. SoTL work fits well within the typical definition of scholarly activity, which focuses on the process and peer review acceptance through presentations and publications in journals and conferences recognized as noteworthy. Hutchings and Shulman (1999) discuss this issue and propose an important distinction between what they call "scholarly teaching" and "the scholarship of teaching." The latter includes the public presentation of work that can be critiqued by others in the field and work that adds to our knowledge of issues surrounding student learning. At other institutions there is a need to broaden the definition of scholarship to include creative inquiry not only in the scholarship of research but also in the scholarship of teaching. This broadened definition will hopefully sway those initially not including pedagogical research within the definition of scholarship worthy of recognition and reward through tenure and promotion.

Glassick, Huber, and Maeroff (1997) discuss how institutions of higher learning rarely provide specific guidelines one can use to define what professional activities would count as scholarly work. Interestingly, despite this lack of clarity, when scholarship involves teaching red flags seem to appear that make some question the scholarly standards of such work. However, if clear standards are identified, most would recognize that SoTL fits well within those standards. Glassick and colleagues identify six standards to use when determining whether activities should be considered as scholarly works. These standards include: clear goals, adequate preparation, appropriate methods, significant results, effective presentation, and reflective critique. These goals are applicable to any type of scholarly activity. If conducted correctly, pedagogical research should meet all six goals. If possible, including examples of acceptable scholarly activity within materials reviewing the tenure and promotion process, which includes SoTL, would provide the "stamp of approval" needed to get some faculty started in this line of research. Fortunately, how scholarship is defined has changed at many institutions, and one can more easily focus on both teaching and scholarship simultaneously by conducting pedagogical research and in turn integrating one's teaching into research.

A different problem with regard to scholarship is often found at institutions focused primarily on teaching and not scholarship. Here we have faculty who often teach many courses with little time to spare for scholarship, and yet teaching excellence is expected. Administrative support is needed to help find the balance with teaching release or grants to assist faculty with their scholarly endeavors outside the classroom. The result would be beneficial for all involved; productive faculty able to be involved in scholarly pursuits and their scholarship would provide answers about how to be more effective teachers and in turn improve student learning.

A director of a teaching and learning center can certainly play an important role in having SoTL identified as scholarship worthy of recognition during important personnel decisions. One needs to be become familiar with the standards used to assess scholarly activity on campus and then work to help others recognize how pedagogical research fits within those standards. Often, it is simply a matter of the programming needed to educate the community about SoTL and how it is different from one's expected teaching responsibilities. Hutchings and Shulman (1999) point out that, just like any other type of scholarship, SoTL activities vary in quality and impact. A director of a center should discuss with faculty and administrators the important distinction between an instructor first beginning to conduct SoTL research who might discuss his or her findings at an on-campus SoTL workshop and others who go through the peer-review process and have their work accepted for presentation at a national conference, or published in a journal or book.

The Role of Assessment

You've made strong arguments for the need for a teaching and learning center on campus, and for the value of scholarship of teaching and learning both for professional development of the faculty and for the improvements of teaching effectiveness and in turn student learning. Now, it is time to provide the evidence. We all have heard that assessment has become an integral part of higher education, where educators, in order to receive the support needed to continue a program, are being asked to supply data to illustrate that program goals are being achieved. As we all know too well, administrators like to use their resources effectively and know that any initiative is making a difference. Providing evidence of effectiveness can lead to continued support from those in charge of the funds. Lewis, Carter, and Patrick (2004) can provide you with not only reasons why you should conduct a self-assessment, but also the important steps to follow to make your assessment successful. These factors include creating a center that is woven within the academic community, evaluating the campus before creating the center to determine a baseline measure, and knowing your goals and what you'll be evaluating after a certain time period. For example, are you interested in measuring the number of faculty who participated in your programs or the number of faculty conducting pedagogical research on campus? Lewis and colleagues also recommend that you keep track of what is going on at your institution, and finally to use the results of your self-assessment to illustrate to those on campus, as well as others in the field, what types of changes you find on you campus as a result of your efforts.

It is through the assessment process that one attempts to show a connection between the programming offered, the initiatives resulting from the programming, and in turn an improvement in teaching effectiveness and student learning. Certainly an easy step to take would be to keep data on the number of faculty attending the different programs sponsored by the center, allowing you to illustrate interest. At many institutions, faculty are asked to provide a report of all professional activity during each academic year. One could easily include a question on that report that pertains to any work related to the scholarship of teaching and learning. Examining the change in numbers of faculty involved in pedagogical research would certainly be one way to assess whether you have reached the faculty on your campus. This would also allow assessment of the scholarship activity related to SoTL. Are faculty providing presentations at regional and/or national meetings? Are faculty disseminating their findings to others in the field through the publications? Answers to all of these questions will allow you to determine the percentage of faculty at each level involved in SoTL work, and the types of activities on your campus that are directed at improving instruction, learning, and course administration. These questions would provide answers about SoTL activity on campus.

The University of Wisconsin System conducted an assessment and provides us with a great example of the questions used to assess SoTL initiatives on all of their campuses (Ciccone & Myers, 2006). These questions are listed in box 5.3. Reviewing this table, you'll see that questions addressed the impact of SoTL campus initiatives on faculty interest, involvement, and activity in SoTL, teaching practices, student learning, teaching and learning discussions among colleagues, awareness of SoTL programming, and the perceived value of SoTL in general. You'll notice that the questions assessed not only how involved faculty are in SoTL, but also the impact of SoTL at many levels including personally, within the classroom, within the department, and at the institution.

Using this assessment tool, Ciccone and Myers found that SoTL initiatives led to significant changes on their campus, with greater faculty involvement and interest in SoTL, application of SoTL in the classroom, and more dialogue among faculty about teaching and learning just to name a few. Evidence of this type of positive influence is exactly what a director would like to be able to present to campus administrators. This type of assessment not only provides information concerning the impact of programming on campus, it also provides valuable information as to where future efforts should be focused. For example, in the UW assessment, they found less of an impact of SoTL initiatives at the departmental level, with respondents indicating the need to create more SoTL dialogue within their departments as well as greater acceptance of SoTL as valuable scholarly activity in promotion and tenure decisions. In response, perhaps more programming is needed to provide a greater understanding of what exactly SoTL is and how this type of scholarship goes beyond typical pedagogical behaviors and is scholarly activity equal in merit to traditional research within one's discipline.

Box 5.3: Scholarship of Teaching and Learning (SOTL) Impact Survey Questions

I read more research and literature on teaching and learning since becoming involved in SoTL initiatives and research.

I am more interested in teaching and learning issues and questions since becoming involved in SoTL initiatives and research.

I talk more to my colleagues about teaching and learning questions and issues since becoming involved in SoTL initiatives and research.

My involvement in reading and doing SoTL work has an influence on my students' learning through my teaching.

I think I am a better teacher since becoming involved in SoTL initiatives.

I value my own and others' SoTL research more now than I did before I got involved in SoTL initiatives or in doing SoTL research.

I am more interested in doing additional research on teaching and learning questions and issues since becoming involved in SoTL initiatives and research.

I plan to continue to do SoTL research now that I have become involved in SoTL initiatives.

I tell my students about the results of my SoTL work.

I teach differently because of the results of my SoTL work.

I incorporate the results of SoTL research into the design and teaching of my courses.

I have changed the content of my course based on SoTL work I have read or completed.

I endeavor to involve my students in my SoTL work.

I have endeavored to get one or more colleagues in my department involved in doing SoTL work.

I have talked with one or more of my colleagues about my SoTL work.

I have formally presented my SoTL research findings to my departmental colleagues.

My departmental colleagues use the results of my SoTL work in their teaching.

My departmental colleagues value SoTL research.

SoTL work is now considered in tenure and promotion cases in my department.

I have mentored one or more of my departmental colleagues in a SoTL project.

SoTL work is now considered in tenure and promotion cases across my university.

Continued

There is a campus-wide SoTL colloquium or event at least once a year on my campus.

There is a teaching and learning center on my campus that coordinates SoTL initiatives and research.

SoTL work is valued on my campus.

I have mentored one or more non-departmental colleagues on a SoTL project.

Most faculty and academic staff on my campus are aware of the SoTL movement.

Most administrators on my campus are aware of the SoTL movement.

On my campus, SoTL work is connected with institutional initiatives affecting student learning.

My disciplinary society has a SoTL interest group or division.

There are SoTL papers paneled at my national disciplinary conference.

I have presented my SoTL research at a national disciplinary conference meeting.

I have presented my SoTL research at a regional disciplinary conference meeting.

I have presented my SoTL research at a state disciplinary conference meeting.

What is your discipline?

Enter the approximate number of years you have been involved with SoTL initiatives or research.

Indicate the approximate number of SoTL research projects you have undertaken.

Indicate the approximate number of SoTL research projects you have completed and presented.

Indicate the approximate number of SoTL research projects you have completed and published.

What is your position?

What is your employment status?

What is your gender?

What is the name of the college/university where you are employed?

The level of courses I teach are

Please tell us anything else you would like us to know about the ways your SoTL experience or research have had an impact.

Sources for SoTL Support or Funding

A director of a teaching and learning center will likely be familiar with the Carnegie Academy for the Scholarship of Teaching and Learning (CASTL). This program, sponsored through the Carnegie Foundation for the Advancement of Teaching in conjunction with the American Association of Higher Education, assists institutions in creating a culture that supports SoTL. Through the CASTL affiliates program and Institutional Leadership program, institutions are provided with the support needed to get SoTL initiatives started or maintained. This support does not come in the form of funding, but instead provides the important support of sharing an extensive knowledge base, providing collaboration with others involved in similar initiatives on their campus, and creating the visibility and recognition for your institution as a campus committed to SoTL. An institution must apply to become part of the affiliate program, with information and applications available through the CASTL website using the program area link (http://www.carnegiefoundation.org). You'll find there a list of requirements needed for your institution to be considered. Essentially, an institution needs to demonstrate a commitment to SoTL through activities on campus that support and promote SoTL, recognition for those involved in this type of scholarship, with specific goals identified, evidence of administrative support, and an assessment plan to review the impact of all SoTL initiatives. A limited number of institutions are accepted to the leadership program, and at times membership is closed to new institutions. The Institutional Leadership Program allows institutions to choose a particular theme of interest (e.g., undergraduate education and SoTL, mentoring scholars of SoTL) with an emphasis on facilitating collaboration among institutions.

As is true for any area of research, one often looks for funding available to support the research endeavor. Although the support provided by organizations like CASTL is invaluable, many programs often inherently require funding to exist. As a faculty member interested in finding funding for research, you should start through your campus teaching and learning center. We found that many teaching centers listed grant programs on their website. Though each internal funding resource will list specific criteria used for obtaining funds, most support any form of scholarship that focuses on instructional development. Examples include funds to encourage evidence based studies into issues of teaching and learning, new modes of

---

Box 5.4: Private Organizations with SoTL Funding Opportunities

The Andrew W. Mellon Foundation
The Coleman Foundation
The Corning Incorporated Foundation
Ford Foundation
Henry Luce Foundation
Learn and Serve America Service Learning grants
Library and Information Science Education Grant
NEA Foundation for the Improvement of Education (NFIE)
Spencer Foundation

---

instruction, the development of new instructional and learning materials, or examining how to encourage greater student engagement. The amount of funding varies greatly. For both directors of centers as well as faculty members interested in SoTL, there are many funding agencies with directives applicable to SoTL including federal agencies such as the National Institute of Health (NIH), the National Foundation for the Improvement of Education (NFIE), the National Science Foundation (NSF) Research on Learning and Education, the Department of Education – Institute of Education Sciences, and Department of Education – Office of Postsecondary Education. External funding opportunities are also available through a number of private organizations, including but not limited to agencies listed in box 5.4.

What Else Is Available through Faculty Development Centers?

Many campus teaching and learning centers provide excellent online resources available not only to their faculty members, but to any faculty member searching for guidance in the area of SoTL. We found excellent websites that included teaching handbooks (e.g., http://www.teaching.iub.edu/handbook_toc.php) from which one can learn everything from planning a course to specifics of different teaching techniques and finally how to assess student performance. Although there are too many to include here, we've listed a number of center websites that we found particularly helpful in the appendix. You'll find a table of contents and services at each website that can provide an incredible amount of information at a click of the mouse. These sites can be particularly useful for a new director of a teaching and learning center wishing to find out what is available elsewhere and what types of workshops are offered, and they provide links to many resources. Faculty interested in SoTL will find many examples of research endeavors of faculty across the country that could be a source of ideas for their own pedagogical research program.

Of the many services available at teaching and learning centers nationwide one in particular is the teaching consult, which we have not yet discussed here. These meetings are often driven by the individual needs of the faculty members with the focus as diverse as that of faculty needs. At times, a faculty member might have a more general concern about his or her teaching style and might want to learn how to assess the effectiveness of that style. At other times, a faculty member who most often uses lectures in the classroom might want to learn how to create effective classroom discussions. Others might be interested in starting a pedagogical research program. A director of a center must be ready for these types of requests, and a faculty member should be aware that this type of service is often available.

Potential Challenges Identified by Those Who Have Come Before You

Though many goals have been achieved and many SoTL centers are providing the guidance and support needed for faculty members on many campuses, those involved in these centers have also identified ongoing challenges. Many of these challenges fall under the need to maintain ongoing institutional support. One difficult task is to create the initiative to start an SoTL center and get administrators on board to see the need to make it a priority. A completely different challenge is to maintain the initial support and for the administration to recognize the value of the early accomplishments or goals achieved through the center. Along the same line with regard to administrative support, some of these challenges involve the need for greater resources. For instance, directors are always interested in increasing the numbers who utilize the resource, and one way to do so is to provide incentives to participate. This incentive can come in the form of funding to conduct pedagogical research or in the form of administrative recognition of this type of research for scholarly activity or for teaching development when one is under any type of review. However, this has been a recognized challenge for many.

Administrative support challenges have also been encountered with regard to the staffing needs. Far too often a center is directed by someone who has too many responsibilities to take on the role as director of a teaching and learning center. Again, administrative recognition of the value of the center for the faculty, students, and really the institution as a whole, will hopefully eventually lead to staffing levels appropriate to achieve the goals identified for the institution. In addition to people, space has also been recognized as a challenge for SoTL centers. Many centers start off within the space of other programs or even in the space of a faculty member's office that is part of his or her department. This type of sharing or multi-purpose office space can only work for so long. Once a center develops, a dedicated space is often required to continue to accomplish the goals identified. Often the initial role of the center is minimal as the resource begins to grow; however, once many on campus see the value of these resources, the need for a dedicated space becomes more and more essential for success.

Finally, administrative support with regard to including this type of scholarship when reviewing faculty for tenure and promotion is one challenge identified by some directors. This gets back to how scholarship is defined, and the challenge is likely due to lack of information about the field of SoTL and how this type of research is analogous to research within other fields that administrators already recognize as valuable. This challenge can also include the problem of administrators not recognizing the value of how SoTL can work in their favor when it comes to recognition of the college or recruitment of new faculty.

Having a teaching and learning center is clear evidence that the institution values teaching and learning and assisting faculty with improving their teaching, and having this as a resource particularly for new faculty sends a signal that they are not alone when first starting out in the world of academics. The challenges of being new to the academic world are recognized, and in turn resources are provided to increase the likelihood of success.

Appendix: Useful References

Recommended Books for Pedagogical Book Group Discussions

Allitt, P. (2004). *I'm the teacher, you're the student: A semester in the university classroom.* Philadelphia, PA: University of Pennsylvania Press.

Bain, K. (2004). *What the best college teachers do.* Cambridge, MA: Harvard University Press.

Baiocco, S. A., & DeWaters, J. N. (1998). *Successful college teaching: Problem solving strategies of distinguished professors.* Boston, MA: Allyn and Bacon.

Boice, R. (2000). *Advice for new faculty members.* Boston, MA: Allyn and Bacon.

Bok, D. (2008). *Our underachieving colleges: A candid look at how much students learn and why they should be learning more.* Princeton, NJ: Princeton University Press.

Fink. L. D. (2003). *Creating significant learning experiences.* San Francisco, CA: Jossey-Bass.

McKeachie, W. J. (1991). *Teaching tips: Strategies, research, and theory for college and university teachers.* Boston, MA: Houghton Mifflin Company.

Menges, R. J. (1999). *Faculty in new jobs.* San Francisco, CA: Jossey-Bass.

Palmer, P. J. (1998). *The courage to teach.* Francisco, CA: Jossey-Bass.

Parini, J. (2004). *The art of teaching.* New York, NY: Oxford University Press.

Provitera-McGlynn, A. (2001). *Successful beginnings for college teaching: Engaging your students from the first day.* Madison, WI: Atwood Publishing.

Weimer, M. (1990). *Improving college teaching.* San Francisco, CA: Jossey-Bass.

Weimer, M. (2002). *Learner-centered teaching: Five key changes to practice.* San Francisco, CA: Jossey-Bass.

Suggestions to Include in Your Library of Teaching Center Resources

Andrews, M. L., & Becker, W. E. (Eds.). (2004). *The scholarship of teaching and learning in higher education.* Bloomington, IN: Indiana University Press.

Angelo, T. A., & Cross, K. P. (1993). *Classroom assessment technique: A handbook for college teachers s* (2nd ed.). San Francisco, CA: Jossey-Bass.

Bain, K. (2004). *What the best college teachers do.* Cambridge, MA: Harvard University Press.

Banta, T. W. (1993). *Making a difference.* San Francisco, CA: Jossey-Bass.

Banta, T. W., Lund, J. P., Black, K. E., & Oblander, F. W. (1996). *Assessment in practice: Putting principles to work in college campuses.* San Francisco, CA: Jossey-Bass.

Berk, R. A. (2006). *Thirteen strategies to measure college teaching.* Sterling, VA: Stylus.

Bligh, D. A. (2000). *What's the use of lectures*. San Francisco, CA: Jossey-Bass.

Boyer, E. L. (1990). *Scholarship reconsidered: Prioirites of the professoriate*. New York, NY: Carnegie Foundation for the Advancement of Teaching.

Braskamp, L. A., & Ory, J. C. (1994). *Assessing faculty work: Enhancing individual and institutional performance*. San Francisco, CA: Jossey-Bass.

Buskist, W., & Davis, S. F. (Eds.). (2006). *Handbook of the teaching of psychology*. Malden, MA: Blackwell.

Cambridge, B. L. (Ed.). (2004). *Campus progress: Supporting the scholarship of teaching and learning*. Washington, DC: American Association for Higher Education.

Chism, N. V. N. (1999). *Peer review of teaching*. Bolton, MA: Anker.

Cross, K. P., & Steadman, M. H. (1996). *Classroom research*. San Francisco, CA: Jossey-Bass.

DeZure, D. (Ed.). (2000). *Learning from Change*. Sterling, VA: Stylus.

Diamond, R. M. (1998). *Designing and assessing courses and curricula*. San Francisco, CA: Jossey-Bass.

Diamond R. M. (Ed.). (2002). *Field guide to academic leadership*. San Francisco, CA: Jossey-Bass.

Gillespie, K. H., Hilsen, L. R., & Wadsworth, E. C. (Eds.). (2002). *A guide to faculty development*. Bolton, MA: Anker.

Glassick, C. E., Huber, M. T., & Maeroff, G. I. (1997). *Scholarship assessed: Evaluation of the professoriate*. San Francisco, CA: Jossey-Bass.

Grasha, A. F. (2002). *Teaching with style: A practical guide to enhancing learning by understanding teaching and learning styles*. Pittsburgh, PA: Alliance.

Hatch, T., White, M. E., Raley, J., Austin, K., Capitelli, S., and Faigenbaum, D. (2006). *Into the classroom*. San Francisco, CA: Jossey-Bass.

Huber, M. T., & Hutchings, P. (2005). *The advancement of learning: Building the teaching commons*. San Francisco, CA: Jossey-Bass.

Huber, M. T., & Morreale, S. P. (Eds.). (2002). *Disciplinary styles in the scholarship of teaching and learning: Exploring common ground*. Washington, DC: American Association for Higher Education and The Carnegie Foundation for the Advancement of Teaching.

Hutchings, P. (Ed.). (2002). *Ethics of inquiry: Issues in the scholarship of teaching and learning*. Menlo Park, CA: Carnegie Foundation for the Advancement of Teaching.

Hutchings, P. (Ed.). (2000). *Opening lines: Approaches to the scholarship of teaching and learning*. Menlo Park, CA: Carnegie Foundation for the Advancement of Teaching.

Kreber, C. (Ed.). (2001). *Scholarship revisited: Perspectives on the scholarship of teaching*. San Francisco, CA: Jossey-Bass.

Lewis, K. G. (Ed.). (2001). *Techniques and strategies for interpreting student evaluations*. San Francisco, CA: Jossey-Bass.

Maki, P. L. (2004). *Assessing for learning: Building a sustainable commitment across the institution*. Sterling, VA: Stylus.

McKinney, K. (2007). *Enhancing learning through the Scholarship of Teaching and Learning: The challenges and joys of juggling*. Bolton, MA: Anker.

Nitko, A. J., & Brookhart, S. M. (2007). *Educational assessment of students* (5th ed.). Upper Saddle River, NJ: Pearson Education.

Orlich, D. C., Harder, R. J., Callahan, R. C., Trevisan, M. S., & Brown, A. H. (2007). *Teaching strategies: A guide to effective instruction*. Boston, MA: Houghton Mifflin.

Pellegrino, J. W., Chudowsky, N., & Glaser, R. (Eds.). (2001). *Knowing what students know*. Washington, DC: National Academy Press.

Richlin, L. (2006). *Blueprint for learning*. Sterling, VA: Stylus.

Savory, P., Burnett, A. N., & Goodburn, A. (2007). *Inquiry into the college classroom: A journey towards scholarly teaching*. Bolton, MA: Anker.

Seldin, P. (2004). *The teaching portfolio: A practical guide to improved performance and promotion/tenure decisions* (3rd ed.). Bolton, MA: Anker.

Seldin, P., Ambrose, S. A., Annis, L., Armour, R. A., Austin, A. E., Baldwin, R. G., et al. (1995). *Improving college teaching*. Bolton, MA: Anker.

Suskie, L. (2004). *Assessing student learning*. Bolton, MA: Anker.

Wehlburg, C. M., & Chadwick-Blossey, (Eds.). (2004). *To improve the academy*. Bolton, MA: Anker.

Wiggins, G., & McTighe, J. (2005). *Understanding by design expanded* (2nd ed.). Alexandria, VA: Association for Supervision and Curriculum Development.

Centers of Teaching and Learning Websites

The Scholarship of Teaching and Learning at Illinois State http://www.sotl.ilstu.edu/

Scholarship of Teaching and Learning at Indiana University Bloomington http://www.indiana.edu/~sotl/

Center of Teaching Excellence at University of Illinois at Urbana-Champaign http://www.oir.uiuc.edu/Did/SOTL/index.htm

SoLT Home http://www.issotl.org/tutorial/sotltutorial/home.html

Center for Excellence in Teaching at Georgia Southern University http://academics.georgiasouthern.edu/cet/sotl.htm

Office of Faculty and Staff Development at Citnecc Teaching and Learning Center http://cit.necc.mass.edu/ofsd/sotl.shtml

Scholarship of Teaching and Learning at Western Carolina University http://www.wcu.edu/sotl/

Scholarship of Teaching and Learning at the International Journal for the Scholarship of Teaching and Learning http://www.georgiasouthern.edu/ijsotl/sotl.htm

Scholarship of Teaching and Learning Initiative at University of Wisconsin Oshkosh http://www.uwosh.edu/sotl/profconnections/index.php

Scholarship of Teaching and Learning at University of Wisconsin River Falls http://www.uwrf.edu/sotl/SOTL%20Readings%201final.html

Center for Teaching at Vanderbilt http://www.vanderbilt.edu/cft/resources/teaching_resources/reflecting/sotl.htm

The Center for Teaching and Learning at Truman State University http://tctl.truman.edu/facultysupport/SoTL/

Scholarship of Teaching and Learning at Faculty Center for Teaching and Learning http://www.fctl.ucf.edu/ResearchAndScholarship/SoTL/

Scholarship of Teaching and Learning at University of Wisconsin-La Crosse http://www.uwlax.edu/sotl/

Mentoring Newer Scholars of Teaching and Learning at Rockhurst University http://www.cfkeep.org/html/snapshot.php?id=52928921

Faculty and Organizational Development at Michigan State University http://fod.msu.edu/OIR/Sotl/sotl.asp

SoTL at University of Houston Clear Lake http://prtl.uhcl.edu/portal/page?_pageid=351,1227518and_dad=portaland_schema=PORTALP

Network for Excellence in Teaching at University of Wisconsin-Eau Claire http://www.uwec.edu/NET/index.htm

Center for Teaching and Learning at Mesa Community College http://ctl.mc.maricopa.edu/_resources/sotl/index.html

Transform at University of Minnesota http://www1.umn.edu/ohr/transform/index.html

Teaching and Learning Center at University of Wisconsin- Parkside http://www.uwp.edu/departments/teaching.center/index.cfm

Innovative Learning and Teaching at Ohio Learning Network http://www.oln.org/ILT/sotl.php

Middlesex Community College's Carnie Academy for the scholarship of Teaching and Learning http://www.middlesex.mass.edu/carnegie/default.htm

References

Al-Hilawani, Y. A., & Sartawi, A. A. (1997). Study skills and habits of female university students. *College Student Journal, 31*, 537–544.

Almer, E. D., Jones, K., & Moeckel, C. (1998). The impact of one minute papers on learning in an introductory accounting course. *Issues in Accounting Education, 13*, 485–497.

Anderson, L. W., & Krathwohl (Eds.) (2001). *A taxonomy for learning, teaching, and Assessing: A revision of Bloom's taxonomy of educational objectives.* New York: Longman.

Angelo, T. A., & Cross, K. P. (1993). Classroom assessment techniques: A handbook for college teachers (2nd ed.). San Francisco: Jossey-Bass.

Arreola, R. A. (1995). *Developing a comprehensive faculty evaluation system: A handbook for college faculty and administrators on designing and operating a comprehensive faculty evaluation system.* Bolton, MA: Anker Publishing Co.

Ausubel, D. P. (1968). Educational psychology: A cognitive view. New York: Holt, Rinehart and Winston.

Bain, K. (2004). *What the best college teachers do.* Cambridge, MA: Harvard University Press.

Balch, W. R. (1998). Practice versus review exams and final exam performance. *Teaching of Psychology, 25*, 181–185.

Balch, W. R. (2001). Study tips: How helpful do introductory psychology students find them?. *Teaching of Psychology, 28*, 272–274.

Banta, T. W., Lund, J. P., Black, K. E., & Oblander, F. W. (1996). *Assessment in practice: Putting principles to work in college campuses.* San Francisco: Jossey-Bass.

Bartlett, F. C. (1932). *Remembering: A study in experimental and social psychology.* Cambridge: Cambridge University Press.

Becker, W. E., & Andrews, M. L. (Eds.) (2004). *The scholarship of teaching and learning in higher education: Contributions of research universities.* Bloomington, IN: Indiana University Press.

Belenky, M. F., Clinchy, B. M., Goldberger, N. R., & Tarule, J. M. (1986). *Women's ways of knowing: The development of self, voice, and mind.* New York: Basic Books.

Berardi-Coletta, B., Buyer, L. S., Dominowski, R. L., & Rellinger, E. A. (1995). Metacognition and problem solving: A process-oriented approach. *Journal of Experimental Psychology: Learning, Memory, Cognition, 21*, 205–223.

Berk, R. A. (2006). *Thirteen strategies to measure college teaching.* Sterling, VA: Stylus.

Berliner, D. C. (2006). Educational psychology: Search for essence throughout a century of influence. In P. A. Alexander & P. H. Winne (Eds.), *Handbook of educational psychology* (pp. 3–28). Mahwah, NJ: Lawrence Erlbaum.

Bernstein, D., Burnett, A., Goodburn, A., & Savory, P. (2006). *Making teaching and learning visible: Course portfolios and the peer review of teaching.* San Francisco: Jossey-Bass.

Bligh, D. A. (2000). *What's the use of lectures?* San Francisco: Jossey-Bass.

Bloom, B. S., Englehard, M., Furst, E., Hill, W., & Krathwohl, D. (1956). *Taxonomy of educational objectives, handbook I: Cognitive domain.* New York: McKay.

Bloom, H. S., & Lipsey, M. W. (2004). Some food for thought about effect size. Retrieved on January 19th, 2008 from http://www.wtgrantfoundation.org/usr_doc/FoodforThought.pdf.

Bol, L., Warkentin, R. W., Nunnery, J. A., & O'Connell, A. A. (1999). College students' study activities and their relationship to study context, reference course, and achievement. *College Student Journal, 33*, 608–622.

Borkowski, J. G., Carr, M., Rellinger, E., & Pressley, M. (1990). Self-regulated cognition: Interdependence of metacognition, attributions, and self-esteem. In B. F. Jones & J. T. Guthrie (Eds.), *Dimensions of thinking and cognitive instruction* (pp. 53–92). Hillsdale, NJ: Lawrence Erlbaum Associates.

Borkowski, J. G., & Muthukrishna, N. (1992). Moving metacognition into the classroom: "Working models" and effective strategy teaching. In M. Pressley, K. R. Harris, & J. T. Guthrie (Eds.), *Promoting academic competence and literacy in* school (pp. 477–501). San Diego, CA: Academic.

Boyer, E. L. (1990). *Scholarship reconsidered: Priorities of the professoriate.* San Francisco: Jossey-Bass.

Bransford, J. D., Brown, A. L., & Cocking, R. R. (Eds.) (1999). *How people learn: Brain, mind, experience, and school.* Washington, DC: National Research Council, Committee on Developments in the Science of Learning, National Academy Press.

Braskamp, L. A., & Ory, J. C. (1994). *Assessing faculty work: Enhancing individual and institutional performance.* San Francisco: Jossey-Bass.

Braxton, J., Luckey, W., & Holland, P. (2002). *Institutionalizing a broader view of scholarship through Boyer's four domains.* ASHE-ERIC Higher Education Report, 29(2). San Francisco: Jossey-Bass.

Brewer, C. (2004). Near real-time assessment of student learning and understanding in biology courses. *BioScience, 54(11)*, 1034–1039.

Brezis, M., & Cohen, R. (2004). Interactive learning in medicine: Socrates in electronic clothes. *QJM: An International Journal of Medicine, 97*, 47–51.

Brown, A. L. (1978). Knowing when, where, and how to remember: A problem of metacognition. In R. Glaser (Ed.), *Advances in instructional psychology* (Vol. 1, pp. 77–165). Hillsdale, NJ: Lawrence Erlbaum Associates.

Brown, A. L., & Campione, J. C. (1977). Training strategic study time apportionment in educable retarded children. *Intelligence, 1*, 94–107.

Brown, W. F., & Holtzman, W. H. (1955). A study-attitudes questionnaire for predicting academic success. *Journal of Educational Psychology, 46*, 75–84.

Buskist, W. (2004). Ways of the master teacher. *APS Observer, 17(9)*, 23–26.

Buskist, W., & Davis, S. F. (Eds.) (2006). *Handbook of the teaching of psychology.* Malden, MA: Blackwell.

Buskist, W., & Keeley, J. (2005). The Teacher Behaviors Checklist (TBC): A psychometrically sound and practical and teaching evaluation instrument. Paper presentation at the annual meeting of the American Psychological Association.

Buskist, W., Sikorski, J., Buckley, T., & Saville, B. K. (2002). Elements of master teaching. In S. F. Davis & W. Buskist (Eds.), *The teaching of psychology: Essays in honor of Wilbert J. McKeachie and Charles L. Brewer* (pp. 27–39). Mahwah, NJ: Erlbaum.

Cambridge, B. L.(Ed.) (2004). *Campus progress: Supporting the Scholarship of Teaching and Learning.* Washington, DC: American Association for Higher Education.

Cano, F. (2006). An in-depth analysis of the Learning and Study Strategies Inventory (LASSI). *Educational and Psychological Measurement, 66, 6*, 1023–1038.

Carini, R., Kuh, G., & Klein, S. (2006). Student engagement and student learning: Testing the linkages. *Research in Higher Education, 47*, 1–32.

Carney, R. N., & Levin, J. R. (1998). Do mnemonic memories fade as time goes by? Here's looking anew! *Contemporary Educational Psychology, 23*, 276–297.

Carrell, L. J., & Menzel, K. E. (1997). The impact of preparation and motivation on learning performance. *Communication Education, 46*, 262–272.

Cavanaugh, J. C., & Borkowski, J. G. (1979). The metamemory-memory "connection": Effects of strategy training and maintenance. *The Journal of General Psychology, 101*, 161–174.

Cavanaugh, J. C., & Perlmutter, M. (1982). Metamemory: A critical examination. *Child Development, 53*, 11–28.

Chapman, K. J., Meuter, M. L., Toy, D., & Wright, L. (2006), Can't we pick our own groups? The influence of group selection method on group dynamics and outcomes. *Journal of Management Education, 30(4)*, 557–569.

Chen, Z., & Daehler, M. W. (2000). External and internal instantiation of abstract information facilitates transfer in insight problem solving. *Contemporary Educational Psychology, 25*, 423–449.

Chi, M. T. H., de Leeuw, N., Chiu, M., & LaVancher, C. (1994). Eliciting self-explanations improves understanding. *Cognitive Science, 18*, 439–477.

Chick, N. L., Hassell, H., & Haynie, A. (2007) Reading for complexity: Recognizing and valuing ambiguity in literature. Retrieved on January 28th, 2008 from http://www.cfkeep.org/html/snapshot.php?id=93751660356067.

Chism, N. V. N. (1999). *Peer review of teaching.* Bolton, MA: Anker.

Chizmar, J. F., & Ostrosky, A. L. (1998). The one-minute paper: Some empirical findings. *Journal of Economic Education, 29*, 3–10.

Ciccone, T., & Myers, R. (February, 2006). *Report on the impact of Scholarship of Teaching and Learning on the UW-System.* Presentation at the International Society for the Teaching & Learning (ISSOTL) Conference, Washington, DC.

Claxton, C. S., & Murrell, P. H. (1987), *Learning Styles: Implications for Improving Educational Practices.* ASHE-ERIC Higher Education Report No. 4, Washington, DC: Association for the Study of Higher Education.

Cohen, J. (1988). *Statistical power analysis for the behavioral sciences* (2nd ed.). Hillsdale, NJ: Lawrence Earlbaum Associates.

Cohen, K. (2006, March). *Instruction in the protection of human research subjects.* Presentation at a one-day training workshop, Madison, WI.

Cox, M. (2001). Faculty learning communities: Change agents for transforming institutions into learning organizations. In D. Lieberman & C. Wehlburg (Eds.), *To improve the academy, 19* (pp. 69–93). Bolton, MA: Anker.

Cox, M. (2004). An introduction to faculty learning communities: Utilizing FLCs to solve problems and seize opportunities. In M. D. Cox & L. Richlin (Eds.) *New directions for teaching and learning, 97.* San Francisco, CA: Jossey-Bass.

Daniel, D. B. (2005). How to ruin a perfectly good lecture: Presentation software as a teaching tool. In B. Perlman, L. I. McCann, & W. Buskist (Eds.), *Voices of experience: Memorable talks from the National Institute on the Teaching of Psychology* (pp. 119–139). Washington, DC: American Psychological Society.

Davis, B. G. (1993). *Tools for teaching.* Indianapolis: Jossey-Bass.

Davis, S. F., & Buskist, W. (2006). What teachers need to know about teaching and learning. In W. Buskist & S. F. Davis (Eds.), *The handbook of the teaching of psychology* (pp. 3–10). Malden, MA: Blackwell.

DeBord, K. A., Aruguete, M. S., & Muhlig, J. (2004). Are computer-assisted teaching methods effective? *Teaching of Psychology, 31*, 65–68.

Dewey, J. (1910). *How we think.* Boston: D. C. Heath.

Diamond, R. M. (1998). *Aligning faculty rewards with institutional mission: Statements, policies, and guidelines.* Bolton, MA: Anker.

Diamond, R., & Adam, B. (2000). *The disciplines speak II: More statements on rewarding the scholarly, professional, & creative work of faculty.* Washington, DC: American Association for Higher Education.

Dickinson, D. J, & O'Connell, D. Q. (1990). Effect of quality & quantity of study on student grades. *Journal of Educational Research, 83,* 227–231.

Dorner, D. (1979). Self reflection and problem solving. In F. Klix (Ed.), *Human and artificial intelligence* (pp. 101–107). Berlin: Deutscher Verlag der Wissenshaften.

Dunlosky, J., & Lipko, A. R. (2007). Metacomprehension: A brief history and how to improve its accuracy. *Current Directions in Psychological Science, 16,* 228–232.

Dunlosky, J., & Nelson, T. O. (1997). Similarity between the cue for judgments of learning (JOL) and the cue for test is not the primary determinant of JOL accuracy. *Journal of Memory and Language, 36,* 34–49.

Edgerton, R. (2005). Foreword. In K. O'Meara & R. E. Rice (Eds.), *Faculty priorities reconsidered: Rewarding multiple forms of scholarship* (pp. xi–xvi). San Francisco: Jossey-Bass.

Elliot, A. J., McGregor, H. A., & Gable, S. (1999). Achievement goals, study strategies, and exam performance: A mediational analysis. *Journal of Educational Psychology, 91,* 549–563.

Entwhistle, N., & Tomlinson, P. (Eds.) (2007). Student learning and university teaching. *British Journal of Educational Psychology,* Monograph Series II.

Ericsson, K. A., & Simon, H. A. (1993). *Protocol analysis.* Cambridge, MA: MIT Press.

Field, A. (2005). *Discovering statistics using SPSS.* Thousand Oaks, CA: Sage.

Fink, L. D. (Ed.) (1984). New direction for teaching and learning: No. 17. In *The first year of college teaching.* San Francisco: Jossey-Bass.

Fink, L. D. (1995). Evaluting your own teaching. In P. Seldin (Ed.). *Improving college teaching.* Bolton, MA: Anker Publishing Co.

Fink, L. D. (2003). *Creating significant learning experiences: An integrated approach to designing college courses.* San Francisco: Jossey-Bass.

Fischer, K. W., Daniel, D. W., Immordino-Yang, M. H., Stern, E., Battro, A., & Koizumi, H. (2007). Why Mind, Brain, and Education? Why now? *Mind, Brain, and Education, 1,* 1–2.

Fisher, R. P., & Craik, F. I. M. (1977). The interaction between encoding and retrieval operations in cued recall. *Journal of Experimental Psychology: Human Learning and Memory, 3,* 701–711.

Flavell, J. H. (1971). First discussant's comments: What is memory development the development of? *Human Development, 14,* 72–278.

Flavell, J. H. (1977). *Cognitive development.* Englewood Cliffs, NJ: Prentice-Hall.

Flavell, J. H. (1979). Metacognition and cognitive monitoring: A new area of cognitive developmental inquiry. *American Psychologist, 34*, 906–911.

Fleming, V. M. (2002). Improving students' exam performance by introducing study strategies and goal setting. *Teaching of Psychology, 29*, 115–119.

Fletcher, J. D. (2003). Evidence for learning from technology-assisted instruction. In H. F. O'Neil, Jr. & R. S. Perez (Eds.), *Technology applications in education: A learning view* (pp. 79–99). Mahwah, NJ: Lawrence Erlbaum.

Flora, S. R., & Logan, R. E. (1996). Using computerized study guides to increase performance on general psychology examinations: An experimental analysis. *Psychological Reports, 79*, 235–241.

Foos, P. W., Mora, J. J., & Tkacz, S. (1994). Student study techniques and the generation effect. *Journal of Educational Psychology, 86*, 567–576.

Gettinger, M., & Seibert, J. K. (2002). Contributions of study skills to academic competence. *School Psychology Review, 31*, 350–365.

Gillespie, K. H. (2002). *A guide to faculty development: Practice advice, examples, and resources*. Bolton, MA: Anker.

Gilligan, C. (1982) *In a different voice: Psychological theory and women's development*. Cambridge, MA: Harvard University Press.

Gillstrom, A., & Ronnberg, J. (1995). Comprehension calibration and recall prediction accuracy of texts: Reading skill, reading strategies, and effort. *Journal of Educational Psychology, 87*, 545–558.

Glassick, C. E., Huber., M. T., & Maeroff, G. I. (1997). *Scholarship assessed: Evaluation of the professoriate*. San Francisco: Jossey-Bass.

Glenberg, A. M., & Epstein, W. (1985). Calibration of comprehension. *Journal of Educational Psychology, 87*, 545–558.

Glenberg, A. M., Sanocki, T., Epstein, W., & Morris, C. (1987). Enhancing calibration of comprehension. *Journal of Experimental Psychology: General, 116*, 119–136.

Grasha, A. F. (1996). *Teaching with style: A practical guide to enhancing learning by understanding teaching and learning styles*. Pittsburgh, PA: Alliance.

Grasha, T. (1990) The naturalistic approach to learning styles. *College Teaching, 38(3)*, 106–113.

Gray, P., Froh, R., & Diamond, R. (1992). *A national study of research universities: On the balance between research and undergraduate teaching*. New York: Syracuse University Center for Instructional Development.

Greenwald, A. G., & Gillmore, G. (1997) Grading leniency is a removable contaminant of student ratings, *American Psychologist, 52*, 1209–1217.

Greimel-Fuhrmann, B., & Geyer, A. (2003). Students' evaluation of teachers and instructional quality – Analysis of relevant factors based on empirical evaluation research. *Assessment and Evaluation in Higher Education, 28(3)*, 229–238.

Gurung, R. A. R. (2003). Pedagogical aids and student performance. *Teaching of Psychology, 30,* 92–95.

Gurung, R. A. R. (2004). Pedagogical aids: Learning enhancers or dangerous detours? *Teaching of Psychology, 31,* 164–166.

Gurung, R. A. R. (2005a). How do students really study (and does it matter)? *Teaching of Psychology, 32,* 238–240.

Gurung, R. A. R. (2005b). In-class learning assessment strategies. In W. Buskist & S. F. Davis (Eds.), *Handbook of the teaching of psychology* (pp. 285–289). Boston: Blackwell.

Gurung, R. A. R., Haynie, A., & Chick, N. (Eds.) (in press). *Signature pedagogies across the disciplines.* Arlington, VA: Stylus.

Gurung, R. A. R., & Daniel, D. (2005). Evidence-based pedagogy: Do pedagogical features enhance student learning? In D. Dunn & S. L. Chew (Eds.), *Best practices for teaching introductory psychology* (pp. 41–56). Mahwah, NJ: Erlbaum.

Gurung, R. A. R., & Martin, R. (2007). Predicting textbook reading: The textbook assessment and usage scale. Manuscript under review.

Gurung, R. A. R., Martin, R., Jarvis, P., & Creasey, G. (2007, August). *Code of conduct: Internationalizing the ethics of SoTL.* Poster session presented at the annual meeting of the International Society for the Scholarship of Teaching and Learning, Sydney, Australia.

Gurung, R. A. R., & Vespia, K. M. (2007). Looking good, teaching well? Linking liking, looks, and learning. *Teaching of Psychology, 34,* 5–10.

Hacker, D. J., Dunlosky, J., & Graesser, A. C. (1998). *Metacognition in educational theory and practice.* Mahwah, NJ: Lawrence Erlbaum Associates.

Hadwin, A. F., & Winne, P. H. (1996). Study strategies have meager support: A review with recommendations for implementation. *The Journal of Higher Education, 67,* 692–715.

Harrison, G., Andrews, J., & Saklofske, D. (2003). Current perspectives on cognitive learning styles. *Education Canada, 43,* 44–47.

Hart, J. T. (1965). Memory and the feeling-of-knowing experience. *Journal of Educational Psychology, 56,* 208–216.

Harvey, V. S. (1995). Teaching study skills. In A. Thomas & J. Grimes (Eds.), *Best practices in school psychology* (3rd ed., pp. 931–942). Washington, DC: National Association of School Psychologists.

Hatch, T. (2006). *Into the classroom: Developing the scholarship of teaching and learning.* San Francisco: Jossey-Bass.

Hattie, J., Biggs, J., & Purdie, N. (1996). Effects of learning skills interventions on student learning: A meta-analysis. *Review of Educational Research, 66,* 99–136.

Hines, L. (2005). Interactive learning environment keeps Modesto students engaged. *T H E Journal, 33(2),* 40–41.

Hood, A. B. (Ed.) (1986). *The Iowa Student Development Inventories.* Iowa City: Hitech Press.

Huba, M. E., & Freed, J. E. (2000). *Learner-centered assessment on college campuses.* Allyn & Bacon.

Huber, M. T. (2001). *Disciplinary styles in the scholarship of teaching: Reflections on the Carnegie Academy for the Scholarship of Teaching and Learning.* Washington, DC: American Association for Higher Education.

Huber, M. T., & Hutchings, P. (2005). *The advancement of learning: Building the teaching commons.* San Francisco: Jossey-Bass.

Huber, M. T., & Morreale, S. P. (Eds.) (2002). *Disciplinary styles in the scholarship of teaching and learning: Exploring common ground.* Washington, DC: American Association for Higher Education and the Carnegie Foundation for the Advancement of Teaching.

Hutchings, P. (2000) Approaching the Scholarship of Teaching and Learning. In P. Hutchings (Ed.) (2000). *Opening lines: Approaches to the scholarship of teaching and learning* (pp. 1–10). Menlo Park, CA: The Carnegie Foundation for the Advancement of Teaching.

Hutchings, P. (2002). Ethics and aspiration in the scholarship of teaching and learning. In P. Hutchings (Ed.) *Ethics of Inquiry: Issues in scholarship of teaching and learning* (pp. 1–18). Menlo Park, CA: Carnegie Publications.

Hutchings, P. (2007) Theory: The elephant in the Scholarship of Teaching and Learning room. *International Journal for the Scholarship of Teaching and Learning, 1(1),* 1–4.

Hutchings, P., & Shulman, L. S. (1999). The scholarship of teaching: New elaborations, new developments. *Change, 31(5),* 10–15.

James, W. (1899/2006). *Talks to teachers on psychology and to students on some of life's ideals.* New York: Elibron Classics.

Jones, C. H., & Slate, J. R. (1992), "Technical manual for the study habits inventory" (unpublished manuscript), Arkansas State University, Jonesboro, AR.

Jones, T. A., & Schallert, T. (1994). Use-dependent growth of pyramidal neurons after neocortex damage. *Journal of Neuroscience, 14,* 2140–2152.

Keeley, J., Smith, D., & Buskist, W. (2006). The Teacher Behaviors Checklist: Factor analysis of its utility for evaluating teaching. *Teaching of Psychology, 33,* 84–90.

Kemmis, S., & McTaggert, R., (1990). *The Action Research Planner.* Melbourne, Australia: Deakin University Press.

Kennedy, E. J., Lawton, L., & Plumlee, E. L. (2002). Blissful ignorance: The problem of unrecognized incompetence and academic performance. *Journal of Marketing Education, 24(3),* 243–252.

Kiewra, K. A., DuBois, N. F., Christian, D., & McShane A. (1988). Providing study notes: Comparison of three types of notes for review. *Journal of Educational Psychology, 80,* 595–597.

King, P. M., & Kitchener, K. S. (1994). *Developing reflective judgement: Understanding and promoting intellectual growth and critical thinking in adolescents and adults.* San Francisco: Jossey-Bass.

Kinzie, J. (2007). *Measuring and managing student engagement: Why it matters in the first year of college. Madison, WI: Opid Spring Conference.*

Kitsantas, A. (2002). Test preparation and performance: A self-regulatory analysis. *Journal of Experimental Education, 70*, 101–113.

Klass, G., & Crothers, L. (2000). An experimental evaluation of web-based tutorial quizzes. *Social Sciences Computer Review, 18*, 508–515.

Kluwe, R. H. (1982). Cognitive knowledge and executive control: Metacognition. In D. R. Griffin (Ed.), *Animal mind – human mind* (pp. 201–224). New York: Springer-Verlag.

Kobayashi, K. (2006). Combined effects of note-taking/-reviewing on learning and the enhancement through interventions: A meta-analytic review. *Educational Psychology, 26*, 459–477.

Kolb, B. (1995). *Brain Plasticity and Behavior.* Hillsdale, NJ: Lawrence Erlbaum Associates.

Koriat, A., & Bjork, R. A. (2005). Illusions of competence in monitoring one's knowledge during study. *Journal of Experimental Psychology: Learning, Memory, and Cognition, 31*, 187–194.

Kratzig, G. P., & Arbuthnott, K. D. (2006). Perceptual learning style and learning proficiency: A test of the hypothesis. *Journal of Educational Psychology, 98*, 238–246.

Kuh, G. D. (2004). The contributions of the research university to assessment and innovation in undergraduate education. In W. E. Becker & M. L. Andrews (Eds.), *The scholarship of teaching and learning in higher education: The contributions of research universities* (pp. 52–59). Bloomington, IN: Indiana University Press.

Kuh, G. D., Kinzie, J., Schuh, J., Whitt, J., & Associates. (2005). *Student success in college: Creating conditions that matter.* San Francisco: Jossey Bass.

Kuhn, D. J. (1988). An assessment of the study habits and skills of students in postsecondary science courses. *Community/Junior College Quarterly of Research and Practice, 12*, 197–204.

Lewis, K. G. (2001). *Techniques and strategies for interpreting student evaluations: New Directions for Teaching and Learning, No. 87.* San Francisco: Josey-Bass.

Lewis, S., Carter, K., & Patrick, H. (2004). Why do self-assessment? In B. L. Cambridge (Ed.). *Campus progress: Supporting the scholarship of teaching and learning* (pp. 32–43). Washington, DC: American Association for Higher Education.

Locke, N. M. (1940). The student skills inventory: A study habits test. *Journal of Applied Psychology, 24*, 493–504.

Lodico, M. G., Ghatala, E. S., Levin, J. R., Pressley, M., & Bell, J. A. (1983). The effects of strategy monitoring training on children's selection of effective memory strategies. *Journal of Experimental Child Psychology, 35,* 73–277.

Lynch, D. (2006). Motivational factors, learning strategies and resource management as predictors of course grades. *College Student Journal, 40,* 423–428.

Maclean, M. S., & Mohr, M. M. (1999). *Teacher-Researchers at Work.* Berkeley, CA: National Writing Project.

Magliano, J. P., Little, L. D., & Graesser, A. C. (1993). The impact comprehension instruction on the calibration of comprehension. *Reading Research and Instruction, 32,* 49–63.

Magolda, M. B. B. (1992). *Knowing and reasoning in college: Gender-related patterns in students' intellectual development.* San Francisco: Jossey-Bass.

Maki, P. L. (2004). *Assessing for learning: Building a sustainable commitment across the institution.* Sterling, VA: Stylus.

Maki, R. H. (1995). Accuracy of metacomprehension judgments for questions of varying importance levels. *American Journal of Psychology, 108,* 327–344.

Maki, R. H. (in press). Predicting performance on text material: Delayed versus immediate predictions and test. *Memory and Cognition.*

Maki, R. H., & Berry, S. (1984). Metacomprehension of text material. *Journal of Experimental Psychology: Learning, Memory, and Cognition, 10,* 663–679.

Maki, R. H., & Serra, M. (1992a). The basis of test predictions for text material. *Journal of Experimental Psychology: Learning, Memory, and Cognition, 18,* 116–126.

Maki, R. H., & Serra, M. (1992b). Role of practice test in the accuracy of test predictions on text material. *Journal of Educational Psychology, 84,* 200–210.

Marsh, H. W., and Roche, L. A. (2000). Effects of grading leniency and low workload on students' evaluations of teaching: Popular myth, bias, validity or innocent bystander? *The Journal of Educational Psychology, 92(1),* 202–228.

Masters, J. (1995). The history of action research. In I. Hughes (Ed.), *Action Research Electronic Reader.* The University of Sydney, online. Retrieved March 15th, 2007 from www.behs.cchs.usyd.edu.au/arow/Reader/rmasters.htm.

Mayer, R. E. (2001). *Multimedia learning.* New York: Cambridge University Press.

Meyers, R. (2007). Guidelines for human research participants in scholarship of teaching and learning research. University of Wisconsin System Leadership Site for the Scholarship of Teaching and Learning. Retrieved February 9th, 2008 from http://www4.uwm.edu//leadershipsite/index.cfm.

McDaniel, M. A., & Einstein, G. O. (2005). Material appropriate difficulty: A framework for determining when difficulty is desirable for improving learning. In A. F. Healy (Ed.), *Experimental cognitive psychology and its applications. Decade of behavior.* (pp. 73–85). Washington, DC: US: American Psychological Association.

McKeachie, W. J. (1997). Student ratings: The validity of use: *American Psychologist, 52*, 1218–1225.

McKernan, J. (1991). *Curriculum action research: A handbook of methods and resources for the reflective practitioner.* London: Kogan Page.

McKinney, K. (2007). *Enhancing learning through the Scholarship of Teaching and Learning: The challenges and joys of juggling.* Bolton, MA: Anker.

Menges, R. J., Weimer, M., & Associates. (1996). *Teaching on solid ground: Using scholarship to improve practice.* San Francisco: Jossey-Bass.

Metcalfe, J. (2006). Principles of cognitive science in education *APS Observer, 19*.

Metcalfe, J., & Greene, M. J. (2007). Metacognition of agency. *Journal of Experimental Psychology: General, 136*, 184–199.

Milgram, S. (1963). Behavioral study of obedience. *Journal of Abnormal and Social Psychology, 67*, 371–378.

Mills, G. E. (2007). *Action research: A guide for the teacher researcher.* Upper Saddle River, NJ: Pearson.

Mohamed, A. A. (1997). Differences among low-, average-, and high-achieving college students on learning and study strategies. *Educational Psychology, 17*, 171–177.

Motes, M. A., & Wiegmann, D. A. (1999). Computerized cognition laboratory. *Teaching of Psychology, 26*, 62–65.

Murrell, P. A., & Claxton, C. S. (1987). Experiential learning theory as a guide for effective teaching. *Counselor Education and Supervision, 27*, 4–14.

National Research Council (2001). *Knowing what student know: The science and design of educational assessment.* Washington, DC: National Academy Press.

Nelson, T. O., & Dunlosky, J. (1991). The delayed-JOL effect: When delaying your judgments of learning can improve the accuracy of your metacognition monitoring. *Psychological Science, 2*, 267–270.

Nesbit, J. C., Winne, P. H., Jamieson-Noel, D., Code, J., Zhou, M., MacAllister, K., Bratt, S., Wang, W., & Hadwin, A. (2006). Using cognitive tools in gStudy to investigate how study activities covary with achievement goals. *Journal of Educational Computing Research, 35*, 339–358.

Neville, H. J. (1995). Effects of experience on the development of the visual systems of the brain on the language systems of the brain. Paper presented in the series Brain Mechanisms Underlying School Subjects, University of Oregon, Eugene.

Nist, S. L., Simpson, M. L., Olejnik, S., & Mealey, D. L. (1991). The relation between self-selected study processes and test performance. *American Educational Research Journal, 28*, 849–874.

Noppe, I. (2007). PowerPoint presentation handouts and college student learning outcomes. *International Journal for the Scholarship of Teaching and Learning, 1*. Retrieved March 20th, 2007 from http://www.georgiasouthern.edu/ijsotl.

Olivares, O. J. (2002). An analysis of the study time-grade association. *Radical Pedagogy*, 4, np. Retrieved on June 24th from http://radicalpedagogy.icaap. org/content/issue4_1/06_Olivares.html.

O'Meara, K, & Rice, R. E., (2005). *Faculty priorities reconsidered: Rewarding multiple forms of scholarship*. San Francisco: Jossey-Bass.

Onwuegbuzie, A. J., Slate, J. R., & Schwartz, R. A. (2001). Role of study skills in graduate-level educational research courses. *Journal of Educational Research*, 94, 238–246.

Palmer, P. J. (1998). *The courage to teach: Exploring the inner landscape of a teacher's life*. San Francisco, CA: Jossey-Bass.

Paris, S. G., & Winograd, P. (1990). How metacognition can promote academic learning and instruction. In B. F. Jones & L. Idol (Eds.), *Dimensions of thinking and cognitive instruction* (pp. 15–51). Hillsdale, NJ: Lawrence Erlbaum Associates.

Pellegrino, J. W., Chudowsky, N., & Glaser, R. (2001). *Knowing what students know: The science and design of educational assessment*. Washington, DC: National Research Council.

Perry, W. G. (1970). *Forms of intellectual and ethical development in the college years: A scheme*. New York: Holt, Rinehart and Winston.

Plant, E. A., Ericsson, K. A., Hill, L., & Asberg, K. (2005). Why study time does not predict grade point average across college students: Implications of deliberate practice for academic performance. *Contemporary Educational Psychology*, 30, 96–116.

Pressley, M., & Afflerbach, P. (1995). *Verbal Protocols of Reading: The Nature of Constructively Responsive Reading*. Hillsdale, NJ: Lawrence Erlbaum Associates.

Pressley, M., Yokoi, L., van Meter, P., Van Etten, S., & Freebern, G. (1997). Some of the reasons why preparing for exams is so hard? What can be done to make it easier? *Educational Psychology Review*, 9, 1-38.

Prince, J. S., Miller, T. K., & Winston, J. B., Jr. (1974). *Student Development Task Inventory*. Athens, GA: Student Development Associates.

Proctor, B. E., Hurst, A., Prevatt, F., Petscher, Y., & Adams, K. (2006). Study skills profiles of normal-achieving and academically-struggling college students. *Journal of College Student Development*, 47, 37–51.

Rice, R. E. (2005). "Scholarship Reconsidered": History and context. In K. O'Meara & R. E. Rice (Eds.) *Faculty priorities reconsidered: Rewarding multiple forms of scholarship* (pp. 17–31). San Francisco: Jossey-Bass.

Richlin, L. (2001). Scholarly teaching and the scholarship of teaching. In C. Kreber (Ed.), *Scholarship revisited: Perspectives on the scholarship of teaching* (pp. 57–68). New Directions for Teaching and Learning. No. 86. San Francisco: Jossey-Bass.

Richlin, L. (2006). *Blueprint for learning: Constructing college courses to facilitate, assess, and document learning.* Sterling, VA: Stylus.

Rinaldi, C., & Gurung, R. A. R. (2005). Does matching teaching and learning styles optimize learning? *Teaching Forum,* np. Retrieved March 27th, 2007 from www.uwosh.edu/programs/teachingforum/public_html/?module= displaystory&story_id=648&format=html.

Robbins, S., Carlstrom, A., Davis, D., Langley, R., Lauver, K., & Le, H. (2004). Do psychosocial and study skill factors predict college outcomes? A meta-analysis. *Psychological Bulletin, 130(2),* 261–268.

Roediger, H. L., & Karpicke, J. D. (2006). Test-enhanced learning: Taking memory tests improves long-term retention. *Psychological Science, 17,* 249–255.

Rohrer, D. & Pashler, H. (2007). Increasing retention without increasing study time. *Current Directions in Psychological Science,* 16, 4, 183–186.

Savory, P., Burnett, A. N., & Goodburn, A. (2007). *Inquiry into the college classroom: A journey toward scholarly teaching.* Bolton, MA: Anker.

Schneider, W. (1985). Developmental trends in the metamemory-memory behavior relationship: An integrative review. In D. L. Forrest-Pressley, G. E. MacKinnon, & T. G. Waller (Eds.), *Metacognition, cognition, and human performance* (Vol. 1, pp. 57–109). New York: Academic.

Schoenfeld, A. H. (1987). What's all the fuss about metacognition? In A. H. Schoenfeld (Ed.), *Cognitive science and mathematics education* (pp. 189–215). Hillsdale, NJ: Lawrence Erlbaum Associates.

Schwartz, B., & Reisberg, D. *Learning and memory.* New York: W. W. Norton and Company.

Seldin, P. (2004). *A practical guide to improved performance and promotion/tenure decisions* (3rd ed.). Bolton, MA: Anker.

Shulman, L. S. (1987). Knowledge and teaching: Foundations of the new reform. *Harvard Educational Review, 57(1),* 1–22.

Shulman, L. S. (2002). *Ethics of Inquiry: Issues in scholarship of teaching and learning.* Menlo Park, CA: Carnegie Publications.

Shulman, L. S., & Hutchings, P. (September/October, 1999). The Scholarship of Teaching: New elaborations, new developments, *Change Magazine,* 10–15.

Snooks, M. K., Neeley, S. E., & Williamson, K. M. (2004). From SGID and GIFT to BBQ: Streamlining midterm student evaluations to improve teaching and learning. In C. M. Wehlburg & S. Chadwick-Bossey (Eds.), *To improve the academy* (pp. 109–113). Bolton, MA: Anker.

Sorcinelli, M. D. (2002). Ten principles of good practice in creating and sustaining teaching and learning centers. In K. H. Gillespie (Ed.). *A guide to faculty development: Practice advice, examples, and resources* (pp. 2–9). Bolton, MA: Anker.

Stanley, B., Slate, J. R., & Jones, C. H. (1999). Study behaviors of college preparatory and honors students in the ninth grade. *High School Journal, 82,* 165–71.

Stenhouse, L. (1975). *An introduction to curriculum research and development.* London: Heinemann Education.

Stevens, D. D., & Levi, A. J. (2005). *Introduction to rubrics: An assessment tool to save grading time, convey effective feeback and promote student learning.* Sterling, VA: Stylus.

Strage, A., Baba, Y., Millner, S., Scharberg, M., Walker, E., Williamson, R., & Yoder, M. (2002). What every student affairs professional should know: Student study activities and beliefs associated with academic success. *Journal of College Student Development, 43,* 246–266.

Thompson, S. B., Nelson, C. E., & Naremore, R. C. (2001) Online SoTL Tutorial. Retrieved January 25th, 2008 from www.fctl.ucf.edu/ResearchAndScholarship/SoTL/whatIsSOTL/content/SoTL-Tutorial.pps.

Tversky, A. (1973). Encoding processes in recognition and recall. *Cognitive Psychology, 5,* 275–287.

Tweed, R. G., & Lehman, D. R. (2002). Learning considered within a cultural context: Confucian and Socratic approaches. *American Psychologist, 57,* 89–99.

Vasquez, K. (in press). Learning styles as self-fulfilling prophecies. In R. A. R. Gurung & L. Prieto (Eds.), *Getting culture: Incorporating diversity across the curriculum.* Sterling, VA: Stylus.

Walvoord, B. E. (2004). *Assessment clear and simple: A practical guide for institutions, departments, and general education.* San Francisco: Jossey-Bass.

Walvoord, B. E. (2004). What it really takes. In B. Cambridge (Ed.). *Campus progress: Supporting the Scholarship of Teaching and Learning* (pp. 78–87). Washington, DC: American Association for Higher Education.

Walvoord, B. E., Anderson , V. J., Breihan, J. R., McCarthy, L. P., Robison, S. M., & Sherman, A. K. (1996). Making traditional graded tests and assignments serve contemporary needs for assessment. In T. W. Banta, J. P. Lund, K. E. Black, & F. W. Oblander (Eds.). *Assessment in practice: Putting principles to work on college campuses* (pp. 278–280). San Francisco: Jossey-Bass.

Washington, H. A. (2007). *Medical apartheid: The dark history of medical experimentation on Black Americans from colonial times to the present.* New York: Random House.

Watson, R. I. (1961). A brief history of educational psychology. *The Psychological Record, 11,* 209–242.

Weaver, C. A. III, & Bryant, D. S. (1995). Monitoring of comprehension: The role of text difficulty in metamemory for narrative and expository text. *Memory and Cognition, 23,* 12–22.

Weimer, M. (2006). *Enhancing scholarly work on teaching and learning: Professional literature that makes a difference.* San Francisco: Jossey-Bass.

Weinstein, C. E., & Palmer, D. R. (2002). *Learning and Study Strategies Inventory (LASSI): User's manual* (2nd ed.). Clearwater, FL: H & H Publishing.

Wiggins, G., & McTighe, J. (2005). *Understanding by design expanded* (2nd ed.). Alexandria, VA: Association for Supervision and curriculum development.

Wingate, U. (2006). Doing away with "study skills." *Teaching in Higher Education, 11*, 457–469.

Winne, P. H., & Jamieson-Noel, D. (2002). Exploring students' calibration of self-reports about study tactics and achievement. *Contemporary Educational Psychology, 27*, 551–572.

Wood, P. (1983). Inquiring systems and problem structure: Implications for cognitive development. *Human Development, 26(5)*, 249–265.

Wrenn, C. G. (1933). *Study-habits inventory.* Oxford: Stanford University Press.

Wright, D. L. (2002). Program types and prototypes. In K. H. Gillespie (Ed.). *A guide to faculty development: Practice advice, examples, and resources* (pp. 24–34). Bolton, MA: Anker.

Wyatt, D., Pressley, M., El-Dinary, P. B., Stein, S., Evans, P., & Brown, R. (1993). Comprehension strategies, worth and credibility monitoring, and evaluations: Cold and hot cognition when experts read professional articles that are important to them. *Learning and Individual Differences, 5*, 49–72.

Zhao, C. M., & Kuh, G. (2004). Adding value: Learning communities and student engagement. *Research in Higher Education, 45(2)*, 115–138.

Zimbardo, P. G. (1973). On the ethics of intervention in human psychological research: With special reference to the Stanford prison experiment. *Cognition, 2*, 243–256.

Index